SECURING THE PEACE

SECURING THE PEACE

THE DURABLE SETTLEMENT OF CIVIL WARS

Monica Duffy Toft

PRINCETON UNIVERSITY PRESS   PRINCETON AND OXFORD

Copyright © 2010 by Princeton University Press
Published by Princeton University Press, 41 William Street,
Princeton, New Jersey 08540
In the United Kingdom: Princeton University Press, 6 Oxford Street,
Woodstock, Oxfordshire OX20 1TW

Library of Congress Cataloging-in-Publication Data

Toft, Monica Duffy, 1965–
Securing the peace : the durable settlement of civil wars / Monica Duffy Toft.
    p. cm.
Includes bibliographical references and index.
ISBN 978-0-691-14145-9 (hardcover : alk. paper)—ISBN 978-0-691-14146-6
(pbk. : alk. paper) 1. Conflict management. 2. Pacific settlement of
international disputes. 3. Civil war—Prevention I. Title.
JZ6368.T64 2009
303.6′4—dc22   2009014401

British Library Cataloging-in-Publication Data is available
This book has been composed in Sabon

Printed on acid-free paper. ∞

press.princeton.edu

Printed in the United States of America

1 3 5 7 9 10 8 6 4 2

To Sam and Ingrid

Contents

Tables and Illustrations

Preface

THIS BOOK WAS born in frustration. As I was finishing my first book, I questioned whether my theory on the origins of ethnic wars could explain the outcome of these wars. As I began reading the literature, I was struck by the fact that most of it was devoted to the study of negotiated settlements. This would have been fine, but it turns out that as a type of civil war settlement, negotiated settlements not only are rare but also often break down. I was struck by the fact that so much intellectual effort had been expended on a mere two dozen or so cases, while another hundred or so had been left unexamined. As a scholar and someone interested in bringing about and securing peace, I found this state of scholarship deeply unsatisfying, and I decided to figure out why it is that negotiated settlements are so precarious, and to do so by examining whether other types of settlements—victories—might help us to understand why.

I approached the problem of post–civil war peace and stability based on training that I received as a graduate student at the University of Chicago. Three important lessons have stayed with me.

First, empirical data and methodologies are the handmaidens of good theory. Without a solid theoretical basis, the best data and the newest methodologies on their own will not advance our understanding. Theory reigns. Think for a moment about Samuel Huntington's thesis on the clash of civilizations. There is no sophisticated methodology, but there is a compelling theory (whether it is correct is another question): no longer will states clash, but cultures. Huntington develops the theory and provides an array of simple but compelling empirical data to investigate the logic of that theory. We are still debating Sam's bold claims nearly two decades later.

Second, theories should be as parsimonious and simple as possible. Yes, I am an international relations scholar, and this mantra hails from the days of Kenneth Waltz and structural realism, but it also happens to be a worthy goal in any field of inquiry. Simplicity and parsimony in theory are beautiful, and a sense of satisfaction emerges when you realize that broad phenomena can be explained with a small set of factors or indicators. This is not to say that nuance does not exist across these phenomena, and that often it is nuance that might be doing some of the work in the analysis, but it is to say that there is something compelling about trying to explain a lot with only a little bit of logic and information. This might explain why rational choice theory, with its narrow conceptions of rationality and operational guidelines, remains so appealing in a variety

of disciplines. Although it does not capture all dynamics of human behavior perfectly, calculated self-interest does seem to dominate in many
economic, political, and social interactions (note that this statement is
coming from someone who studies ethnicity, religion, and nationalism,
where self-interest is often shelved in favor of group interest).

Third, the best research examines big questions. As one of my advisors
used to say, "You want to go for the artery, not the capillary." Think
big. It sounds simple, but it often turns out to be difficult to achieve.
So, returning to the research of this book, I realized that one of the reasons I was frustrated with the existing literature (and policy making) was
that not only were researchers unnecessarily circumscribing the number
of cases they were examining, but it meant that they were also crafting
theories to explain only a narrow set of cases. A *general* theory of civil
war termination and durable peace is not possible if only one type of
settlement is examined. Thus, from the outset, I attempted to develop a
general theory of civil war termination to explain the entire set of cases
and associated dynamics of post–civil war environments. I leave the question of whether I have succeeded to the reader.

As with most major research projects, this one could not have been
completed without the help of many colleagues and research assistants,
and much financial support. Results of this project have been presented
over the years in a number of brownbag luncheons, seminars, and conferences, including at Harvard University at the Kennedy School's Belfer
Center International Security Program brownbag seminar (on at least
two occasions), at the John M. Olin Institute's National Security Fellows
seminar, and at Columbia University, Georgetown University, the University of Chicago, and Yale University. I have also presented earlier versions
of this work at a number of academic conferences, including those of the
International Studies Association and American Political Science Association. Although some colleagues in these venues were offended (yes, offended) by the notion that "victory" might serve as a viable alternative to
negotiated settlement, all were incredibly helpful in pushing the analysis
and forcing me to hone it. (I should admit that the early working title and
presumption was "Peace through Victory," a bit more provocative—and
inaccurate—than the current title and analysis.)

Over the years I have had the fortune of excellent research assistance,
including that of Ben Ansell, Katie Gallagher, Aishwarya Lakshmi, Debo-
rah Lee, and Elias Wolfberg. I am especially thankful to Jeff Friedman,
who helped out early on with research as a recently graduated Harvard
College student and then again in the final push to complete the manuscript as a recently admitted Ph.D. student at the Kennedy School, as
well as to Janet Lewis for her insightful research on Uganda and Gwen
McCarter for her willingness to track down even the most obscure refer-

ence. Special thanks go to Meghan Tinsley, who helped to ensure that the manuscript was as polished as possible.

Several colleagues have provided helpful feedback and critical comments along the way. They include Marie Besançon, Charles Call, Francis Deng, Page Fortna, Caroline Hartzell, Stathis Kalyvas, Roy Licklider, William Rose, Nicholas Sambanis, William Stanley, R. H. Wagner, and Libby Wood. Generous funding for this research was provided by the Smith Richardson Foundation and, at Harvard University, the Davis Center for Russian and Eurasian Studies, the Kennedy School, and the Weatherhead Center for International Affairs. I thank my indexer David Prout, copy editor Anita O'Brien, and the team at Princeton University Press including Leslie Grundfest, and especially my editor, Chuck Myers.

My husband and colleague Ivan has suffered through every iteration of the argument and evidence presented in this book, all with far more grace than I could endure. Finally, I dedicate this book to our children, Sam and Ingrid, who have had to put up with long work hours and a sometimes (I'm sorry) impatient and distracted mom. For what is good in this book, I thank you all.

SECURING THE PEACE

Chapter 1.

Introduction: Civil War Termination in Historical and Theoretical Context

CIVIL WARS ARE NASTY, brutish, and long. Sometimes, civil wars that seem ended recur. They are the most common sort of large-scale violence, resulting in massive and often catastrophic killing and destruction. The civil war in Rwanda was accompanied by genocide, and in Afghanistan, the Taliban are resurging against domestic and international opponents. Civil war plagues Colombia, the Democratic Republic of Congo, Iraq, Somalia, Sri Lanka, and Sudan, while it threatens to reemerge in full force in Lebanon and Nigeria.

Why do some civil wars end, and stay ended, while others reignite? Under what conditions do civil wars end in an enduring and constructive peace—a peace that does not hamper positive postwar social, political, and economic development? Is it something in the nature of the agreements themselves, or perhaps in the nature of the way the war ends, that makes the crucial difference?

These questions are important because although much has been written about civil wars (how and why they start, how costly they are, when they are likely to expand across state boundaries, and how to end them), there has been little attention paid to the significant issue of the relationship between how a civil war ends and the likelihood that a constructive peace will be sustained. Furthermore, though recent works begin to explore the subject both empirically and qualitatively, we have yet to develop a general theoretical framework for understanding the conditions that lead to a stable, democratic, and prosperous peace.

Civil wars, especially those in the last sixty years, have most often ended in one of two ways: (1) with outright military victory by one side over its rival(s); or (2) with a negotiated settlement that preserves belligerents physically and undertakes to ratify by contract an acceptable postwar distribution of valued resources. I argue that each resolution type has its advantages and disadvantages, and that combining the stronger elements of each will make it possible to design civil war settlements that are both enduring and constructive. In sum, I offer a general explanation of civil war termination outcomes and introduce a strategy of "mutual benefit and mutual harm" for achieving durable peace.

Mutual Benefit, Mutual Harm

If we look at most negotiated settlements, we find that their chief strength lies in the promise of two sorts of direct benefit to former combatants. On the negative benefit side, combatants who contract to avoid further armed conflict immediately benefit by avoiding the risk of physical destruction (both of themselves and of their collective or private property), and by lifting the cloud of anxiety that invariably accompanies conflicts when pursued by violent means. On the positive benefit side, most negotiated settlements include provisions for development and reconstruction aid, and for the redistribution of offices in postwar government. Recent negotiated settlements to civil wars make it clear that, taken together, most well-meaning third parties tend to assume that the benefits of peace (narrowly defined), and the positive benefits promised following a cease-fire, are sufficient conditions for what they hope will become an enduring and constructive peace settlement. I disagree. I will show that a key weakness of negotiated settlements lies in their general lack of a credible guarantee to harm or punish defectors should one or more of the contracting parties renege on its commitments. In ending a civil war, the negotiated provision of a promised benefit without the provision of a credible threat of punishment leaves negotiated settlements vulnerable either to outright cheating or to tactical cease-fires in which one or all parties simply use the respite to rearm in hopes of achieving original or expanded political objectives. This may explain why negotiated settlements are both advocated more often as an ideal means to end civil wars, and why empirically they are more likely to break down, resulting in a renewed (and at times escalated) violent conflict.

In contrast, and again empirically, civil wars ended by military victory are much more likely to stay ended. This striking difference forces consideration of a number of important theoretical and policy questions. For example, when we want to know whether, as a matter of policy, we should work toward better-negotiated settlements or toward military support of one side that would hasten a military victory, we must closely examine questions of relative cost. This raises the immediate problem of which side to choose, and the question of whether there in fact exists a "good" side to aid over a "bad" or "worse" side. Most parties to a civil war have both legitimate and illegitimate grievances and motivations. Whereas negotiated settlements have the virtue of appearing to save lives (a crucial cost), military victories appear to suffer from the opposite drawback in that they imply greater loss of life. I use the word "appear" because, in many cases, the promise of an outright victory of arms by one side may actually save lives, either by forcing the losing side to surrender more quickly (once prospects of support or intervention by a third party vanish) or by preserving peace over a longer period of time. At this juncture, two key questions thus follow: (1) Are lives the only or most crucial cost to take into consideration when evaluating the utility of outcomes? (2) By what mechanism do military victories tend to result in an enduring peace?

The first question must be answered in the negative: certainly, casualties involving both combatants and noncombatants are a crucial cost consideration, but so are quality-of-life issues. The latter category includes factors such as basic human rights, political liberties, and prospects for economic survival and prosperity after the immediate threat of physical violence has ebbed. Although the concern of preserving lives is surely a worthy goal and a necessary consideration, it should never serve as a sufficient consideration for evaluating the utility of potential policy options.

In contrast, several answers to the second question (concerning the mechanisms by which military victories result in enduring peace) seem appropriate. These answers involve issues that range from the nature of the political objectives sought, to the destructiveness of the war itself, to the relative power of the actors following the cessation of conflict. In fact, military victories have the advantages and disadvantages of negotiated settlements in an inverted form: while they excel in terms of the guarantee of providing harm to survivors on the losing side (potential defectors to the peace), they are weak in their promise of affording benefits to losers. Because the threat of physical harm in reprisal for violating the peace is generally a more immediate one than the threat of other harms (e.g., economic and social), military victories, ceteris paribus, result in a higher likelihood of enduring peace.

Two crucial issues follow from the argument above. First, we cannot infer from the strong correlation between (1) military victory as a civil war termination profile and (2) enduring peace as an outcome that military victory should be promoted *in general* as an ideal resolution to civil wars.[1] This is because victory is determined by legitimacy as well as by resources (e.g., access to cash, arms, and allies), and no necessary connection exists between possession of resources and legitimacy. Supporting military victory as a generally preferred civil war termination outcome would therefore sometimes result in a "better" outcome (greater justice alongside less loss of life and overall destruction) and sometimes produce a "worse" outcome (injustice, regardless of loss of life). This serves as another avenue by which one can question the practice of measuring the utility of a policy option only in terms of physical loss of life. Second, a large-n analysis of civil wars reveals an even more interesting empirical puzzle: when we disaggregate "military victory" and consider the impact of victories made by incumbents and rebels separately, military victories by rebels tend to be far more stable. This clearly implies that, no matter how military victories achieve this effect, something more nuanced than "they save or cost more lives than negotiated settlements" must be at work.

In sum, negotiated settlements are stronger in their promise of benefits to former combatants but weaker in their promise of harm to those who violate the peace. Military victories are stronger in their promise of harm to former combatants on the losing side, and weaker in their promise of benefits. Empirically, military victories, as a war termination type, correlate strongly with enduring peace. As noted above, however, we cannot infer from this that of the two policy options, military victories are to be generally advocated, because they carry with them the promise of other costs that may outweigh the benefits of peace and savings in terms of lives lost and property destroyed.

The central argument of this book is that it is both possible and necessary to develop a hybrid strategy for ending civil wars in a constructive manner, one that incorporates the strengths of both the negotiated settlement and military victory termination profiles. While negotiated settlements tend to emphasize the provision of goods, such as political offices and the distribution of resources, credible mechanisms that establish the threat of harm to perpetrators of violence—and most notably reforming the security sector—are often given little to no consideration. There are several reasons for this. First, a credible threat of harm most often implies a credible threat of military intervention. As most military interventions since the end of the Cold War (save perhaps NATO's intervention in Kosovo in 1999) have gone badly, negotiated settlements appear to offer the promise of halting violence without risking body bags. Second, rebuilding the armed forces and police of a state does not produce the same visceral appeal as does feeding starving children, housing returning refugees, or handling war crimes and human rights violations.[2] Third, the security sector may be implicated in the worst excesses of the war, in which case the people would be disinclined to reconstitute security institutions, thereby reempowering them with a capacity that could be used for future repression and civil war.

But by building on an existing collection of excellent and well-developed literature on the rise of the "state" as a form of political association, as well as literature on state- and nation-building, I show that security sector reform (SSR) offers the potential for both enduring and constructive peace.[3]

The next section presents an empirical overview of civil wars and the nature of their ends since 1940, and an explanation of why the study of civil wars and civil war termination is so important. Thereafter, the chapter introduces keys terms and lays out the plan of the rest of the book.

TABLE 1.1
Number of Civil Wars Started in Each Decade, 1940–2000

Decade	Number	Percent of all civil wars (1940–1990)	Cumulative total
1940	21	16	16
1950	23	18	34
1960	23	18	52
1970	25	19	71
1980	17	13	84
1990	20	16	100
Total	129	100	

An Empirical Overview of Civil Wars and Their Termination

Perhaps the most common observation since the end of the Cold War has been that, while interstate wars continue to decline in frequency, civil wars and ethnic conflicts are on the rise. Examining the number of civil wars that began in each decade, as shown in Table 1.1, we find no real pattern of a decrease or increase in this type of conflict. Between 1940 and 2005 there were a total of 130 civil wars.[4] Of these, 11 were ongoing as of 2008 and 2 (Sudan and the Philippines) "ended" only recently; these 13 cases were dropped from the statistical analysis.[5] The average number of intrastate wars that started in each decade is about 22, with a high of 25 new wars in the 1970s and a low of 17 in the 1980s.

If we examine the number of civil wars ended per decade, we do see that the 1990s saw far more wars ending than in previous decades. Table 1.2 highlights the increase in peace that followed the collapse of the Soviet Union and the end of U.S.-Soviet rivalry. In the 1990s 37 civil wars, or one-third of all wars that began during the entire period (1940–1999), came to an end. Most civil wars were ended by a military victory (79 wars, or 70 percent), followed by negotiated settlements (22 wars, or 19 percent), with cease-fires/stalemates (12 wars, or 11 percent) accounting for the fewest terminations. During this period, military victories were nearly four times more common than negotiated settlements and seven times more common than cease-fires/stalemates. However, when civil war termination types are broken down by decade, some interesting trends emerge:[6]

TABLE 1.2
Number of Civil Wars Ended in Each Decade, 1940–1990

Decade	Number	Percent of all civil wars (1940–1990)	Cumulative total
1940	13	12	12
1950	20	18	30
1960	14	12	42
1970	21	19	61
1980	8	7	68
1990	37	33	101
Total	113	101	

Note: Due to rounding, the percent and cumulative totals exceed 100.

Figure 1.1 shows that the manner in which civil wars end has changed dramatically since 1940. Whereas military victory was the dominant mode of ending civil war for most of the period—ending from between three-fourths of and all wars up through the 1980s—by the 1990s military victory ended only four out of ten such conflicts. Moreover, while negotiated settlements ended only a handful of wars between 1940 and 1989 (a total of 7), by the 1990s they were just as common as victories, accounting for 41 percent of all civil wars ended in that decade. A total of 37 wars ended in the 1990s, including 15 ended by negotiated settlement, 15 by military victory, and 7 by a cease-fire/stalemate.

The data in table 1.2 and figure 1.1 raise two immediate questions. First, what was it about the 1990s that might account for the increase in civil wars ending by negotiated settlement? Second, if ending civil wars by negotiated settlement has become the preferred policy (as shown clearly in fig. 1.1), should it remain so?

Two factors can explain the increase in peace observed in the 1990s. First, the end of the Cold War deprived the United States and Soviet Union of the incentive to provide cheap (or free) arms to combatants in proxy wars. Even for those combatants who wished to continue fighting, this provided an unavoidable lull in hostility during which new sources of revenue to support further weapons acquisitions could be arranged (e.g., in Sierra Leone and Angola). Second, as the sole remaining superpower, the United States came under increasing pressure to take moral responsibility for ongoing civil wars, as it possessed the diplomatic, eco-

**Percentage of wars
ended by type**

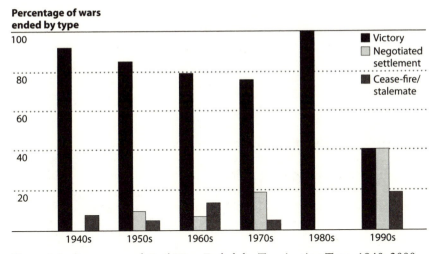

Figure 1.1. Percentage of Civil Wars Ended, by Termination Type, 1940–2000

nomic, or military capacity to halt many such conflicts outright. This pressure, which has continued to exist, encouraged the United States (and some of its allies) to intervene in order to stop the progress of ongoing civil wars. The positive case for intervention arose especially with regard to conflicts where the benefits of a resolution were expected to be high (e.g., those like the former Yugoslavia in the early 1990s, whose destructiveness threatened a U.S. national interest, such as stability in Europe), or to conflicts where the costs of achieving a resolution were expected to be low, such as Somalia in 1993.

The question of whether a general policy of intervening to halt civil wars by negotiation is good policy is at the center of the present inquiry. While there are a number of arguments for ending civil wars by negotiated settlement, two in particular stand out: a negotiated settlement would result in (1) fewer deaths than a war ended by decisive victory,[7] and (2) a reduced likelihood of the need for military intervention by third parties facilitating the negotiations (and for volunteering postwar reconstruction resources). According to the logic of the first argument, without a settlement the combatants would go on killing each other, perhaps even escalating the quality of violence along with the quantity. By negotiating an armistice followed by settlement, negotiated settlements should therefore save a greater number of lives than could be preserved by allowing combatants to fight to a decisive outcome. The logic of the second argument is that the economic costs of postwar reconstruction can be shared more easily—and sustained without a loss of public support—than can the costs in soldiers' lives. Although both cash and lives represent real costs, citizens experience the price of lost loved ones in a much more intense and direct manner than they experience the opportunity costs associated with a larger aid package. States therefore have a strong interest in limiting costs to those of an economic sort (and perhaps a risk of diplomatic prestige or reputation) and will be more loath to risk the lives of soldiers, except in cases where leaders have calculated that a military operation will be low-risk (again, as the United States did in Somalia in 1993).

But there are problems with both arguments. If it is true, for example, that a war interrupted may save lives, it is equally true that combatants have strong incentives to avoid sharing power or other values with their adversaries. Furthermore, in the absence of committed intervention by a third party, combatants may simply use an armistice as an opportunity to recover and rearm in preparation for a future fight. In other words, negotiated settlements may have an increased likelihood of saving lives in the short term, but they may cost more lives in the long term. By contrast, decisive victories make rearming by the losing side improbable. In addition, if combatants nearing defeat cannot assume that a third party will be available to save them, they may give up sooner, thus sparing lives by shortening the war.[8]

The second argument for negotiated settlements as a preferred policy—regarding the reduced likelihood of the need for a third-party military force—seems stronger.[9] Nonetheless, the problem has been well canvassed both in theory[10] and in empirical studies: after an armistice is signed, combatants are sensitive not simply to the factual elements of commitments but also to their *credibility*. Because former combatants also understand the relative priority of lives over cash, this "commitment problem" focuses on each postwar actor's assessment of the likelihood that third parties will risk lives as well as cash in order to deter or punish defection from the terms of the settlement. It seems likely, in other words, that interested third parties who take measures to lower their risk of military intervention may, ipso facto, signal their lack of commitment and, again ipso facto, increase the likelihood of defection from the contract and reignition of the war. It is important to note that this is not tantamount to saying that a credible commitment to risk lives is sufficient to bring about enduring peace; rather, it is one necessary factor in doing so.

The data analysis presented in chapter 4 lends considerable support to my critique of negotiated settlements as a default policy option, which holds that they do not in fact save lives as compared to decisive military victories.[11] Wars ended by military victory were nearly twice as likely to remain settled as those ended by a negotiated settlement or a cease-fire/

stalemate. Whereas only 13 percent (ten out of seventy-nine) of wars between 1940 and 2000 ending in military victories recurred, 23 percent (five out of twenty-two) of wars ending in negotiated settlements recurred, and 33 percent (four out of twelve) of wars that ended in cease-fires/stalemates recurred. Put differently, wars ended by negotiated settlement are two times more likely to reignite than those ended by military victory.

Embedded within this finding about the relative stability of military victories is another striking fact: victories achieved by rebels (as opposed to governments) are the most stable. In other words, if enduring peace is to be preferred as an outcome, the winning party matters. While 17 percent of wars (eight out of forty-seven) ending in a government victory recurred (less than negotiated settlements and cease-fires/stalemates), only 6 percent of wars (two out of thirty-two) won by rebels recurred. While we should logically expect cease-fires/stalemates to be the most precarious of all termination profiles, surprisingly, the data show that there is no statistical difference between a negotiated settlement and a stalemate breaking down. This is not to say that the terms of negotiated settlements are evolving and improving, or that this finding may not change. Nevertheless, the results of the present study and of others confirm this state of affairs.[12]

Definitions

This section introduces the key terms of the book, including both what is meant and what is *not* meant by my use of the expressions "civil war," "military victory," "negotiated settlement," "security sector," "enduring peace," and others.

Civil War

A civil war is a fight that occurs within the boundaries of an internationally recognized state. There must be at least two sets of organized combatants with the capacity to physically harm one another. According to these parameters, genocide, in which one side murders the other (where the "other" is generally unarmed—or armed but not organized), would thus not be considered a civil war in this analysis. In addition, one of the combatants must be a state (since the focus of analysis here is the civil war, I typically refer to the state as either the "incumbent government" or the "center"). This would preclude consideration of communal conflicts in which the state is not involved in the actual fighting (although it might be involved in trying to end the fighting). Finally, there must be a substantial number of deaths over a defined period. The threshold of deaths used here—at one thousand battle-related deaths per year on average—is that used by the Correlates of War Data Set.[13] Thus, to cite one important example, the conflict in Northern Ireland would not be included in the analysis, although lessons about terminating violence might nevertheless be learned from that case.

Military Victory

Military victories are situations in which one side in a war is defeated, with the other party emerging as the victor. Although the losing side is not necessarily required to formally accept defeat, there is nevertheless an understanding that it will not have the privilege to be part of the government unless the victor allows it to do so. The victor, in other words, determines the type and composition of any postwar government and will determine whether and how survivors on the defeated side will participate.

My analysis further disaggregates military victory into two types: rebel victory and government victory. Rebel victories occur when the opposition defeats the incumbent government, as in the case of Bangladesh when it successfully seceded from Pakistan. In contrast, government victories involve cases in which the state defeats an opposition group. China's defeat of Tibet, the Greek government's defeat of communist rebels, and Sri Lanka's recent triumph over the Tamil Tigers are examples of this type.

Negotiated Settlement

While military victories leave governance to the winning side, negotiated settlements allow both sides to participate and call for a permanent cessation of violence. Negotiated settlements involve agreement on how the parties will "explicitly regulate or resolve their basic incompatibility."[14] They typically include provisions about the future composition of the government, elections, disarmament and demobilization of the fighters, refugee repatriation, and issues of justice, human rights, and accountability during the course of the war. Not all peace agreements contain all of these provisions. In fact, most do not. What they have in common, however, is a shared agreement to end the fighting and an understanding that each party will participate in a future government. Examples of civil wars ended by negotiated settlements include the Salvadoran civil war, which was ended by the Chapultepec Accords, and the first Lebanese civil war, which was ended by the Tai'f Accords.

Cease-fire/Stalemate

Similar to negotiated settlements, cease-fires/stalemates involve a common understanding and agreement that the violence must be halted. However, whereas negotiated settlements aim to establish a permanent cessation of hostilities, cease-fires/stalemates are nothing more than an agreement to stop the violence. Although one or both sides might desire a permanent end, the agreement does not stipulate this. Rather, it simply states that each side will cease firing on the enemy. In some instances, this might require handing in weapons or disclosing caches in close proximity to the battlefields, but it also might not. Each side may retain the capacity to reengage in battle should conditions warrant such action. Furthermore, cease-fires/stalemates stipulate nothing about the postwar environment, largely because the war has not formally ended. Cases of this sort include the two wars fought in the early 1990s in Georgia between the Georgian government and proponents of independence for Abkhazia and South Ossetia. Both wars were ended by formal cease-fires.

Enduring Peace

Peace is a tricky concept, much like power. One knows it when one sees it, but it is difficult to define generally or theoretically. In this book, when I refer to peace I mean (1) a cessation of violence, but I add (2) a general lack of willingness to pursue economic, political, or social objectives by means of violence. A cease-fire or stalemate would therefore not be the same thing as peace because one or both parties remain willing to pursue their objectives by means of organized violence, although the capability to do so may be temporarily lacking.[15]

By extension, then, enduring peace would be a peace that lasts at least ten or, ideally, twenty years. Similar to "peace" as defined above, however, I add a second condition or meaning to the term "enduring" (which in general implies only a duration or time component). An "enduring peace" in this analysis means not only peace that lasts a long time, but also peace that holds the possibility of an improved quality of life for *all* survivors of a civil war. By quality of life I mean minimalist conceptions of personal security and sustenance. This definition makes sense because a lack of the means to achieve personal security and sustenance perhaps stands as the most common reason individuals (followed by groups) choose to take up arms in the first place. War is a nasty, dirty, difficult business, and rational human beings seek to avoid it when possible. But when faced with the threat of death or arbitrary imprisonment or starvation, they will often pursue a small chance at winning a violent contest rather than refuse to take up arms while still suffering death or the loss of loved ones as a consequence.

Enduring peace is therefore the goal an ancient philosopher such as Plato might have identified as "the good life." It is an ambitious goal in many cases, not least because people often group themselves into imaginary communities and arrogate *only* to those communities the right to obtain such security and prosperity as is available. But it is the only goal that makes sense to pursue because, as will become clear as we proceed, falling short of enduring peace involves the prospect of recurring war. And the destructive consequences of civil wars today—even wars in distant, underdeveloped countries—can no longer be contained. Their impact causes harm far beyond the conflict zone in both time and space.

What Is the "Security Sector"?

While there is no common definition of the security sector, according to the United Nations Development Programme (UNDP) the security sector refers to institutions that have the authority to order the threat of force or use force to protect the state and civilians.[16]

When the security sector is discussed, it is usually referenced in tandem with the justice sector. So, for example, a recent working paper highlighted six different categories of actors that fall under the justice and security sectors. These include (1) criminal justice organizations; (2) management and oversight bodies; (3) military and intelligence services; (4) noncore institutions (e.g., customs agencies); (5) nonstatutory security forces (militias not sponsored by the state); and (6) civil society.[17] Other publications do not include the fifth and sixth elements, yet they claim that the nonstatutory forces are nevertheless "very relevant to SSR priorities in many countries."[18]

As is evident, security sector reform (SSR) is often linked with institutions that "as one integrated whole are responsible for the provision of an accountable, equitable, effective, and rights respecting public service for the state and the people living in it."[19]

To date, policy makers attempting to undertake SSR have sought three objectives. The first task is to restore order and neutralize nonlegal, nonstatutory insurgents. The second task is to rebuild the security forces such that these forces can take responsibility for the maintenance of public order. The third task is to build security-related institutions that monitor and support the security forces. These include interior and defense ministries, national and local police agencies, and an effective judicial sector. The ultimate goal of SSR is governance and, at a minimum, the ability to maintain order through the use of force, if necessary. Furthermore, SSR is in general envisioned as a long-term development project, one that extends well past one round of elections, resulting in the "building up of accountable, efficient and effective security forces."[20]

Although SSR has been conceptualized and promoted as part of a comprehensive effort to mitigate violence and promote development and good governance, in this book I define the security sector in a narrower manner. I focus on the armed elements of the security sector, especially the agents capable of imposing order *by force*. Depending on the particular historical and institutional exigencies in a given state, these might include military, paramilitary, and police forces (those authorized to bear arms).

In terms of defining SSR for the analysis, this is done in one of two ways, depending on the method at hand. For the statistical analysis, I relied mainly on data compiled by Barbara Walter for her data set on third-party guarantees.[21] These data include whether a given negotiated settlement provided for the reconstitution and restructuring of a country's armed forces, while in others it might include the full (re)constitution and training of forces, in essence reform of the security sector. Each of the cases and its respective security forces were assessed independently and then coded for (1) whether the agreement included provisions for a military pact, and (2) whether that pact was implemented. In Mozambique, a new national army was created that included equal numbers of forces from each side, while in Cambodia, the Paris Peace Agreement mandated troop and equipment reductions on both sides. The second way SSR is defined and operationalized is more particular to the case studies themselves. In the four case studies, SSR is assessed in terms of the forces that were in place and those that were being demanded by the combatants at the end of the war. So, for example, in the case of the El Salvador, security sector reform involved dismantling the repressive government security forces that were loyal to the government and creating a new national police force; in Sudan, reform of the existing army was seen as crucial (yet did not happen). The point here is that different states have different configurations for which institutions are responsible for imposing order, and therefore which aspects of the security sector need to be reformed. As noted above, the security sector is often bundled up with judicial institutions and, to the extent that we have seen SSR in action, the lines between sectors have been blurred. By restricting analysis to the core of the security sector—the capacity to prevent and cause physical harm—we obtain a clearer picture of the relative utility of different institutional actors at various times in the reconstruction process. We may think of postwar environments as the first stage in a long process that may eventually eliminate many of the soldiers and police necessary or useful at this early stage.

Methods

Two primary methods are used to assess postwar environments and enduring peace. First, I employ statistical methods, using a variety of well-vetted databases (some "off the shelf" and others compiled by me) to both explore and test key propositions regarding civil war terminations and long-term outcomes since 1940. The statistical analysis performs three functions. First, it assesses the type of termination in relation to the durability of peace: negotiated settlements correlate with war recurrence, while military victories by rebels do not. It also assesses whether there is a correlation between different types of outcomes in relation to longer-term changes in levels of autocracy and democracy, as well as economic growth, over two decades. Finally, the statistical analysis gives a preliminary assessment of whether reforms to the security sector provide a plausible alternative to third-party guarantees in relation to war recurrence. These series of tests are not to be taken as proving causality, so much as to see whether there is a positive correlation in support of the proposition that a settlement needs to promise credibly both benefits and harms to sustain peace.

Although we can infer causality from these, statistical associations by themselves are not definitive. I therefore use a series of qualitative case studies to assess further the causal logic of my argument regarding durable peace following civil war.[22] Part of the statistical analysis sets up a three-cornered fight in which third-party guarantees are compared with SSR against the empirical data, while the case studies are structured as two-cornered fights with the argument about security sector reform and the need for a balance of harm and benefit set against historical evidence. These case studies do not constitute three-cornered fights because none of the selected cases involves third parties tasked with the job of enforcing the peace (as a way to control for this factor). In sum, because SSR is such a complex and multidimensional phenomenon, for which there are no direct indicators available in any existing data set, the statistical analysis and its use of proxies should be seen as a plausibility probe, while the case studies allow for the study of SSR in particular, but controlled, historical contexts. The combination of both suggests that the argument advanced here about security sector reform and the notion of benefits and harms is productive for further scholarly analysis and policy in keeping civil wars ended. In other words, SSR should be seen as a policy recommendation strongly supported by the available evidence.

The chosen case studies focus on how civil war ended and what occurred after the initial fighting stopped. They include three countries and four cases: El Salvador (1980–1992), Uganda (1980–1984), and Sudan (1955–1972 and 1983–2005). They were chosen because they include variation on both independent (type of termination) and dependent (recurrence) variables. Additionally, third parties were not involved in enforcing the peace. I chose the Salvadoran civil war as a "least likely" case because it ended in a negotiated settlement that has, in fact, endured. This case study is crucial because the negotiated settlement in question contained comprehensive provisions for SSR, including the building of a new national police force. What is striking about this case is that although economic grievances over land distribution and poverty were key to this fight, these issues were not central features of the settlement. The new government guaranteed a sufficient balance of benefit and harm to former combatants. Uganda is a case in which enduring peace resulted from a rebel victory. This case is crucial because it demonstrates that despite being victorious over its opponent, the new government gradually opened the political space. Consequently, not only did peace emerge, but the government also became less autocratic over time, inviting former combatants into the administration. Sudan is the most complicated case in the study. Not only is it the longest and most brutal of the conflicts examined here, but its civil war also reignited. I contend that the breakdown was due in part to a lack of SSR (i.e., no mutual harm) and argue that the most recent settlement (the Comprehensive Peace Agreement signed in 2005) is in danger of failing, in part because the provisions outlining the reform of the security sector are not being carried out.

I do not examine cases of cease-fire/stalemate, for two reasons. First, there are so few cases of cease-fires/stalemates that it is difficult to generalize about them either statistically or theoretically. Focusing on cases of military victory and negotiated settlements therefore seemed more useful, both on a theoretical level and in terms of generating policy recommendations. Second, because length is an issue, I felt that the combination of a statistical analysis and four cases would sufficiently test the validity of my theory as compared to competing arguments.

Data used in the case studies come from secondary and some primary sources. All four cases are old enough that there are now excellent secondary historical accounts of their events. Yet each case remains sufficiently contemporary that accounts of events in local newspapers, speeches of key actors, and other sorts of data that might be needed are readily accessible.

Why Study Civil War Outcomes?

Civil wars generally do not concentrate their destructive impact to the same degree that the world wars of the last century did. Moreover, they are unlikely to involve the use of nuclear weapons, though chemical have been used in some civil wars, including conflicts that took place recently. Yet, collectively and over time, the civil wars that began and ended in the twentieth century are just as deadly, and in some cases, more so.

Civil wars cannot be dismissed as mere "remnants of war."[23] They have been and continue to be by far the most common type of large-scale killing among humans and have demonstrated the capacity to cause disruption not only on the local level (as in the Great Lakes region of Africa) but also in the global arena (as in Afghanistan). Although contrary to some conventional wisdom, the number of civil wars has not increased precipitously since the end of the Cold War. Rather, what has increased is our awareness of the particularly destructive nature of civil wars. This comes alongside an understanding that technology has made the world smaller and closer, a situation that allows more people in more regions to feel the effects of civil wars. We now recognize that, although some civil wars take place far from the advanced-industrial world, those distant locales are much closer today for all intents and purposes, and that the violence coming from far away can have a serious impact on our own health and well-being.[24] Afghanistan is the most obvious example. After decades of violence that pitted the Cold War blocs against one another, the end of the Cold War allowed the rise of an extremist and isolated government that harbored terrorists bent on destroying those it viewed as enemies to its beliefs and traditions. The global war on terrorism is rooted in what was once a local fight that became international, then local, and then international again.

Given that civil wars have the capacity to disrupt regional and even international stability, it is incumbent upon us to understand how to end these wars—to end them constructively and to end them for good. This book is dedicated to that understanding.

Conclusion

In sum, this book is about how civil wars end, and what both combatants and interested or well-meaning third parties can do to facilitate enduring peace. A small amount of the large body of literature on civil wars focuses on a possible connection between how a war is ended (e.g., by outright victory of one side or another, or by negotiated settlement) and whether an initial peace endures. My argument is that most of the work done toward theorizing about the likelihood that civil wars will stay ended has been initiated by policy makers who are either too busy solving immediate problems to generalize the solutions they innovate or too institutionally or organizationally unfamiliar with the security sector to develop and execute an ideal termination and reconstruction strategy.

The theory presented here as vital to enduring peace is a settlement that provides in the first place a credible threat of harm or punishment to those who defect from the treaty, and in the second place a credible delivery of benefits. This represents the theory of "mutual benefit and mutual harm." As such, my policy recommendations focus on SSR first, followed by a closely linked and targeted set of economic, political, and perhaps even social reforms.

Plan of the Book

Chapter 2 introduces both a brief history of SSR to date as well as an analysis of competing explanations for why negotiated settlements might fail. I outline the logic of competing arguments and then present my own explanation for why negotiated settlements have tended to fail, and why military victories have tended to succeed in producing enduring peace.

Chapter 3 introduces the theory of mutual benefits and mutual harms and spells out the logic behind why some settlements are more stable than others.

Chapter 4 focuses on broad empirical features of civil wars, including how to think about what civil wars cost and a large-n analysis of the relationship between civil war termination profiles and the duration, reignition intensity, widening potential, postconflict political liberalization, and post-conflict economic development associated with civil wars. The book's main hypotheses are given an initial, large-n test here.

Chapters 5–8 explore four historical cases of civil war and trace key actors, conflict issues, conflict terminations, and postconflict outcomes. Chapter 5 includes a study of El Salvador from 1980 to 1992. Uganda is examined in chapter 6. In chapter 7 I analyze the civil war in Sudan that took place from 1955 to 1972, and in chapter 8 I examine Sudan's relapse into civil war from 1983 to 2005. Taken together, the case study analyses provide a second test of my theory of mutual harm and mutual benefit. On balance, SSR emerges as a clear policy option where enduring peace is the desired outcome.

Finally, chapter 9 presents the conclusions of the book. It includes a discussion of the theoretical and policy implications of the findings as well as practical analyses of the U.S. engagement in Iraq. Not only does this case have significant importance to policymaking in the United States and elsewhere, but it also offers additional insights into and support of the theory that the other cases do not. The discussion of Iraq shows the centrality of security in why and how that country succumbed to civil war after Saddam Hussein was ousted from power. It further shows how the United States and its coalition allies attempted security sector reform, and how concern for the immediate short-term security environment overwhelmed the struggle for establishing more permanent security institutions. In addition, the conclusion includes my thoughts on the future prospects of stability, democracy, and prosperity in Sudan.

Civil War Termination in Perspective

PRIOR TO WORLD WAR II, most civil wars ended when one side decisively defeated its rival, which surrendered, was destroyed, or, more rarely, fled. Sometimes the winning side had help from the outside; at other times it accomplished victory using only its own resources. Since 1940, and particularly since 1990, negotiations aimed at preventing the defeat or destruction of a given party have become increasingly common to the extent that, as of the time of this writing, they constitute a new norm.

A good first question would then be: "What does a typical negotiated settlement entail?" An examination of postwar negotiated settlements confirms that beyond the immediate goal of halting violence, the objective of most such settlements is to establish a solid, representative set of institutions with power shared between warring factions. In most cases, negotiated settlements include extensive provisions for establishing executives, legislatures, free and fair elections, judiciaries, and the demobilization, demilitarization, and reintegration (DDR) of armed forces. The goal of this process is to reintegrate soldiers into society by giving them cash and other resources. Security sector reform is generally given only secondary consideration, or, if provisions regarding the police and armed forces are written into the agreements, SSR implementation is backed with anemic resources. Moreover, and as the above makes obvious, the goals of DDR and SSR very often tend to be in direct opposition, since DDR aims to reduce the supply of security personnel, whereas SSR aims to retrain and retain them.[1]

As the following pages make clear, SSR is a crucial element to enduring and constructive peace. According to a recent Organization for Economic Cooperation and Development (OECD) report, "The challenge of ensuring [the] security of states and their populations is both most urgent and most difficult in the context of societies seeking to 'rebuild' following war where there is a risk of recreating the conditions that gave rise to the violence in the first place."[2] The results of this research indicate that long-term development of a country is more likely to fail without reform of the security situation. Moreover, the report provides extensive guidance on the recommendation that security reform ought to be developed indigenously, keeping local culture and customs in mind: "As an approach to building stable and democratic civil-security relations, the foreign-brokered peace process is fundamentally flawed.... Donors have tended to focus on short-term objectives, such as securing an early end to hostilities, followed by demobilization, rather than reintegration of ex-combatants, reprofessionalization of the armed forces, and building of institutions of democratic oversight."[3]

Although discussions of DDR are common in academic and policy treatises, SSR continues to receive little consideration in academic research and has only recently become a policy priority among affected policy makers.[4] Although the concept of SSR was coined in the late 1990s, it was not until the U.S. defeat of the Taliban in Afghanistan in 2001 that policy makers set up a fund explicitly for SSR. In doing so, they finally recognized the "vicious circle of security and reconstruction/development,"[5] a situation in which a lack of reconstruction and development progress intensifies security problems, and in which security problems further inhibit meaningful reconstruction and development.

Paradoxically, it was international financial institutions and not NATO or the U.S. military that took the lead on SSR. This is because both the International Monetary Fund (IMF) and the World Bank were chiefly responsible for the economic reconstruction of Afghanistan, and each came to realize through painful experience that SSR would need to be a crucial component of future economic development and responsible governance.

In a 1989 report on sub-Saharan Africa, the World Bank began to stress "governance" as it related to economic growth. According to the report, "underlying the litany of Africa's development problems is a crisis of governance."[6] Aid was failing to promote development due to poor governance, weak political institutions, and inadequate rule of law.

Although the World Bank shifted to focus on issues of governance, that focus came to center on the narrower issues of corruption, lack of transparency, and budgeting. For the security sector, that change meant smaller and more transparent budgets, premised on the idea that large, independent militaries were somehow inimical to economic development.

At the same time, the IMF began to take notice of how a lack of development of the security sector in areas of responsibility impeded its development objectives. In 1989 the managing director of the IMF, Michael Camdessus, argued:

> We publish statistics on public expenditures showing the importance of military expenditure in the budgets and that helps to show the tremendous amount of unproductive spending.... We look at this problem in our discussions with government but taking due consideration, as we are obliged to according to our guidelines for conditionality, of the social and political conditions of the country. We put a finger on this question, and we try to do everything to con-

vince each government that, at the end of the day, a growing and vibrant economy and the productive employment of the population are their best defense. And that finally, in having such economies, you also have the safest way of promoting domestic tranquility.[7]

Excessive spending on armed forces was thus implicated as being unproductive and was said to contribute to instability. At this point, postwar reconstruction success was thought to depend simply on austere budgets and better oversight. Despite a shift in emphasis on governance, reforming the security sector was not yet a key goal for either the IMF or the World Bank.[8] In fact, the economic stabilization programs led to greater instability: "Cuts introduced to resolve fiscal crises and satisfy donors have aggravated the crises of fragile regimes and of their military and security establishments, all the more where military spending has already fallen due to economic decline, resulting in 'demilitarization by default.'"[9]

It became apparent that the emphasis needed to shift away from military budgets and toward the "processes by which resources are allocated to and within the security sector."[10] One international organization that has acknowledged the link between SSR and effective governance is the OECD, whose Development Assistance Committee (DAC) has moved beyond expenditures alone and has sought to improve the performance of the security sector.[11] In its policy statements, the DAC stresses that SSR is a key factor in preventing violent conflict. According to DAC chairman Richard Manning:

> To work effectively on SSR, whole-of-government frameworks and mechanisms are needed—both in donor and developing countries—in order to harness the range of policy and funding instruments available into a common effort. This range includes development co-operation, diplomacy, trade, finance and investment, and defence. Donors also need to develop comprehensive development programming strategies to help with coherence and avoid piecemeal efforts, where possible. And partner country ownership and buy-in is critical. Donors must align work in these contexts behind the developing country's approaches. All external actors need to have a keen understanding of the context and history of partner countries and carefully consider regional dynamics. This requires long-term analysis and engagement.[12]

While it is true that both the World Bank and the IMF have come to recognize in theory the importance of the security sector in achieving their development goals, it is equally true that in practice their policies have tended to fixate on economic expenditures and budgets. The OECD's DAC appears to be the first international financial institution to fully appreciate the role of SSR in its development programs.

The United Nations and SSR

Although international financial institutions first made the link between SSR, economic development, and governance, the United Nations (UN) was also becoming more aware of the link. International military efforts in the mid-1990s were guided by the doctrine of "Peace Support Operations" (PSO), which was a product of Britain's Ministry of Defense. This doctrine located peace operations along a continuum and provided guidelines for intervening forces. Within that context, intervention was seen as progressing from peacemaking to peacekeeping and finally to peacebuilding. SSR was part of the final phase of peacebuilding, consisting primarily of DDR.[13] Success on the part of the intervener relied not only on the attitude of the recipient country toward outside intervention but also on the development of a consensus within that country on the desire for peace. More specifically, a key factor was the desire for peace over other valued ends, such as total control over a government's distribution of resources following a war.

Secretary General Boutros Boutros-Ghali incorporated this PSO doctrine into UN operations in 1995. At this stage, there existed no indication that the United Nations viewed SSR as necessary for the prevention of violence.[14]

But real-world problems eroded the promise of PSO. The start and stop of wars in Angola, Liberia, and Sierra Leone revealed that as conflicts start, end, and begin again, any original consensus breaks down. (Very often, moderate political elites are slain or forced to flee.) Peace was thus not always a natural outcome, and peacebuilding proved to be elusive.

The new doctrine soon came under attack. Critics charged that mismanagement of the security sector was a primary cause of instability, arguing that the topic could no longer be ignored. Consequently, they recommended that the United Nations become more proactive in promoting peace and that it needed to address structural forces. Such a shift in focus included integrating SSR earlier in the process to prevent not only escalation to war but also the backsliding into war that seemed to occur so frequently.

The United Nations has undertaken sustained efforts to analyze its past failures. In 2000 Under-Secretary General Lakhdar Brahimi convened a panel on peace operations. The panel's statement, commonly referred to as the Brahimi Report, called for "a doctrinal shift in the use of civilian police and related rule of law elements in peace operations that emphasizes a team approach to upholding the rule of law and respect for human rights and helping communities coming out of a conflict to achieve national reconciliation." It also called for "bringing demobilization and reintegration programs into the assessed budgets of complex peace operations for the first phase of an operation in order to facilitate the rapid disassembly of fighting factions and reduce the likelihood of resumed conflict."[15] The recommendations of the Brahimi Report represented a new awareness of the importance of SSR in the international military community, while they contrast sharply with the peacekeeping doctrine articulated by Secretary General Boutros-Ghali in 1995.

The United Nations has followed up on the advice of the report. For instance, the Bureau of Crisis Prevention and Recovery (BCPR) is a new program under the United Nations Development Programme. As part of this initiative, the UNDP created a task force within BCPR devoted to Justice and Security Sector Reform (JSSR). The JSSR task force staff is small and continues to formulate its strategy as well as a roadmap for what the UN ought to do in terms of justice and security sector reform.

Although it is too soon to be certain of what the JSSR task force will yield, the fact that the United Nations chose to create this entity is a good sign that SSR will be given proper consideration by the UN in the future. According to BCPR, human development and human security cannot be achieved without effective justice and security structures.[16]

Although the UN has historically been hesitant to engage in the reform and restructuring of militaries, more and more countries are demanding help in this domain. The key question remains whether the international community has the stomach for such work and whether BCPR can carry it out.

At least three tensions exist in the current formulation of SSR at the United Nations, all of which can be observed in a statement made by the agency established to handle it:

> The Bureau for Crisis Prevention and Recovery (BCPR) assists UNDP country offices to set up and provide a quicker and more effective response for natural disaster reduction, justice and security sector reform, small arms reduction, disarmament and demobilization, mine action, conflict prevention and peacebuilding, and recovery. BCPR strives to ensure UNDP plays a pivotal role in transitions between relief and development; promotes linkages between UN peace and security and development objectives; and enhances governments' responsibilities and technical and national capacities to manage crisis and post-conflict situations.[17]

First, BCPR is dedicated to achieving quick response times in crisis situations. SSR, however, requires long-term investment and resources for it to be successful. Second, SSR is only one part of BCPR's mandate, which includes a whole host of pressing issues: natural disaster reduction, small-arms reduction, disarmament and demobilization, mine action, conflict prevention, and peacebuilding. Furthermore, SSR is linked to justice reform. Given the international community's past reluctance to engage in military reform, a potential problem is that a disproportionate share of resources might be directed at the justice sector—more so than at the security sector. While reform of the justice sector is certainly vital, our task is to determine when in a reconstruction timeline it is most appropriate to shift resource priority from security to justice. The five defense attorneys murdered while working on the case of Saddam Hussein should serve as a case in point.

Explaining Civil War Recurrence

A survey of the existing literature on civil war recurrence reveals that SSR is largely missing in the dialogue. The literature is myopically focused on negotiated settlements, a termination type that until recently made up only a fraction of all civil war settlements. Although the literature considers postwar institutions more generally, reform of *security* institutions is largely ignored. Instead, the literature places great emphasis on the expectation of the international community of states to serve as the guarantor of peace and security in societies riddled with conflict and violence. Finally, the extant research tends to examine the immediate aftermath of the war. Or, if a study does examine a longer time frame, the analysis typically ends with the first round of elections. Studies of the longer-term consequences of civil war for democratization and economic development are rare.

Resources and Fear

Most scholars of civil war termination rely on the motivational factors that explain why wars begin and, by extension, why they end. Often these stimuli are resources and fear.[18] Negotiated agreements tend to emphasize resources over fear. The resource question is dealt with empirically and theoretically in the literature with regard to two perspectives: (1) lack of resources and (2) greed for resources. This is true particularly with regard to natural resources. Inequality in resource distribution—or greed for resources—drives two schools of thought on resource-related causes of civil wars.[19] Theoretical approaches to the fear factor derive from interstate and intrastate theory. While one school of thought emerges from concern over physical safety at the end of interstate wars and also at the point of state collapse, the other school revolves around fear for what the future may hold. Both of the fear schools are driven by uncertainty.[20]

Under the resource rubric, the first school of resource "lack" (which generally comprises part of the grievance school in civil wars literature) has been largely researched over the last four decades. This body of work concludes that inequality in income, representation, land, or other resources propels civil war.[21] Later works, however, have suggested that different types of civil wars have different causes.[22] These elements make up the lion's share of what negotiations redress.

A more recent (though widely disputed) claim under the resource rubric is that most civil wars are driven by greed. The "greed school" has been a part of empirical research on civil wars in the last decade and a part of interstate war theory. Introduced by Charles Glaser to explain what drives interstate war strategy, this school of thought was empirically developed by researchers at the World Bank in the mid-1990s to clarify civil wars.[23] According to this argument, civil wars are in essence the product of greed. In this context, governments and opposition groups fight over the spoils of the state. The most famous spoil was diamonds, which came to be referred to as "conflict" diamonds. Disputes in parts of Africa were framed as clashes over the control of diamond mines and the revenue they generate. While oil, drugs, and other natural resources also fell under the greed rubric, it was conflict diamonds that caught the world's attention and prompted the international community to deal with tracking and controlling the distribution of these war spoils as a way to terminate civil wars. Here, it was understood that an ability to reduce revenues from these resources would further yield an ability reduce participants' capacity to wage war.[24]

Although this research did a great service in calling attention to the role of resources in starting and perpetuating civil wars, it suffered in two related ways. First, the explanation was developed in reaction to cases in Africa that perplexed policy makers—most notably Angola, Liberia, and Sierra Leone. There is no denying that in these cases, resources—especially diamonds—helped to fund the fight. Even in this context, however, other motivations were in play. Furthermore, in other cases of civil war beyond Africa, greed played virtually no role; resources had almost nothing to do with why the wars broke out or with how they should be ended. Cases in which motivations other than resources were prominent include the wars in the former Yugoslavia and in Chechnya in the 1990s.

A different and perhaps more applicable argument for SSR lies in the explanation that wars stem from the particular motivation of insecurity or fear (as was the case in the former Yugoslavia and Chechnya). In these and other cases, what drove the belligerents to kill one another was the basic notion of fear. In the literature on civil war origins and termination, fear was explained by way of the "security dilemma." First fully developed by Robert Jervis for work on interstate wars and later applied to civil wars by Barry Posen and James Fearon,[25] the security dilemma describes situations of state collapse (analogous to anarchy in the international system) in which each side's efforts to increase its own security inadvertently threaten the other side. Such threats may in turn motivate the enemy to arm, thus creating a spiral of arming and countermeasures that lead to the outbreak of war, or to a more destructive version of an existing war.[26]

With its driving force of fear, the "spiral model" possesses a powerful logic and does seem to apply to many cases. At the same time, we can identify many other cases in which fear was not the primary motivating factor, or in which fear only partially motivated the belligerents. There, resource lack or greed may have played a partial or significant role as well.

Whether the belligerents are motivated by resource scarcity or by greed for resources, fear has important implications for how to end wars and to keep them ended.[27] If the sides are disadvantaged in terms of resources or are simply greedy, then offering inducements such as control over a mine or a portion of revenues from oil output might be incentive enough to persuade them to end the war and to not reignite it. By contrast, where fear is the core issue, material inducements on their own would prove ineffective as a means to demobilize and disarm a given group or faction. Here, the belligerents would need some sort of security guarantees. In the short term perhaps, such assurances might come from third parties, while in the long term this sense of security might be tied to a belief that the state's police and armed forces will protect them.

In cases where the belligerents are motivated by resource scarcity, greed *and* fear are trickier. They are also more likely to be empirically true. This represents a fundamental oversight in most negotiated settlements and a looming problem for ending civil wars. Most civil wars are fought by belligerents who possess mixed motivations, with individual fighters and groups of fighters likely driven by a combination of greed and fear. In this context, actor motivations are neither trivial nor mutually exclusive. Second, even if combatants begin to fight out of fear, control over resources during the war may then turn them into greedy fighters as the war proceeds.[28] If the war began as a result of either a lack of resources, other grievances, or greed, then the actual fighting is likely to produce a good deal of hatred between the two sides, thus introducing an element of fear on the part of each side that will have to be addressed in order to resolve the war.[29] In other words, any long-lasting solution to a civil war must take into account both greed and fear.

In the next section, I assess previous explanations regarding both greed and fear. After first examining the literature that explains why negotiated settlements fail or succeed, I then turn to two explanations that account for why military victories fail or succeed. These are examined in light of how they address the dominant motivations for why belligerents might end a war and keep it ended. As will become evident, most explanations rely on one motivation or the other, which means that, as a tool for achieving enduring peace, they remain inadequate both conceptually and in terms of policy. Furthermore, because these alternative explanations examine why only one type of settlement succeeds or fails, they cannot be considered general explanations of the stability or fragility of the post–civil war environment.

Negotiated Settlement Failure and Success

When examining the termination of civil wars, one is quickly struck by the fact that negotiated settlements dominate scholarly writing and policymaking. Although the study of the end of civil wars has broadened to some extent—from how to get the parties to the table to how to implement peace agreements—the focus remains on negotiated settlements. This presents a problem for two reasons. First, as observed above, negotiated settlements are precarious; they are far more likely to result in another outbreak of violence than are other types of war terminations. Second, negotiated settlements are a more recent phenomenon, which will thus lead us to be less confident in the general applicability of any lessons learned from them. A more effective approach would be to examine all types of war termination—especially those that are successful—in order to learn more (and perhaps better) lessons that can be applied to current and future civil wars.

Three families of explanations illuminate why negotiated settlements fail to sustain peace following war. Roughly speaking, they investigate (1) the specific terms of settlement and whether these terms are flawed or ambiguous; (2) the process of settlement implementation; or (3) the structure of the environment in which the peace agreement is implemented. More specifically, the first area of consideration looks to the terms of peace agreements themselves, arguing either that elements within the settlement did not address fundamental contradictions that gave rise to violence in the first place or that the settlement included elements that produced an entirely new set of problems that in turn gave rise to new grievances. The second set of explanations argues that the process of implementing the agreement was flawed, which would have consequently led the parties to abandon the terms of the settlement and resume violence. Finally, the third collection of explanations examines the power structure of the environment and how third parties can help the belligerents overcome mutual fear and suspicion.

Flawed Terms of Settlement

Perhaps the most common argument for why peace agreements fail and war resumes is that the agreements themselves contain the seeds of the next war.[30] Because allocation of offices is so closely tied to prosperity and security in many places in the world, the fair and effective redistribution of offices—power sharing—has proven to be the undoing of many negotiated settlements. The more power sharing, so the argument goes, the more stable the peace will be.[31] That is to say, there will be sufficient political resources in place to ensure that grievances are addressed. Allocation of offices is not all that peace agreements have to accomplish, however. They must also establish procedures of justice and restitution, resettle refugees and internally displaced citizens, reestablish a functioning economy and markets, distribute resource revenues, and figure out what to do with former combatants. Many issues therefore exist that might give rise to resentment among the former belligerents.[32] If one side feels that power and resources have not been properly allocated as a result of the peace agreement, then it will likely become frustrated and will seek to change that balance by force, thereby reneging on the terms of the settlement.[33] The bottom line is that the terms of a peace agreement are deemed to hold the seeds of future conflict. Put simply, one must repair the agreements in order to ensure lasting peace.

There are at least two problems with this argument. First, it places too much faith in the autonomous power of "scraps of paper" and the institutions established and regulated by those documents. To be sure, signed agreements and institutions are only as strong as the support they receive from those parties who sign and use them. People alone have the power to make peace agreements matter and work. Thus, although the content is not irrelevant, the mechanisms in place to enforce the specific provisions of an agreement are equally as important as the actual details of the agreement.

On a second and related note, faith in peace agreements and in the resiliency of the institutions they create often causes well-meaning third parties to underestimate the deep-seated fears and anxieties that persist following a war. Roland Paris, a critic of "liberal institutions," encapsulates this problem well: "As with power-sharing pacts, however, electoral systems and constitutional checks on power are particularly difficult following civil war and generally fail to overcome the security dilemmas and fears that shape such transitions."[34] Ultimately, even the best-designed peace agreements will not stop former belligerents from taking up arms if they feel their environment remains insecure, or if at least one side believes it can do better by resorting to war rather than by upholding the terms of peace laid out by the settlement.[35] Bearing in mind that institutions failed to protect their interests and livelihood before the war, it does not come as a surprise that people have little faith in their ability to safeguard them after the war.

Furthermore, war is as likely to resume from the desire to control more of the economic markets and political institutions and from insecurity that might arise should the other side do so as well. This is something that Paris and most other scholars overlook. The most egregious example of this error was in Liberia and the numerous peace accords that were struck in that context throughout the 1990s. A key reason these agreements continued to fail is that rebel leader Charles Taylor was greedy. He wanted more and more control over the political and economic systems of Liberia and repeatedly fomented war as a means to achieve it.[36]

In sum, concern over the content of agreements is necessary, but it is not sufficient to explain the likelihood of agreement failure.

Flawed Implementation

In the literature, the "Charles Taylors" of the world are often called "spoilers," a term explored most fully by Stephen Stedman. According to Stedman, spoilers are committed to prolonging violence and actively work to disrupt both negotiations and peace. In his view, spoilers are a key reason for the failed implementation of peace agreements and for the resumption of violence.[37]

For spoilers, the civil war is not "ripe" enough. Through the continuation of the war, they manage to make more gains than losses, and so long as these conditions remain, they have little incentive to stop spoiling the process and to help implement peace. Stedman maintains that changing their behavior is contingent on changing their incentive structure—something that is, in turn, contingent on the type of spoiler in a given conflict. Under this framework of analysis, he isolates three types of spoilers: those who have limited aims; those who are greedy; and those who have total aims, seeing power as zero-sum in nature. He argues that limited aims and greedy spoilers can be induced or socialized to abide by the terms of an agreement, while total-aim spoilers have to be coerced.

Although Stedman does a nice job isolating a key factor that explains why some peace agreements fail to be implemented or break down, his categorization of spoilers suffers from the same problem as the others. He seems to assume that the spoilers are either greedy or insecure. And in fact, upon close reading, he seems to assume that most are greedy. This is a problem because motivating belligerents to abide by the terms of an agreement is likely to be more difficult if the belligerents are needy, greedy, and insecure.

As we know from Charles Glaser's security dilemma logic, however, attempting to coerce and induce a party that is both fearful and greedy will only make matters worse.[38] Coercion will make them even more insecure, while providing inducements will only make them greedier. The key, then, is to come up with a solution that not only provides for a secure environment but also curbs the appetite of the greedy belligerent.

Third-Party Guarantees or External Balancing of Power

A final set of arguments stresses the structure of the environment in which combatants negotiate. Here, the key assumption is that former adversaries would like to end the violence, but each party fears that the other will renege on the peace contract. Overcoming fear of defection is therefore the operative factor, and the issue of enduring peace comes down to the problem of how third parties can help former belligerents overcome their distrust of each other and abide by their commitments to implement and uphold the terms of their agreements. In situations where upholding commitments proves difficult for different parties, it is useful to turn to neutral third parties as enforcers of the peace.

As an obstacle to rational actors agreeing on a form of settlement short of violence, this "commitment problem" was well summarized by James Fearon and has been explored most fully in the civil war literature by Barbara Walter.[39] Walter and others have attempted to show that peace settlements overseen by third parties are far more likely to succeed than those that lack third-party assistance. Furthermore, peace agreements supported by strong third-party guarantees have the highest chances of success. In short, successful negotiations and agreements vary directly according to the level of commitment offered by third parties.[40] This commitment is measured in terms of number of troops, with those third parties willing to commit at least ten thousand or more troops revealing a strong commitment to protecting the peace. By contrast, a lack of third parties means a greater probability that negotiations will fail and that war will resume. Weak third-party support, which comes in the form of a promise to enforce the peace, means a greater likelihood that negotiations will succeed and less of a chance that hostilities will resume. This scale continues through moderate (i.e., the commitment of at least five hundred troops) to strong third-party guarantees. In this context, the relative strength of guarantees is intended to provide a deterrent that will prevent the belligerents from resorting to violence by helping to alleviate the security dilemma. According to Walter, third parties seek to guarantee the security of all parties while at the same time ensuring that contract provisions are met.[41] Unfortunately, this line of reasoning reintroduces the older notion that security guarantees are a sine qua non of an enduring settlement.[42] The larger theoretical argument consequently suffers on three counts.

First, on an empirical level, insecurity alone (i.e., the commitment problem) is not the sole or even the most common reason why peace agreements fail. There are a number of examples in which peace agreements were undermined not because of inadequate third-party guarantees, but rather because of the maneuverings of the belligerents who used the negotiations as a delaying tactic to increase their strength, or as a hedging strategy to increase their portion of the spoils of war. In other words, Walter's argument could only work in the small subset of cases in which actors were genuinely more fearful of defection than of the costs and risks of continuing to fight. It could not explain the more common situation in which a "peace agreement" is simply another part of a signatory's grand strategy to win the war.[43]

Second, the third-party guarantee argument has not fared well in subsequent empirical analyses. Two later studies have shown that third-party guarantees had little to no impact on the likelihood of successful settlement, although third parties are likely to be able to encourage rebel groups to come to the table for talks.[44] Most third parties were reluctant to provide firm and lasting guarantees, insisting on filling the more limited role of monitoring, verification, and assisting with demobilization. As Stedman explains, "the costs and risks of becoming a direct combatant in a civil war are often too high for implementers."[45] This argument is tested directly against my own in the next chapter.

Third and finally, third-party guarantee arguments apply only to negotiated settlements, which represent only a small portion of war outcomes. Such scenarios cannot account for what does or does not happen in the remaining 80 percent of cases of civil war settlements. It is therefore both difficult to generalize these findings and impossible to rely on them as the basis of any useful foreign policy recommendations.

Of course, this last criticism can be lodged against all three broad categories of explanations, but an additional critique is that most of the implementation and third-party enforcement arguments suffer from the same short time horizon. The reason for this is simply that peace agreements typically stipulate timetables and goals that must be reached by the relevant parties. If such goals are attained, then the process of implementation will be deemed a success and third parties will leave. Research focusing on the substance of peace agreements typically stops engaging in analysis at the time of the first round of elections, which can be held anywhere from one to five years after the end of a war. In fact, most such studies accept that a war has been successfully terminated if the ensuing peace lasts for five years.

But while no rule exists that requires a specific time threshold for peace, and five years seems reasonable, how useful is that particular number? Why not choose one year? I argue that, in fact, anything less than ten years will lead us to experience a false sense of success when we consider the problem of civil war termination. We need longer-term analyses to determine not just whether an agreement was implemented, but whether it led to the creation of self-sustaining institutions, rules, and procedures that help to forestall a reignition of civil war. The true state of political affairs cannot be assessed without this longer view. A case in point is Sudan, which suffered decades of war through the 1950s and 1960s and into the 1970s. In the Sudanese context, the fighting finally came to an end because of negotiations and a peace agreement that held for eleven years. At the end of that period, the northern-dominated government attempted to impose Sharia law on the entire state, including the largely Christian South, which had been one of the belligerents in the first war. War resumed in full force in 1983 and is now in the process of being ended. The point here, then, is that analyses of negotiated settlements would consider the peace agreement that ended the first Sudanese civil war to be a success, since "peace" lasted for more than five years. This is troubling for at least two reasons. First, it artificially truncates political and economic developments, which can take decades, if not generations, to evolve. Second, dealing with such a short time horizon makes it seem as if negotiated settlements lead to a more robust and stable outcome than is actually the case.

To their credit, none of the scholars I cite above argues that his or her explanation is exhaustive. Furthermore, each does a good job of explaining specific cases of civil war recurrence and stability. None of these explanations, however, provides a sufficiently general explanation for negotiated settlement failure or success on its own terms. In addition, given the restriction of their cases to negotiated settlements only, none can explain why peace might be sustained following a military victory.

Military Victory Failure and Success

If it is true that the distribution of war terminations dramatically favors military victories, we must do more than highlight the weaknesses of negotiated settlements in achieving both lasting and constructive civil war terminations. We must also explore *why it is* that military victories correlate much more often with enduring peace than do negotiated settlements. The best explanation for this trend can be reduced logically to two main contenders: (1) radical disequilibrium (the destruction of all but one actor) and (2) equilibrium (a balance of power).

Destruction

Perhaps the simplest argument for why military victories are relatively more stable than negotiated settlements can be based on the number of relevant actors who survive the conflict. If military operations result in the destruction of the enemy, then the number of survivors is confined to the one remaining actor or side. This destruction argument constitutes an important and logically consistent explanation for why a military victory might result in a longer lasting peace and create a more stable foundation for postwar economic recovery.

The logic of this argument is that when the number of relevant actors who have survived a war falls to one (a radical disequilibrium achieved by means of physical destruction), we can expect peace to last because a single actor cannot, by definition, have subsequent conflicts with itself.[46]

Elegant as it is, however, there is a serious problem with this argument: Destruction of the enemy is empirically rare. Consider that by "destroy" we mean physical destruction in the literal sense and not merely forcing the adversary to flee the state, or imprisoning survivors and their leaders. In either of the latter two cases, the seeds of a future resistance (and of possible terrorism or civil war) would remain. The Great Lakes region of Africa—especially Burundi, Congo, and Rwanda—exemplifies this pattern.

Although one can readily think of examples in which winners literally destroyed losers—for example, Rome's destruction of Carthage after the Second Punic War—cases after the Industrial Revolution are rare. In modern times, advances in communications and transportation technology have made it more difficult to isolate and destroy mobilized resistance to state authority.[47] Even absolutist states, such as Stalin's Soviet Union, proved unable to eradicate Chechens or Crimean Tatars (both accused of collaboration with the Germans during World War II), who today largely inhabit their ancestral homelands even after having been murdered, imprisoned, and periodically deported en masse to the Soviet hinterlands.

Balance of Power

An alternative yet related argument has to do with the postwar balance of power. By this logic military victories succeed because, unlike negotiated settlements, they ensure that private information about capabilities and political objectives becomes transparent or public.[48]

Similar to arguments about the causes of interstate wars, the logic of this argument is that wars erupt when two sides are not certain of the true balance of power or misrepresent their true interests in the outcome of a fight.[49] The actual process of fighting allows for the true balance of power to emerge. When one side realizes that it cannot triumph in war because the balance of power does not favor it, it will accept defeat—a defeat that will remain in place so long as the power balance does not shift.

Balance-of-power arguments have been used to explain postwar stability in two ways: first, as a support to those who advocate the separation and partition of populations to end civil wars between ethnic groups; and second, as a support to those who advocate the use of third-party intervention to establish an equilibrium where none existed previously.

The most forceful contemporary proponent of the separation and partition of ethnic groups to secure a lasting peace is Chaim Kaufmann.[50] According to Kaufmann, ethnic civil wars result from the mass mobilization of populations as a result of hypernationalism that, more often than not, leads to the ethnic cleansing of territories. Deep-seated mistrust and insecurity will be ameliorated only if the two sides no longer have any contact with each other. This is achieved through the ethnic "unmixing" of populations, a process that occurs partially as a result of the war's ethnic cleansing, but which also might have to be carried out at the war's end to sustain a semblance of peace. Unless the parties are separated completely, war is likely to break out again. What Kaufmann advocates is a separation in order to balance the two hostile parties against each other. This is another way of saying that, once separated, the relative capabilities of each party are clearer, which thus precludes the need to fight in order to establish which actor would be most likely to win.

Kaufmann recognizes that a balance of power may not be achieved in some situations, while the "clarification" of partition results in an uneven distribution of power. This will perhaps tempt the stronger side to attack the weaker party—or at least levy formerly unacceptable demands. Here, Kaufmann recommends that a third party might have to step in to help balance the sides so that a weaker side will not fall prey to a stronger one. Nevertheless, his basic argument is that ending ethnic civil wars requires a sort of balanced stalemate, where each side stands alone with its own kind poised against the other. Implicit in this argument (and made explicit at points) is that negotiated settlements and peace agreements will not be able to overcome the fear and animosity that exist between the two groups during the implementation of a settlement, especially after blood is spilled.

This additional element—the assertion that each group's *incentive* to escalate to violence may be reduced by partition—makes Kaufmann's argument very compelling. Nevertheless, there exist at least three problems with his theory.[51]

First, at the most general level, there is no reliable evidence that partition reduces the likelihood that a war will reignite. The most extensive examination to date found little empirical evidence to support this claim.[52] Second, Kaufmann's argument applies only to a narrow set of cases: ethnic wars in which fear based on ethnicity is the driving motivation, and in which the ethnic populations can be divided into discrete, compact geographical entities. These conditions do not apply to all or even most civil wars. Third, the international community has long avoided separation and partition as a solution to stabilizing peace. Partition is hardly even recognized as a solution of last resort, and the international community still holds a good deal of faith in power sharing or a loose federation.[53] Thus, regardless of the merits of the separation of ethnic groups on the ground, partition would be a difficult policy to advocate since it is unlikely to gain patrons.

The international community's reluctance to embrace partition as a lasting solution to ethnic civil wars has resulted in an alternative strategy: international peacekeeping. Bosnia and Cyprus are prime examples of this approach. In each case, the international community stepped in and essentially established a power equilibrium, acting as a local hegemon and enforcing the peace. Although efforts have been made to impose or cajole a final resolution in each of these conflicts, such efforts have been stymied, and the international force has stayed far longer than anticipated. Originally, international forces were expected to leave Bosnia within one year. Despite an impressive and comprehensive peace agreement signed in 1995 in Dayton, Ohio, the international community is not likely to be able to leave the region anytime soon.[54] International efforts to enforce or balance forces by separation—as in the peace solution to civil wars—originally had been justified on the grounds that such a plan would save lives by stopping the killing. But while it is true that Serbs, Muslims, and Croats—and Greek and Turkish Cypriots—are no longer killing one another on a large scale, it is also true that what peace does exist is extremely tenuous; none of the underlying issues of the conflict has been resolved. Moreover, the hardliners from each side are now in charge. In essence, the battle lines are still in place, and few people are optimistic that the populations will continue to be able to live in peace and harmony should the international community pull out.

A second and related issue with the international-community-as-balancer strategy is that, as represented by the United Nations, the "international community" possesses only so many resources and personnel that it can offer to deploy in such operations. Indeed, these are not cheap operations. The UN has been in Cyprus since 1964 with 1,248 personnel at a cost of 1.15 billion U.S. dollars through 2002/2003, in addition to an expected additional 45 million in 2003/2004.[55] The NATO-led implementation force (IFOR) in Bosnia in 1995–1996 saw the deployment of some 60,000 troops and a total cost of 5 billion dollars. Replacing IFOR, the NATO stabilization force (SFOR) employed 12,000 troops and cost 20.535 billion dollars through 2002/2003 and 31 million in 2003/2004. In 2004 the EU operation (EUFOR) took over the role of SFOR in Bosnia and Herzegovina, deploying 6,300 troops in December of that year. In 2008 it employed 2,125 troops and operated with a budget of 71.7 million euros. Considering that international balancing does not permanently resolve these wars, that such efforts come with a high price tag, and that the possibility exists of becoming embroiled in a reignited civil war, one might expect that this solution is hardly permanent or widely available enough to yield a lasting cessation of violence.

A final problem with Kaufmann's argument is the need for, and difficulty of, separating and moving at-risk populations into discrete territories. More often than not, the populations are fighting over the same ground, with both parties closely identifying with that ground. Partitioning the groups might clarify their relative power (and thus simplify the task of calculating how much of which type of commitment of resources might best deter aggression or reduce fear). At the same time, however, it would also increase their incentive to fight unless each was satisfied that the acquired territory was valid as ethnic homeland (or that its rival did not control or possess territory deemed to be the other's homeland). Failing to address this important consideration—an extremely difficult task in itself—would almost certainly pave the way for another fight farther down the road.[56]

My Argument: Security Sector Reform First

Although each of the arguments above embraces important factors that need to be addressed in order to lead to stable peace, none provides a sufficient explanation of why negotiated settlements fail or succeed or why military victories fail or succeed. My explanation works by taking into account both greed *and* fear as belligerent motivations.

I argue that both negotiated settlements and military victories contain the key elements necessary for endurance, but also that neither of these by itself is sufficient to achieve this important aim. In short, although negotiated settlements have excelled at providing adversaries with positive incentives (i.e., benefit) to maintain cease-fires and work toward unity, they have proven weak at providing negative incentives (i.e., harm) beyond the vague collective good of "no more violence." Military victories, by contrast, have excelled at providing negative incentives to potential adversaries following a civil war, but, with one striking exception—rebel victories—they have tended to be lacking in their provision of positive incentives.

I hypothesize that negotiated settlements are more likely to result in war recurrence because, although peace agreements typically delineate an acceptable distribution of goods and services from the state, the disposition of military and police are often overlooked in these settlements. While most peace agreements stress demobilization and demilitarization, little effort is made to create, reconstitute, and/or train the military and police. Due to the absence of a reformed set of security institutions, the state does not have the capacity to repress the reemergence of military bands that remain loyal to former belligerents. Furthermore, it fails to integrate former rebels into the state military or police system in order to make them part of the security solution. The state lacks repressive capacity—or the capacity to punish defection—and this lack of harm capacity makes the state susceptible to civil war recurrence. In other words, there is an imbalance of *benefit* and *harm*. Although settlements provide for the provision of benefit, they typically do not provide for the provision of harm.

This is not the case for military victories, where the government or the rebel forces have triumphed and emerge as an effective fighting force. The military retains the capacity to repress and can choose to offer benefits to a broader community of citizens, including former belligerents (e.g., government fighters or opposition rebels) if it so chooses. In the next chapter, I argue that there are logical reasons for why we should expect rebel victories to result in a balance that stresses both benefits and harm, while government victories will stress harm over benefits. I make the case that rebel victories therefore not only are the least likely type of settlement to lead to a recurrence of violence but will also lead to the greatest levels of democratization in the longer-term postwar environment.

As per cease-fires/stalemates, the notion of a balance of benefit and harm between the belligerents is somewhat moot. Because the parties have separated and continue to exist autonomously, an argument based on the notion of a provision of benefits and harms that impact the other side would have difficulty explaining a recurrence of war between them. This is not necessarily a problem for a general theory of civil war termination for at least two reasons. First, cease-fires/stalemates make up the smallest proportion of civil war endings, about 9 percent of all cases. And second, although the argument does not apply specifically to cease-fires/stalemates, its explanatory power is sufficient to illuminate key aspects of cease-fires/stalemates and how they contribute to a recurrence or cessation of violence.

In short, I argue that for settlements to endure and to facilitate liberal political institutions, they must contain credible promises of harm and benefit in order to avoid collapse. Or, if they hold, they will result in increasing authoritarianism—a grievance traditionally cited as being capable of producing war. An imbalance of harm and benefit explains why negotiated settlements fail to maintain the peace more often than military victories do. The next chapter outlines this theory more fully.

Chapter 3

Securing the Peace: Mutual Benefit, Mutual Harm

OVER THE LAST DECADE, the learning curve for negotiated settlements has taught us that the *quality* of peace following a war is the deciding factor in the duration of peace. The key question, then, is this: under what circumstances (i.e., with what qualities) will peace endure following the end of a civil war?

Where the end of violence is followed by injustice, abuse, or neglect, civil war is likely to break out again, whether sooner or later. In contrast, if the end of violence is followed by the rule of law, political liberty, and some meaningful chance at economic and social mobility, peace is more likely both to endure and to be valued as something worth preserving.

Ending civil wars and keeping them ended seems an insurmountable task, especially considering the conditions of a post–civil war state. In that context, the political system has been compromised and perhaps overthrown, the economic and transport sectors have been destroyed, international trade and investment have stopped, and the country has been divided into warring groups that have just undergone massive bloodletting. An objective assessment of such conditions would predict the country at hand to be ripe for renewed violence rather than ready to ensure the end of conflict—notwithstanding mutual exhaustion of the warring factions.

Still, countries do manage to recover from civil war and thrive. The history of state-building is a history of warfare, at both the international and the domestic levels. Most states are the products of a violent birth.[1] Indeed, contemporary America is the product of two major wars: the American Revolution (1775–1783) and the Civil War (1860–1865). Both wars actively disrupted the political and economic systems, yet the country emerged and recovered and continues to enjoy the benefits of a strong constitutional democracy and a vibrant market economy.

Despite a long historical record of violent state birth and subsequent stabilization, we still know relatively little about the process by which states emerge from civil wars and build stable peaceful regimes. This chapter introduces a theory to explain why some states experience lasting peace following civil war, while others succumb to renewed violence over the same issues and with the same belligerents. The theory is premised on the notions of benefit and harm, hypothesizing that rebel victories are the most stable and lead to the greatest levels of democratization because they provide both of these concepts. In contrast, negotiated settlements afford only benefits, government victories tender only harm, and cease-fires fail to result in either benefits for those who have been neglected by the system or harm to the perpetrators of violence and repression.

Securing the Peace

In order to understand why military victories are more stable than nego-tiated settlements, we must understand how the type of civil war settle-ment will configure the mix of incentives—both positive and negative—that the former belligerents face. Strong institutions make for positive postwar outcomes. In turn, strong institutions imply relatively unified action and consolidated resources, leading to a more stable and perhaps more democratic system of government. Although this argument seems as obvious as it is logical, and this type of institution building has been dealt with in both the democratic consolidation literature and work on economics, where security institutions are concerned most contemporary scholars of security and civil war appear to have forgotten it.

This is not the case in the now classic writings of Barrington Moore, Samuel Huntington, and Dankwart Rustow, each of whom argued to varying degrees that the type of transition a state faced would influence (if not determine) the character of its political institutions and future stability.[2] For Moore and Huntington, political violence is the midwife of democracy. A quick, violent transition therefore allows for the emergence of democratic political institutions. A gradual transition, however, leads to highly bureaucratized, authoritarian regimes. The same logic might apply to civil wars, whereby a military victory allows for a rapid transi-tion and thus creates greater prospects for democracy. At the same time, negotiated settlement delays a transition and thereby inhibits the forma-tion of democratic institutions.

Rustow takes a different angle. His argument about political develop-ment and stability puts forth the idea of sequencing. According to him, for a stable political system to emerge (especially a democratic one), national unity must be established first, followed by government authority, and then by political equality. Similarly, Eric Nordlinger argues, "the probabilities of a political system's developing in a nonviolent, authoritarian, and eventu-ally democratically stable manner are maximized when a national identity emerges first, followed by the institutionalization of the central government, and then by the emergence of mass parties and a mass electorate."[3]

This is exactly the sort of strategy that Terrence Lyons recommends for democracy development, but he also recognizes its weaknesses: "Power-sharing pacts and electoral systems are unlikely to improve the chances that elections will advance both war termination and democratization, particularly in the most difficult cases where a return to war is a real risk."[4]

He then goes on to claim that politics needs to be "demilitarized," but he does not discuss what this process entails. Arguing that "the rationale for demobilization and disarmament is the exchange of military capacity for political benefits," Lyons fails to discuss exactly how this exchange is to happen, devoting only two paragraphs in a book on democratic consolidation to the role of the military.[5] Lyons does highlight some factors that might contribute to "deepening democracy" and stability, however. The one that seems to be the most important is persuading the military to refocus its attention on matters of national defense and international security, moving away from intervening in the internal affairs of the state. Larry Diamond points out that this takes a long time, "unless the military has been defeated or shattered."[6] This same argument was made over forty years ago but seems to have been forgotten.

Following a decisive military victory, one side gains control of all state resources and, crucially, the ability to set the political and economic agenda.[7] While it is true that even a relatively unified actor may make mistakes—say, bad economic decisions—it is also generally true that a more unified actor will gain advantages in recovering from mistakes. Moreover, when the winners gain control of the military and police, they gain an advantage in preventing the emergence or re-emergence of organized violence and crime.

In contrast, negotiated settlements by their very design leave a state's offices divided, in terms of both physical infrastructure and human capital. Each side will have some say in a postwar government and may demand partial control of the police and military. Key areas of territory, including international borders, may become porous transit points for arms, drugs, contraband, or recruits. Thus, although the chief public good of nonviolence may be gained through negotiated settlement at a lower short-term cost than through military victory, the resource-consolidation argument implies that this good may come, paradoxically, at the expense of the public good of an effective postwar administration.[8] Adam Przeworski comes closer to setting up a balance between political benefits and military control by modeling the alliance structures that underlie democratic consolidation after the example of the liberalization of an authoritarian regime. According to him, the moderates must ally with the reformers in order to wrestle control of the military away from the hardliners. This alliance must assure the reformers that they will receive a guaranteed share of the vote (i.e., benefits) while also ensuring that the current military structure is no longer able to engage in repression.[9]

State Consolidation: Benefit and Harm

Imagine a state that has just suffered a civil war, and in which the violence has only just come to an end. Perhaps a cease-fire has been arranged, or perhaps each side has sent envoys to negotiate a longer-term agreement. Regardless of the specific circumstances, actors on all sides are calculating the utility of maintaining the cease-fire in comparison to the utility of reinitiating hostilities.

Those calculations can be divided into two broad concerns: benefits (i.e., what the parties have to gain through peace) and harms (i.e., what the parties have to lose through breaking a peace agreement or through continuing the fight). As the concerns apply to both sides of the conflict, a stable situation would involve mutual benefit for adhering to an agreement and mutual harm for defecting from the agreement.

Benefit

Actors who have just survived a civil war and are contemplating the value of nonviolence as weighed against continuing the aggression at a later date are likely to consider how much they will benefit (as individuals and as a group) from nonviolence.

For the purposes of this analysis, "benefits" signify political (in terms of both offices and survival) and economic benefits. The essential issue of benefit distribution is this: who and how many actors will benefit and by how much? Stating it in these terms helps us to see that the most useful way to think about "actors" is to divide them into elites and their supporting publics. This latter group of supporting publics can be expected to benefit immediately and directly by means of an increased likelihood of physical survival. In addition, and less directly, the cessation of organized violence is a precondition for positive economic progress, apart from cases in which a state is "endowed" with highly concentrated and desirable natural resources (such as gold, diamonds, or petroleum). In contrast, elites gain both an increased chance of physical survival and the opportunity to share in the distribution or redistribution of offices. In rare cases (that is, rare by today's standards), they may even be rewarded directly with cash or property, should they agree to support and extend the cease-fire.[10]

Harm

Aside from how much actors will benefit, they are also concerned with how much peace might cost them and what the costs of defection from a peace treaty might be. That is to say, what are the punishments for taking up arms again? For incumbents already in possession of the state's capacity to distribute and redistribute political and economic benefits, the prospects of sharing this capacity amount to a significant positive cost.[11] Similarly, for rebels, accepting less than full control of the state may be calculated as a positive cost as well. In short, every cease-fire has built into it a potential for defection. This implies that well-intentioned third parties who are interested in facilitating enduring peace must consider adding credible enforcement mechanisms—a threat of harm—to any cease-fire or peace agreement. In this book, "harm" therefore means security. As Nicole Ball explains:

> A number of priority tasks . . . [in security] are routinely enshrined in peace agreements. The tasks include the disbanding and disarming of informal security forces and the demobilization of some number of the formal forces, as well as some degree of police reform and judicial system development. Many of the longer-term tasks associated with strengthening good governance in the security sector are more often not mandated by the peace accords and are also not included in efforts to consolidate the peace at the end of the formal peace process.[12]

As Ball notes, reforming the security sector includes the military, paramilitary groups, the local police, and other organizations that support the policy in "delivering accessible justice (judiciary and penal system), intelligence, customs enforcement, and the civil management and oversight authorities."[13] The process of reform begins with an assessment of the current status of the sector and how it accords with current needs. Once this is accomplished, it is then a matter of identifying resources and allocating them in an appropriate manner.

A problem exists in that most agreements do not conduct an assessment of security sector reform in the first place. Ball explains that "donors have traditionally shied way from engagement with the security sector."[14] The security sector can provide both safety to the repressed and punishment to defectors from the agreement. We are thus left with benefits related to safety and harm (e.g., costs) to those who wish to return to fighting.

Why Peace Fails

An examination of peace agreements is illuminating in this regard. Most include extensive provisions for establishing executives, legislatures, free and fair elections, and judiciaries, and for the demobilization and demilitarization of the armed forces. In such contexts, constructing a solid and representative set of institutions is often the primary objective. Means and methods to refashion and reinstitutionalize the military, however, are given only secondary consideration. Or, if provisions regarding the police and armed forces are written into the agreements, then their implementation is provided with deficient resources. The desire is to make soldiers into citizens by giving them money and resources, in order to help them reintegrate back into society—not necessarily to establish a security sector of professional, trained organizations at both the local and the national levels.[15]

Thus, following most negotiated settlements, the military and police are left to fend for themselves. The citizenry faces a similar situation. A pattern seems to be forming, constituted by the eventual reemergence of multiple sets of militaries, militias, or rebellion organizations ready to comply with politicians who can provide resources to sustain them (or have already done so). Charles Call and William Stanley make a good point when they claim that the way civil wars end provides an excellent, yet often overlooked, opportunity for reforming security institutions.[16]

Consider Colombia as a case in point.[17] For decades, that government's policy was not military victory. Instead, the aim was to hurt the rebels— Revolutionary Armed Forces of Colombia (FARC)—enough to bring them to the negotiating table. Following numerous negotiated settlements over a period of decades, the military became frustrated with government negotiations and inadequate levels of funding—funding that the military wanted to use to defeat the rebels decisively.[18] Militias thus splintered off, and the government now faces a whole new series of rebel organizations in addition to FARC, currently sustained by an illicit drug economy. Only now, with American help under Plan Colombia, has the Colombian government committed itself to defeating the rebels (all of them) in an effort to consolidate the state's control over its territory and institutions.

The need to devote attention and resources to the security sector for developing and transition countries in general (instead of only those that have suffered through civil war) was the subject of an intensive review by the Development Assistance Committee of the OECD. According to the DAC report, "security and development are increasingly seen as being inextricably linked which opens the way to mainstreaming security as a public policy and a governance issue."[19]

The DAC report goes on to list the core security actors: the armed forces, police, paramilitary forces, presidential guards, intelligence and security services (both civilian and military), coast guard, border guards, customs authorities, and the reserve of local security units (civil defense forces, national guards, and militias). In addition, the study mentions that nonstatutory security forces such as liberation armies, guerrilla armies, private bodyguard units, private security companies, and political party militias are rarely engaged by donors. The report then claims that "the most critical task facing countries embarking on SSR processes is to build a nationally-owned and -led vision of security. This is the foundation that countries require to develop appropriate security system policy frameworks and the required institutional mechanisms to implement them."[20] The integration of security reform with development has been called the "whole-of-government" approach. In essence, all of this intellectual and policy work is directed toward one objective: integrating and enhancing security in countries around the world. The fact that task forces have been formed and studies have been commissioned is a good indication that security institutions and their reform have been overlooked. What is more, this omission has been a general phenomenon regarding the aid and development assistance provided to countries across the globe. Accordingly, it is not surprising that we now see the same sort of oversight in the reconstitution and consolidation of states as they transition from civil war.

As the DAC report states, "One of the clearest lessons of the past is that when problems in the security system are approached in a piecemeal fashion, without reference to broad goals and underlying structural problems, security-system governance is generally not improved significantly." Furthermore, the study asserts that, "without adequate attention to these political and structural problems, it will be impossible to develop professional security bodies capable of providing the secure environment necessary for sustainable economic development and poverty reduction."[21]

Consider the case of Sierra Leone and Britain's support of "defense diplomacy":

> The emphasis of the UK programme of support for SSR in Sierra Leone shifted dramatically in June 2000 after the upsurge in activity by rebel Revolutionary United Front (RUF) forces. Following their attack on the capital, Freetown, re-establishing a climate of security across the country and conditions in which a sustainable peace settlement could be reached became the Government's priority. With UK support, a large programme to train the new army was put in place which enables capable forces to be rapidly deployed against the RUF, backed by United Nations peace-keepers (today the largest UN peace-keeping mission). By 2001, with the security situation largely under control, attention again turned to various SSR-related tasks such as strengthening the Ministry of Defense, building the capacity of the police forces, and developing a new national security policy.[22]

At the time of this writing, Britain has left, and Sierra Leone now has a military and police force that is professional and capable of maintaining peace in a country that was plagued by decades of civil war.[23]

Yet "monopoly over the legitimate use of force" is unlikely to be sufficient to secure the peace. Enduring peace demands an additional factor: credible mutual benefit. As observed above, contemporary negotiated settlements have fallen short in their ability to credibly threaten signatories with direct punishment if they should defect. In contrast, however, they have been very good at credible promises of benefit to former combatants. Important benefits can be found in the collective goods of (1) no more violence and (2) an opportunity to participate in an electoral process, which is more likely to result in (3) a government that promises to represent and protect the parties' interests in some form.[24] In addition, most contemporary negotiated settlements promise more direct aid, such as reconstruction and food assistance, as well as loans or debt rescheduling.

This is one of the reasons why much of the literature stresses the need for third parties.[25] But whereas the significant difference that third parties make lies in their threat to "harm" one or both sides if the provisions of the settlement are undermined, in reality third parties often limit their engagement to getting active or former combatants to the bargaining table, or to involvement in the immediate stage of implementation. Furthermore, third parties are rarely accorded the right to impose the terms of the settlement through use of force. Or, in some instances, they themselves refuse to do so. Finally, not every war attracts enough international interest to render third parties willing to become and stay engaged, especially militarily. At other times, when they do become engaged, it is typically in small states that require only limited operations.[26] Ultimately, while negotiated settlements do well in terms of benefits, they do poorly in terms of harm. This is why they fail.

All of this leads to an important problem: since we know, a priori, that we cannot justify a general policy of allowing wars to run their course, it makes sense to ask why military victories by incumbents result in less political liberty than victories attained by rebels.

My argument is straightforward. Generally, incumbent governments have, as Max Weber reminds us, a monopoly on the legitimate use of force.[27] It follows that the government will also possess a disproportionately large share of the means of imposing its will on its citizens. Included here are resources such as arms (a material component), police, and, in some cases, soldiers (human capital components). All of this works to point out that rebels generally start out at a disadvantage in terms of all three dimensions. Those rebels who succeed typically do so by compensating for material weaknesses with sheer numbers. By extension—and we know this to be a historical constant—broad social support is a virtual sine qua non of successful rebellion.[28]

That being said, the postwar environment is expected to differ systematically for incumbents who have put down a rebellion and for rebels who have toppled a sitting government. When governments win, they are apt to view much of their population with suspicion, and to take steps to ensure that a future rebellion is impossible. As a consequence, surviving incumbents will be strongly tempted to restrict civil liberties and to establish surveillance regimes. This postwar reaction will be intensified in cases where an identifiable group has been closely linked to rebellion.[29] In such cases, the incumbent government will have reestablished its monopoly on the legitimate use of force while also having restored its control over the means of imposing that force. Moreover, this will take place when the government has survived a rebellion that, in order to have counted as a threat, logically must have attained sufficient social support for the government to resent survivors.

When rebels win, however, the opposite dynamic is in force, with the rebels being more willing to open up or liberalize the political space.[30] There are both domestic and international incentives for rebels to do this. At the domestic level, the former government began with a monopoly on the legitimate use of force, along with a strong advantage in weapons and trained personnel needed to employ them. Perhaps even more important is the status quo bias of the international system, which views the defeat of an incumbent government as a potentially dangerous and destabilizing event that could act as a precedent for future volatility. The social support needed to overwhelm these advantages confers a new legitimacy, one that implies a majority of a state's (or a seceding region's) surviving citizens—citizens who likely risked a great deal to overthrow the government and should be rewarded for doing so.[31] Thus, the rebels should be more willing to allow a wider spectrum of the population to take part in the political process, and for that reason, lower levels of autocracy should follow these victories. At the international level, rebels must enhance their image. One is dealing, after all, with a rebel organization that just overthrew a legitimate government. In light of the situation, one way in which rebels might cast themselves in a more positive light is through the opening up of political institutions. That is to say, they ought to engage in liberalization. Fostering greater democratization enhances their liberal credentials with the international community, but it further ensures that international aid and support will be offered.[32]

In reality, of course, there are many variations of this ideal model of a postwar environment of legitimacy. Third parties, for instance, may provide weapons and experts to rebels to compensate for a government advantage. At the same time, governments often receive outside support as well. In some cases, incumbent governments may be so corrupt and ineffective that their possession of an advantage in terms of arms and international diplomatic support may be relatively easily nullified, and easily overcome by rebel-led social opposition.[33] Finally, although in most states the possession of small arms is restricted to government-authorized personnel, in other countries the average citizen is afforded the right to bear small arms (e.g., Israel, the United States, and Switzerland). This means that incumbent governments cannot rely on the threat of force as the sole basis for their authority; rather, they must instead depend on laws and legitimacy in order to govern effectively.

In sum, the nature of the environments that actors face following civil wars will differ considerably from one case to another. Incumbents will have lost legitimacy and may be tempted to repress civilians in an effort to avoid a repeat of the clash, or in an effort to avenge imagined support of the former rebels. Their victory implies a capacity to harm, while they remain unthreatened by harm and unleavened by a capacity to benefit survivors, save in the general sense of individual physical survival—an aspect that ought not to be underestimated. Conversely, when rebels win, the postwar environment contains both elements of harm and benefit. In terms of harm, the rebels have demonstrated their military capacity, while in terms of benefit, their victory against doubtful odds has secured them legitimacy. Thus, the logic of successful postwar governance and settlements is the same: the credible capacity to harm is paramount, but long-term positive outcomes *beyond* daily physical survival require the credible promise of benefits.

This ideal model of postwar outcomes and incentives leads to a clear association between war termination type and the credible provision of benefit and harm (and the expected outcome of the situation). This association is summarized in table 3.1.

Although very few civil wars "end" in stalemates or cease-fires, those that do can only count as being ended in the sense of an immediate suspension of the threat of further destruction and killing. An attack by either side would provoke retaliation, resulting in a costly war. Should the relevant combatants choose to extend and formalize this respite, either they will move into the "negotiated settlement" column by default or the war will reignite. This immediate suspension of the threat of violence cannot count as a benefit because it could end at any moment.[34] As a result, neither elites nor supporting publics living within the state can enjoy stable expectations regarding their survival, and both groups are therefore unlikely to be able to carry on meaningful economic or social activity. On the other hand, a cease-fire does not require either side to admit fault or to sacrifice the asserted legitimacy of its claims. It should then not be surprising that, overall, cease-fires are more stable than negotiated settlements.

As illustrations of how civil wars have ended since 1940, negotiated settlements are more common than stalemates and cease-fires but less common than military victories. Historically, the structure and process of negotiations have favored credible guarantees of benefits to former combatants, while they have proven equally weak in generating security guar-

TABLE 3.1
Civil War Terminations, Benefit and Harm, and Expected Outcomes

Type of Settlement	Harm	Benefit	Result
Cease-fire/Stalemate	N	N	No Peace
Negotiated settlement	N	Y	Peace withers
Government victory	Y	N	Enduring peace with tyranny
Rebel victory	Y	Y	Enduring peace with democratization

antees. They have also disappointed in the more important element of SSR: enabling the postwar government to reform and reconstruct its own security sector. It is important to note that this feature is more than merely descriptive. That is to say, if more than one actor survives the war, all survivors will face the need to compromise and to share both power and wealth. This "sharing" in turn demands a sacrifice of legitimacy. One might ask: If the cause was truly just, and the costs were therefore necessary and acceptable, then how can we now sacrifice that cause by compromising? Thus, reignition is unlikely when one of two conditions holds: (1) there is a guarantee of long-term, neutral, and skillful occupation aimed at SSR (noting that SSR takes time, even when skillfully implemented); or (2) the surviving combatants remain balanced in their capacity to deal and sustain harm. One case of a successful negotiated settlement can be seen in Guatemala. As William Stanley and David Holiday argue, in that set of circumstances both sides agreed to a cease-fire out of mutual exhaustion.[35] That is, the guerrillas were "fought out" and the government saw no prospect of actually winning. Both parties understood that the balance of power between them meant that they would face a stark choice between two options: either they could continue to impose costs on each other without advancing their respective political objectives, or they could formalize a peace agreement and share power. Because a balance of power existed between the guerrillas and the government, each side was dissuaded from reigniting violence, and peace has thus been sustained. Unfortunately, most negotiated settlements since 1990 have not satisfied either of the above conditions. While such settlements generally fail to consider how the allocation of offices and positions might contribute to a situation in which the parties might be able to harm each other, they also routinely leave out the restructuring and professionalization of the armed forces altogether.

Military victories are the most common way that civil wars end. In spite of that, there has been a clear trend since 1990 toward increasing reliance on negotiated settlements. Although victories by incumbent governments promise stability (i.e., extended nonviolence), because governments who survive a challenge to their authority are likely to view their supporting publics with suspicion, these victories are less likely to result in political liberties (and perhaps economic advances) than are those victories achieved by rebels. The "benefit" provided by an incumbent's military victory is real, but it tends to lead to an increased likelihood of individual physical survival. Rebels, when they win, generally do so against great odds. Overcoming an incumbent government—one that in many cases has outside help—thus awards the rebels an advantage in terms of legitimacy. This gain can also be observed in terms of a "honeymoon" period in which supporting publics may expect improvements in their lives over what they had experienced under the previous government. As such, the expected benefits of life under the new regime are high. In addition, with the new administration having shown itself to be an effective military force, an escalation of dissent would allow the credible threat of harm to create ideal conditions for enduring peace.

If all this is correct, important (though, surprisingly, not new) policy implications follow. First, security is the primary (but not the only) sector demanding reform and resources following a civil war. If SSR is done well, then a negotiated settlement can take on all the positive attributes of an outright military victory (e.g., duration of peace) without having to absorb all of the associated costs (e.g., reignition and political repression). This is true because, both for peace to last and for government to work, the same conditions must hold: the credible threat of harm against violent dissent and criminal activity, and the promise of benefit from compliance and participation. This argument addresses the concerns of both fearful and greedy parties. In other words, it solves the problem of the mixed motives that Charles Glaser identified in his extension of the security dilemma.[36] If a government retains the capacity to both harm and benefit the population, then it can both deter and appease potential opponents. The key is finding the right balance of harm and benefits. The same is true of the agreements needed to end violence and lay the groundwork for enduring peace. Furthermore, this argument shows how peace can become self-sustaining, not having to rely on outside actors. As we know from the literature on economic development, sustained development cannot be achieved by way of outside aid.[37] Rather, aid is helpful only when it is used to support indigenous initiatives based within the country, not those imposed from outside. In other words, it shows a way for states to become the owners of their security and political environment (a concept referred to in the literature as "national ownership"), which is increasingly viewed as vital for enduring peace.

Why Negotiated Settlements Came to Prevail

In addition to the fact that support for negotiated settlements (i.e., being in favor of nonviolence) appears at first glance to be morally superior to support for military victory (i.e., being in favor of violence), a review of third-party participation in civil war peace settlements since 1940 answers the question of why negotiated settlements have gained preferred status and why they have tended to fail.

First, as John Mearsheimer rightly points out, during the Cold War the superpowers were able to simplify their security requirements.[38] Each side imitated and studied the other, with the result that neither party devoted significant resources to understanding the underlying issues of conflict in the developing world. In that context, each side rightly identified the other as the chief threat to its survival, which, though not an irrational strategy, has proven to be a costly move. The true colonial powers, who had invested considerable energy in both creating (in terms of "divide and conquer") and understanding underlying conflict issues in the developing world, did not have the resources to both maintain their colonies and protect themselves against what they perceived to be a growing and credible threat of assault from the Soviet bloc in Europe. They dismantled their colonial offices and, either gracefully (e.g., Britain) or by forced ejection (e.g., France, Spain, Portugal, Netherlands, and Belgium), abandoned their colonies in Asia and Africa.

During the Cold War, under the now widely discredited but then understandable view that allies in the developing world could help to curb the larger bipolar confrontation, each rival camp aimed to support either an incumbent government or an insurgency to military victory. Because the costs of civil and ethnic wars were largely sustained in theater, the most common outcomes were either military victories or stalemates and cease-fires.

Second, and of perhaps greater significance, large advance-industrial states intervening in distant civil wars found themselves increasingly on the losing side. The United States supported the Guomindang in postwar China, but the Guomindang was defeated by Mao Zedong and fled to Formosa (Taiwan today). The trend of weak-actor victories in asymmetric conflicts continued and accelerated such that by the end of the Cold War, weak actors had won a majority of such asymmetric conflicts. Put differently, the costs of military interventions were rising and the policy implications that followed were stark: either alter one's military and domestic political expectations or avoid such interventions altogether.[39]

At the end of the Cold War two things happened. First, the utility of providing sufficient support for an incumbent government or insurgency to obtain military victory declined dramatically. Second, many of the costs of civil and ethnic wars began to reach the developed world.[40] In addition, each side had worked assiduously to shed its human capital regarding the developing world, with soldiers adept at fighting small wars retiring and deliberately taking their wisdom with them, and with experienced diplomats with language skills being brushed aside and ignored in favor of technical intelligence resources. As a result, the puzzling specter of "irrational" combatants trying to kill each other in civil disputes arose. Since the benefits of supporting civil war factions outside resource-rich regions had dropped to zero and the costs of allowing them to continue were rising (with costs being measured not only in terms of refugees, transnational crime, narcotrafficking, and terrorism, but also in terms of "never again" legitimacy), negotiated settlements were left as the default policy option. To outsiders interested in avoiding risky military interventions (or promising them should combatants defect from negotiated settlements), a short-term halt to the violence followed by reconstruction aid seemed sufficient. Negotiated settlements became an ideal policy option.

Furthermore, aside from the calculations of pure interest, there seems to be something normatively desirable about negotiated settlements, which offer the promise of opening markets and liberalizing political institutions. As Roland Paris nicely states, the end of the Cold War witnessed "the perceived triumph of liberal market democracy as the prevailing standard of enlightened governance across much of the world, including places where it had been anathema only a few years earlier."[41] Mark Peceny and William Stanley take these notions a step further, making the case that "liberal social reconstruction," by which they mean the adoption of "liberal norms and practices," can be a sufficient condition for settlement of civil wars.[42] Where Paris's research demonstrates that outside parties press for liberal changes to markets and institutions, Peceny and Stanley show how these associated beliefs and practices have influenced belligerents in civil wars and their desires to settle them. Peace agreements and negotiated settlements are the most apparent manifestation of this system of belief.

Regardless of whether there are practical reasons for negotiated settlements or normative desires to promote liberal institutions, this book seeks to understand the practical implications of these settlements. A key question remains: Is it truly the case that these settlements are a better solution to civil wars?[43] If so, can they be strengthened so as to ensure a durable peace? The next chapter examines these questions by way of statistical analysis of different types of civil war termination, focusing on the impact they have on recurrence, democratization, and economic growth.

Chapter 4

Statistical Analysis of War Recurrence and Longer-Term Outcomes

THIS CHAPTER PRESENTS four empirical tests of the thesis that security sector reform is a key to enduring peace and to the character of the peace that follows civil wars. Here, the aim is to learn whether there exists a statistically significant relationship between types of civil war termination and longer-term outcomes, as well as to examine security sector reform and the effects of third-party interventions on enduring peace.

Examined in the first analysis is the effect of civil war outcome type (the independent variable) on the likelihood of the recurrence of war (the dependent variable). At the center of this study will be the following pair of questions: Does it matter if the war ends in a victory or which party is the victor? Or does a negotiated settlement present a better solution altogether? A logit model will be used to test the argument, to assess whether war recurred, and to examine the factors associated with such recurrence.[1]

The next area of focus highlights how SSR performs in securing the peace as compared to third-party guarantees. Not only is SSR shown to reduce the likelihood of the recurrence of war following a negotiated settlement, but we also see that third-party guarantees may actually *increase* the probability that the war will recur. These statistical findings are important because they show that the key to stabilization may not be necessarily a third party enforcing the peace from the outside; rather, internal institutional developments that include SSR form a vital element in creating a durable peace.

This statistical portion concludes with an analysis of levels of democracy, authoritarianism, and economic growth following civil war in relation to termination types. As is the case with recurrence, the findings indicate that negotiated settlements may not ensure either a more open political space or greater prosperity and economic growth. In fact, states that experience rebel victories are more likely to have greater levels of democratization than states that ended wars through negotiated settlements.

As noted in chapter 1, the total number of wars that qualified for inclusion in the data set is 130. Chapter 1 briefly outlined the precarious nature of negotiated settlements and proposed that, among all civil war termination types, they are the most likely to break down.

Previous chapters also explained that negotiated settlements are frequently seen as the preferred solution to civil wars because they are assumed to (1) reduce the likelihood of a war's recurrence; (2) promote democratization; and (3) promote economic growth. Furthermore, it is presumed that because negotiated settlements stop the violence in the short term, they will lead to lower levels of killing and destruction in the long term. The remainder of this chapter examines these assumptions.

War Recurrence

The first desired outcome of civil war termination is stability. Above all, we do not want a war that ended to recur. Furthermore, we would like to know what factors make this recurrence more or less likely. Is it the case, for instance, that security sector reform surpasses the work of third parties in ensuring that belligerents do not reengage in hostilities?

To obtain a fuller account of the relationship between civil war outcomes and the duration and quality of peace, one must consider not only the key variables, but also a number of control variables. In the literature on civil wars, scholars have already identified some key factors that seem to influence the likelihood of a given type of civil war settlement and its duration. Three such factors stand out and serve as control variables for this analysis. They isolate the following matters of concern: (1) whether the war in question was identity-based; (2) whether the war was a fight over territory; and (3) the death toll of the conflict.

The first two factors involve the quality of the war and the issues over which the combatants fought. Did the fight center on concerns of identity and cultural survival, and/or was territory the focus of the fight? As some research has indicated, identity and territory are often perceived as indivisible and therefore less amenable to negotiation.[2] If that is the case, then we should find that these two aspects negatively correlated with negotiated settlements. In the models presented below, I represent each of these characteristics with a dummy variable.[3]

Factor three considers the intensity of the fight. William Zartman, for instance, argues that hurting stalemates should make the involved parties more willing to negotiate.[4] According to Zartman, we should therefore expect to see high casualty counts and long wars associated with negotiated settlements. In the model below, I consider the intensity of the fight using two measures: the natural log of total war-related deaths and the natural log of war-related deaths per month.[5]

Though gross domestic product (GDP) per capita is already well tested as a factor showing the likelihood of civil war, the data set includes countries that have already waged civil wars and established some kind of peace.[6] Here, data show that when a state is more prosperous, it will be less likely to be plagued by an internal war. General prosperity may then help to increase the probability of an enduring peace after a civil war. While the first model is tested with and without GDP per capita, the later models included in this chapter test for prosperity after wars and as controls. The theory and subject presented here are applicable for the period after civil war has ceased and thus are not concerned with which particular factors lead up to which kind of war endings. In other words, the factors that might encourage a negotiated settlement or a military victory are not tested because they are not the dependent variable. Instead, recurrence is the object of the theoretical underpinning. Because there were several cases in which the war recurred multiple times (e.g., Burundi), all of the regressions include the "cluster" command in STATA to control for state, a standard operation for estimating within-cluster correlation based on the values of a variable. Clustering and not clustering on state had no impact on the results.

The best tool to assess the relationships among these various factors is a logit model. Table 4.1 presents the impact of the five types of war termination—military victory, negotiated settlement, cease-fire/stalemate, military victory by government, and military victory by rebels—on civil war recurrence. In that context, "0" indicates no recurrence and "1" indicates recurrence. These factors serve as the dependent variable.[7] This table demonstrates both the effects of war termination types and the impact of the control variables mentioned above on war recurrence. Given that the coefficients of a logit model are not directly interpretable as unit changes on the dependent variable (as they would be in a linear regression), the table includes "first differences"—factors that demonstrate the effect of war termination types on the probability of war recurrence while holding the alternate independent and control variables at their mean.[8]

The data presented in table 4.1 reveal that military victory reduces the likelihood of war recurrence by 24 percent, while negotiated settlements increase the chances of recurrence by 27 percent. Both findings are statistically significant, and the impact of negotiated settlements is stronger than any variable in model 2 besides conflict intensity. Establishing a control by using dummy variables for conflicts between the 1940s and the 1990s actually increases the strength of the results. In other words, there is no pre–Cold War or post–Cold War effect on a termination type's effect on the likelihood of war recurrence.[9] Military victory doubles the dampening effect, meaning that regardless of time period, military victory decreases war recurrence by 28 percent. Negotiated settlements remain about the same if we control for Cold War effects, while cease-fires/stalemates increase war recurrence by 24 percent. Moreover, if we disaggregate the information on which side prevailed in the military victory, we find that

TABLE 4.1
Logit Results of Civil War Termination Type on Recurrence

	Model 1	Model 2	Model 3	Model 4	Model 5	First Differences
Military victory	−1.935*** (.607)	−	−	−	−	−0.238***
Negotiated settlement	−	1.850*** (.853)	−	−	−	0.273***
Stalemate/ cease-fire	−	−	1.248* (.770)	−	−	0.200*
Military victory: government	−	−	−	−0.578 (.585)	−	−0.055
Military victory: rebels	−	−	−	−	−1. 466** (.879)	−0.111**
Identity	2.348** (.819)	2.236*** (.843)	2.273*** (.794)	2.361*** (.901)	2.030*** (.742)	0.181***
Territorial war	−0.997* (.684)	−0.416 (.707)	−1.077* (.747)	−0.723 (.638)	−0.828* (.616)	−0.037
LN average deaths per month	0.739*** (.204)	0.762*** (.209)	0.497*** (.176)	0.564*** (.190)	0.528*** (.165)	0.283***
LN total deaths	−0.395** (.171)	−0.422*** (.176)	−0.233 (.184)	−0.302** (.171)	−0.211 (.181)	−0.152***
Constant	−2.813** (1.439)	−4.537*** (1.812)	−4.040*** (1.526)	−3.641*** (1.479)	−3.919*** (1.676)	−
Pseudo–R2	0.242	0.209	0.182	0.168	0.197	

N = 116 in all models
Notes: One–tailed t–tests *** p < .01 ** p < .05 * p < .10
Standard errors in parentheses. Clustered on state. They are Huber/White robust standard errors.

All of the models were tested using additional controls. In none of the models did regime type, duration, or the incidence of third-party military intervention achieve significance; nor did they affect the coefficients and significance of other variables. When economic development was measured by the natural log of a country's per capita GDP in the year prior to a civil war, it did affect the significance of termination type: military victory in model 1 moves to two-star significance, while both negotiated settlements and rebel military victories drop below the one-star threshold. But in no model is the economic indicator significant itself, and its adverse effect on other variables is probably due to the fact that per capita GDP data are missing for more than half of the observations in the data set.

military victory by rebels decreases the likelihood of recurrence by 11 percent, while the effect of government military victories turns out not to be statistically significant at the 0.15 level.

A complex set of relationships thus emerges from the logit analysis. The bottom line is that this study confirms the hypothesis that a negotiated settlement may be an undesirable outcome *if we seek to prevent war recurrence*. Military victories, on the other hand, appear to reduce the likelihood of war recurrence. More important, the results show that military victory by rebels has an even greater dampening effect on war recurrence than does military victory by governments.

Before moving on to assess security sector reform in relation to recurrence, it is worth noting that two other prominent data sets display less of a correlation between war termination and recurrence: Sambanis and Doyle report that 17 percent of military victories recur versus 20 percent of negotiated settlements, while Fearon and Laitin's data show that 12 percent of victories collapse versus 9 percent of negotiated settlements.[10] In neither of these sets are rebel victories more stable than government victories. Several coding differences across these data sets account for these different results.

First, and most important, Sambanis and Doyle and Fearon and Laitin do not code several negotiated settlements that ultimately failed. Fearon and Laitin do not account for Iraq's settlement with the Kurds in 1970; Angola's 1994 Lusaka Protocol between UNITA and the MPLA; and the Philippines's 1996 peace deal with the Moro Liberation Front. Sambanis and Doyle include Angola (1994) but none of the others. In all of these cases, the parties signed formal documents that established a process to end hostilities and include all combatants as part of the government. They are clear instances of failed negotiated settlements.

Second, Sambanis and Doyle and Fearon and Laitin have lower conflict intensity thresholds than the data used for this book. There are twenty wars in Sambanis and Doyle and thirteen wars in Fearon and Laitin that had fewer than one thousand battle-related fatalities. These wars demonstrate a higher rate of successful negotiated settlements than do more intense conflicts. (Removing these conflicts from Sambanis and Doyle, for instance, raises the percentage of peace deals that fail from 20 percent to 25 percent.) Since this book is primarily concerned with mechanisms for preventing mass violence, it is theoretically justified to exclude conflicts below this thousand-fatality threshold.[11]

Third, while Sambanis and Doyle consider a number of wars of independence (e.g., Chechnya, Biafra, Burma, Southern Sudan, Western Sahara, and Yemen), they exclude a number of others (Algeria, Cameroon, Guinea-Bissau, Indonesia, Madagascar, Malaya, Morocco, Mozambique, Namibia, and Tunisia). These wars make up a substantial fraction of post–World War II armed conflict. Almost all of them were won by rebels, and none of them recurred.[12]

Finally, there are a number of instances where the data sets differ on matters of interpretation about how to aggregate or disaggregate certain conflicts. Sambanis and Doyle, for instance, consider Afghanistan to have undergone three separate wars from 1978 to 2001, and Guatemala to have undergone separate civil wars from 1966 to 1972 and 1978 to 1994. Both Sambanis and Doyle and Fearon and Laitin consider the Sandinista and Contra uprisings in Nicaragua to be separate conflicts, and both code separate Congolese civil wars in 1996–1997 and from 1998 onward. None of these conflicts is separated in the data examined here, based on the judgment that their combatants were essentially the same, that they were fighting over the same issues, and that the war could not be considered "terminated" by any means in the interim. This is a qualitative decision about what constitutes a civil war. But since this book aims to identify processes that produce stable peace, it makes sense to maintain a stringent standard for what constitutes the "end" of civil violence.

Security Sector Reform versus Third Parties

The previous logit analysis only tells us that military victories are more stable than negotiated settlements. Although this provides some support for the notion that a monopoly on the use of force is vital, because rebel organizations and governments that win seem better able to keep the peace, the statistical analysis does not reveal what might increase the stability of the peace after a negotiated settlement. For our purposes, such an analysis might examine whether security sector reform is the key to stabilizing peace after negotiated settlements.

In other words, we would like to know how effective SSR might be at maintaining peace in general. Will states that experience SSR following a negotiated settlement be less likely to experience a return to war than those cases in which SSR is absent? Furthermore, does SSR outperform third-party guarantees from organizations such as the United Nations in securing peace?

A logit analysis tests the efficacy of SSR in maintaining constructive peace. Again, recurrence of war is the dependent variable. The dummy variable for wars based or not based on identity is included as a control, along with the logged rate of casualties per month, since both of those variables were significant in every model tested in table 4.1. The model also includes the negotiated settlement variable that indicates how a war ended. It is coded "1" if the war ended by negotiated settlement and "0" if it ended by other means.

The SSR variable is a combination of two variables from Barbara Walter's "Civil War Resolution" data set.[13] Here, SSR consists of two different measures from that data set that serve as dummy variables. The first of these measures outlines the disposition of the armed forces after war and whether the combatants will form a new army that requires quotas from each party.[14] Although it does not indicate the nature or the extent of reforms of the armed forces, nor does it mention the state of the police, this model nevertheless serves as a good proxy of whether any consideration of the disposition of the armed forces was part of the settlement. If the settlement includes a military pact, it is coded "1," whereas if it does not, it is coded "0." The second variable indicates the extent to which a settlement is implemented. It is a categorical variable with four values: no negotiation, active formal negotiation, a signed settlement, and a successfully implemented settlement.[15] For this analysis, the combination SSR variable includes only those cases in which a successfully implemented settlement was present. If the settlement was well executed, the variable was coded "1." Unsuccessful implementations were "0." The SSR variable combines both of the variables with a value of "1"; if a settlement both included a military pact and was successfully implemented, then SSR was coded "1," while it was coded "0" if that was not the case.

In table 4.2, the logit models that test for the efficacy of SSR in sustaining a peace also employ a variable from Walter's data set indicating whether a third-party security guarantee was an element of the war settlement.[16] This variable also acts as a dummy variable and is coded "1" if a third-party security guarantee existed or "0" if no such assurance was given. The third party promises to enforce the terms of the peace treaty after the belligerents sign it, and these promises can be either verbal or written. These variables were coded using the criteria outlined above and were integrated into the new Civil War Data Set presented here and updated to include more recent cases.

While the first model does not include third-party guarantees, the second does. Here, the second model was employed to calculate "first differences," or the percentage probability with which each variable affects the endurance of peace while all other variables remain at their means. The results are reported in table 4.2.[17]

Table 4.2 reveals that security sector reform reduces the likelihood of war recurrence by 13 percent—a finding that is statistically significant in both estimations. This is the only factor in table 4.2 that appears to dampen the possibility of war recurrence. Furthermore, third-party guarantees are shown to have a positive relationship with war recurrence, increasing the likelihood that a war will recur by 7 percent. (This relationship is not statistically significant, however, given that by themselves they are not significant as variables.) Although third-party guarantees do

TABLE 4.2
Logit Results Testing Security Sector Reform on Recurrence

	Model 1	Model 2	First differences
Security sector reform	–2.091*	–2.295**	–0.131**
	(1.355)	(1.372)	
Identity	2.123***	1.981***	0.213***
	(0.854)	(0.826)	
Negotiated settlement	1.993***	1.648**	0.280**
	(0.856)	(0.829)	
LN average deaths per	0.516***	0.488***	0.218***
month	(0.185)	(0.196)	
Third-party guarantees	—	0.430	0.074
		(0.822)	
Constant	–7.054***	–6.487***	—
	(1.862)	(1.914)	
N	116	93	
Pseudo R2	0.180	0.169	

Notes: *** $p < .01$ ** $p < .05$ * $p < .10$
Standard errors in parentheses. Clustered on state. One-tailed t-tests.
First differences for logged intensity are calculated using the change between an observation one standard deviation below the mean and one standard deviation above the mean.
   In nine out of ten cases where SSR was implemented, the civil war did not recur. One reason that this variable only reaches the 0.10 threshold of significance is that it has so few observations. (If SSR were successful in all ten cases, it would not be possible to use it as a variable in logit regression.)

not always increase the probability of war recurring, they clearly do not help to secure the peace. Both wars ended by negotiated settlement and conflicts based on identity remain troublesome, with each of these factors increasing the probability that violence will at some point resume.

   Thus, *in general,* the status of the security sector and its reform appear to be vital. This analysis indicates that the internal balance of power may be more important for the longer-term stability of a state than are the guarantees of outside third parties.

   Although it is clear that war recurrence plagues negotiated settlement, a powerful argument exists to support settlements of this kind: a recurring war is actually less deadly over the long term than allowing the war to end in a military victory. In other words, not only do fewer people die in the short term with a negotiated settlement because the violence is stopped with the resolution, but the same also holds true in the longer term. That the recurred wars result in fewer casualties is a normatively

TABLE 4.3
The Difference of Means of Death Counts on Negotiated Settlement

	Military victory (2) mean (N)	Negotiated settlement (1) mean (N)	Pr |T| > |t|	T-test
Total deaths average	118,113 (80)	145,048 (23)	0.7077	0.3760
Total deaths average per capita	0.0089 (63)	0.0174 (22)	0.1001	1.6628
Battle deaths average	71,226 (73)	54,348 (22)	0.7108	−0.3719
Battle deaths average/per capita	0.0042 (59)	0.0063 (21)	0.3409	0.9582
Duration in months	65.7 (81)	172.9 (23)	0.000	4.5576

appealing argument and one that deserves to be considered. After all, if it were the case that fewer deaths overall resulted from negotiated settlements, then perhaps they are ultimately a better outcome. To evaluate this argument, we should verify that is indeed the case.

To assess whether negotiated settlements end in fewer deaths, the four factors of average total battle deaths, average total deaths, average battle deaths per capita, and average total deaths per capita were all analyzed against the two options of negotiated settlement (coded as "1") and military victory (coded as "2") for significance using a two-sample t-test. The same investigation also analyzes the death variables against war recurrence. In addition, war duration in years was tested in terms of its significance in negotiated settlements and in recurrence.[18]

The findings show that there were significantly more deaths in negotiated settlements than in military victories as measured by total deaths per capita (table 4.3). This relationship is statistically significant. In the case of recurring wars (table 4.4), there were considerably more total deaths on average, but this finding does not quite reach statistical significance. The numbers of total battle deaths per capita were not much greater in the case of recurring wars as opposed to nonrecurring wars. Wars that recur and wars that end in negotiated settlements are significantly longer than ones that end in military victory.

Moreover, negotiated settlements not only are more likely to recur than other termination types but are significantly more deadly when they do. The five failed negotiated settlements in this data set (Angola, Iraq, Lebanon, the Philippines, and Sudan) led on average to 0.015 total deaths per capita compared to 0.011 for all recurred civil wars; and an average of 0.005 per capita battle deaths compared to a mean of 0.003 for all recur-

TABLE 4.4
The Difference of Means of Death Counts on Recurring Civil Wars

	Recurrence (0) mean (N)	Recurrence (1) mean (N)	Pr |T| > |t|	T-test
Total deaths average	135,897 (88)	258,377 (14)	0.2034	−1.2802
Total deaths average capita	0.01007 (70)	0.01120 (14)	0.8485	−0.1916
Battle deaths average	85,512 (80)	70,517 (14)	0.8042	0.2486
Battle deaths average capita	0.00543 (65)	0.00276 (14)	0.3330	0.9743
Duration in months	97 (89)	180 (14)	0.0184	−2.3970

rences. By both measures, the recurred negotiated settlements were roughly 50 percent more deadly than the global mean.[19] If war recurrence—with its corresponding increase in deaths, sacrifices in opportunity costs, renewed destruction of infrastructure, and possible escalation of violence—represents a high cost, then negotiated settlements appear to be more costly than simply allowing two parties in a civil war to fight until one side surrenders.

At the same time, there may be other costs or benefits associated with negotiated settlements. The Civil War Data Set allows for some important comparisons in this area. What if, for example, despite the higher hazard rate of war *recurrence* following negotiated settlements, the postwar environment following a negotiated settlement promotes greater democratization and economic growth? In other words, what if we face a trade-off between a greater probability of violence reemerging (and its intensification) and the potential for a free, stable government along with prosperity? The next section reveals that, unfortunately, a trade-off of this kind does not exist. In general, negotiated settlements lead neither to greater democratization (i.e., less authoritarianism) nor to economic growth.

The Fate of Postwar Politics and Economics

What impact, if any, might war termination type have on the nature of postwar political institutions? The Civil War Data Set allows us to test whether there is in fact a relationship between the two.

TABLE 4.5
Mean Polity Scores for All States
Involved in Civil Wars

Mean polity score	
Five years prior	−3.63 (n = 73)
One year prior	−2.53 (n = 80)
Year war started	−2.63 (n = 82)

In order to track regime types by differences in war termination types, changes in the level of democratization were estimated based on the POLITY variable from the Polity IV Project data.[20] The POLITY variable ranges from −10 to 10, with a score of −10 corresponding to the most severe authoritarian regimes with no democratic qualities, while a score of 10 corresponds to the most democratic regimes with no authoritarian qualities. In the Civil War Data Set, four variables capture the average polity score following each war's termination at increments of five, ten, fifteen, and twenty years after the cessation of hostilities.[21] An additional set of variables was created to measure the difference between polity scores five, ten, fifteen, and twenty years after war termination compared to the polity one year prior to the outbreak of war.[22]

Before presenting the analysis, it is important to report some statistics about the level of democratization or authoritarianism among the states that experience civil war.

Generally speaking, civil war begins in states that display few democratic qualities. An assessment of the average polity scores before and at the outset of war in fact indicates a sizable degree of authoritarianism.[23] For example, five years prior to the start of civil war, the mean score for these states was −3.63 and a slight *decrease* in authoritarianism as war approached (see table 4.5).[24]

These average polity scores are significantly lower than those for all states in the international system. Between 1990 and 2000, the average polity score for all states that were members of the United Nations was 1.96, or nearly five points higher.[25] Hence, civil wars tend to occur within authoritarian states.

Given the evidence above that civil wars tend to arise in authoritarian states, the next step is to determine whether certain types of civil war outcomes are associated with varying degrees of authoritarianism. In other words, is it the case that military victories are more likely in states that are less democratic? Is there a systematic difference in polity scores across the different types of settlements at the start of the war? Table 4.6

TABLE 4.6
Polity Scores by Termination Type before and at the Start of the Civil War

War Termination Type	Average Polity Score		
	Five years before	One year before	Year of war
Military victory	−4.26*	−3.44**	−3.31*
Negotiated settlement	−3.40	−2.47	−3.33
Cease-fire/stalemate	4.00***	2.89***	2.89***
Military victory: government	−4.16	−3.09	-2.43
Military victory: rebels	−4.41	−4.05	−5.11**

Notes: ***p < .01, ** p < .05 * p < .10
One-tailed t-test for significance of difference in means.

presents the mean polity score five years before the war broke out, one year before, and the year of the war.[26]

This table shows that a negotiated settlement is not significantly related to a state's polity score. Statistically speaking, democracies and authoritarian states are equally likely to experience a negotiated settlement. That is not the case, however, with cease-fires/stalemates, which were associated with states that are more democratic.[27] The opposite is true for military victories; the mean polity score for cases of military victory was substantially different (i.e., more authoritarian) than for those cases not ended by military victory. It is important to note that when government and rebel victories are disaggregated, the overall correlation between military victory and enduring peace is driven by rebel victories. What this means is that wars ended through rebel victory tend to occur within more authoritarian states.

While these are important findings, they do not answer the question of whether the level of autocracy increases or decreases within states following the termination of the war.[28] This problem can be solved with data on average change in polity scores following the termination of a war. The findings produced here prove to be quite interesting.

Figure 4.1 illustrates the average change in polity scores five to twenty years after the war came to an end.[29] One can observe that negotiated settlements are more likely to be associated with increasing levels of authoritarianism as more time passes since the end of the war. Although negotiated settlements do result in an initial decrease in autocracy, as evidenced by an average increase of five points in the average polity score, this change

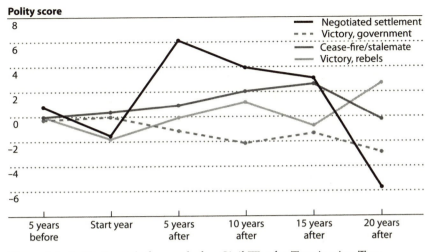

Figure 4.1. Polity Score before and after Civil War, by Termination Type

shortly gives way to an opposite trend (and a trend that is statistically significant). This finding reinforces the results presented above on the subject of war recurrence. Cases that are susceptible to a recurrence of war seem to sink precipitously into authoritarianism as governments crack down in an attempt to avert another round of violence.

Cease-fires do not seem to have an impact on the level of autocracy or democracy. Typically, the level of repression a state had at the beginning of a war is a good indication of what it will have after the war. Nonetheless, we need to be careful examining this trend given that there are so few cases (thirteen) to test.

Though military victories on the whole do not exhibit much of an impact on regime type, a significant pattern emerges when those victories are disaggregated by government versus rebel victories. As figure 4.1 illustrates, when the government wins, repression increases by one to two POLITY points over the following decades. This makes sense considering that the government—the *same* government that just suffered a civil war—is wary of opening up the political arena.

Rebel victories paint a more positive picture. Put simply, following rebel victory, democratization increases. Within ten years, autocracy has decreased by more than one point, and by twenty years that amount has more than doubled. This trend on the whole is statistically significant compared to other termination types (though the slight increase in authoritarianism at the fifteen-year mark is not).

Although still within the authoritarian range, these countries demonstrate that repression eases for a good portion of the citizenry following a rebel victory. In fact, states where rebel victories have taken place perform better on average than all of the other types on the democratization front when measured twenty years after the end of conflict—a finding that is statistically significant.

Given this result, the cliché image of a civil war—which typically depicts a corrupt and tyrannical government opposed by freedom-loving rebels—may not be entirely unfounded. Under this model, when the "repressive" government wins, it goes on creating reasons for legitimate grievances, on the part of either survivors from the previous skirmish or an entirely new set of actors. When "good" rebels win, by contrast, reforms tend to be dramatic and far-reaching, resulting in fewer grievances among survivors.

In sum, the relationship between polity scores and termination types provides further evidence that negotiated settlements may not be the best way to secure democracy following a civil war, for this type of settlement is associated with increasing authoritarianism over time. While this finding is striking on its own merits, it is also important for at least four other reasons. First, it suggests that more "democratic" processes do not necessarily lead to more democratic outcomes. In spite of a dramatic increase in the average polity score five years after wars terminated by negotiated settlements, this positive shift does not last (and it is mirrored in the other types of settlements as well). In all likelihood, what is being captured here is the effect of elections, mandated by the settlement itself and giving rise to the increase in the polity coding. Years later, however, once the first round of elections has come to pass and third parties have departed, it seems that repression starts to increase. This is consistent with the finding presented above that negotiated settlements are more apt to lead to a recurrence of the war. Generally speaking, political dynamics seem to move in a decidedly negative direction. Second, any general explanation of the relationship among war termination types, durable peace, and robust reconstruction will have to contend with this finding, especially if democracy promotion and inclusion are the reasons that negotiated settlements are sought, which does seem to be the case. According to one accounting, three-fourths (twenty-five of thirty-three) of UN peacekeeping missions that started between 1989 and 1998 involved some sort of democracy promotion. Third, although negotiated settlements are precarious in terms of both recurrence and authoritarianism, these findings suggest, if only tentatively given the few number of cases, that cease-fires may be a better path, even if they are not a permanent solution. Finally, although military victories in general may not have a positive impact on postwar civil liberties and freedom, military victories by rebels are associated with significantly reduced levels of authoritarianism.

Per capita GDP

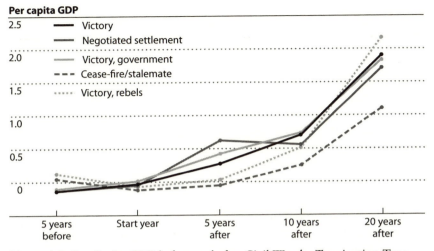

Figure 4.2. Per Capita GDP before and after Civil War, by Termination Type

Postwar Economic Reconstruction

Since the statistics show that negotiated settlements do not necessarily lead to greater democratization, the next question is whether negotiated settlements lead to prosperity. This question can be answered if we use GDP as a proxy for economic development. Following the end of a civil war, GDP can measure the impact that a given war termination type has on the speed and magnitude of postwar economic reconstruction. Figure 4.2 shows percent change in GDP at points five, ten, and twenty years after the wars terminated, with the year prior to the outbreak of war serving as the benchmark. That is, the percent change in GDP five years after war termination is the GDP at the five-year benchmark minus GDP from the year prior to the outbreak of war, divided by the latter figure. Likewise, the percent change in GDP ten years after war termination is the GDP at the ten-year benchmark minus GDP from the year prior to the outbreak of war, divided by the latter.[30]

The data presented in figure 4.2 show that economic growth or decline is unrelated to the type of civil war settlement. Most states that suffered civil wars followed the same trajectory, showing little divergence from that common trend. The most deviation that does occur is present among states with wars that ended with military victories by rebels. In these cases, the states suffered a decline in GDP immediately following the war. However, by the time ten years had passed, they recovered and displayed the same level of economic performance.

TABLE 4.7
Summary of Tests on War Termination Types

	War recurrence?	*Democratization?*	*Economic growth?*
Rebel victory	No	Yes	No
Government victory	No	No	No
Negotiated settlement	Yes (and recurrences are more violent)	No	No

In sum, this combination of statistical analyses reveals that the type of settlement does impact the prospects for peace and democratization, but not necessarily for prosperity. First and foremost, war is significantly more likely to recur after negotiated settlements. Second, negotiated settlements are no more likely to lead to democracy than are other types of settlements. In fact, rebel victories seem to be a better avenue for this. Third, economic growth trends seem to be uncorrelated with the type of termination. These findings are summarized in table 4.7.

Every war ends uniquely, and even a decisive military victory can be seen as a kind of negotiated settlement. However, reducing the complexity of civil war endings shows that there is a general pattern correlating how wars end with the peace that follows.

The destruction argument explains why negotiated settlements are more fragile than military victories. This is because in military victories, the destruction of the adversary's capacity leaves only one belligerent standing. However, that does not answer the question of why cease-fires/ stalemates are more stable than negotiated settlements or why military victories by rebels lead to more robust outcomes.

Robert Harrison Wagner's argument that decisive military victories have a positive utility is strongly, though not unconditionally, supported.[31] Peace following a decisive military victory does last longer. By contrast, negotiated settlements seem to cause postwar governments to become less democratic over time. In those cases, the more time that passes beyond the point of settlement, the less democratic the nature of postwar political regimes will become.

Several important policy implications follow. First, axiomatically supporting negotiated settlements may be not sound policy because in general they do not seem to last. In addition, as observed here, when civil wars reignite, they frequently escalate the violence in either quantity or quality. If we take the paramount values to be stability, democracy, and development, then this analysis implies that negotiated settlements as a default policy option is problematic, while victory as an option should be given consideration. But axiomatically supporting victories suffers from the same defect as the idea of always "giving war a chance": there may be cases in which the cause of the rebels or governments is in fact unjust, and this must be balanced against the desirability to foster a stable, productive, and politically liberal postwar order.

The next chapter traces the logic of the argument about SSR and benefits and harms through an important historical case: El Salvador. For the purposes of this book, the case of El Salvador is important because it represents a successful negotiated settlement after a long civil war. The case allows for a close examination of agreement content and an analysis of why it resulted in a lasting peace given the criteria presented for enforcement. As the next chapter demonstrates, provision for comprehensive security sector reform helps to explain why peace has endured.

Chapter 5

El Salvador: A Successful Negotiated Settlement

THE CIVIL WAR IN El Salvador officially ran from 1980 to 1992. In 1992 the government of El Salvador and the rebel Farabundo Martí National Liberation Movement (FMLN) signed the Chapultepec Peace Accords, ending the twelve-year conflict. El Salvador's transition from conflict to peace is considered to be "among the most successful implementations of a peace agreement in the post–Cold War period."[1] After the accords were signed, the cease-fire held, FMLN guerrillas disarmed and officially joined El Salvador's political system as the nation's second-largest political party, and the elections held in 1994 were, at the time, the sole example of free and fair elections in a postwar environment.[2]

Considered in light of the arguments made in this book, El Salvador's postconflict success is even more remarkable because it was brought about through a negotiated settlement. Peace talks began after a major FMLN assault on San Salvador in 1989, which convinced both sides that they had reached a "strategic stalemate."[3] Historically, however, civil wars concluded by negotiation and stalemate have produced outcomes that are less peaceful and less democratic than civil wars resolved by military victory.[4]

The hypothesis advanced here for why military victories hold better than negotiated settlements is that military victories *generally* result in a robust security sector. Victorious armies are typically large, disciplined, and well equipped, and, almost by definition, they are more effective than the forces they defeated. Therefore, when civil wars end by military victory, victorious armies are able to assert their authority and keep the peace. When civil wars end through negotiated settlement, however, the security sector tends to be divided and therefore less capable of keeping the peace. This pattern emerges for two reasons. First, winning and losing have powerful social implications: the victors gain legitimacy, and the defeated lose legitimacy. By extension, violence subsequent to defeat is criminal when undertaken by losers, and lawful when undertaken by winners. Winners end up with a monopoly, not on the use of violence, but on the use of *legitimate* violence—the sine qua non of a government. Second, when two or more intact and therefore quasi-legitimate military organizations exist, there is no monopoly on the legitimate use of vio-

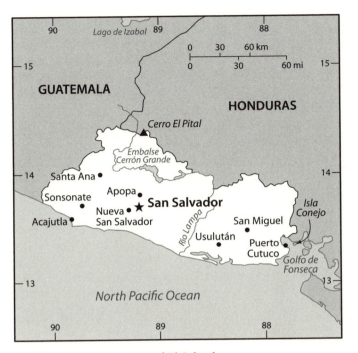

Figure 5.1. Location Map of El Salvador

lence, and both sides retain a physical and sociological capacity to re-ignite conflict. Thus, differences in security sectors may help explain why military victories produce peace more consistently than negotiated settlements following civil wars.

If this hypothesis is correct, then an ideal negotiated settlement must establish a robust and efficacious security sector. The Chapultepec Accords, which ended the Salvadoran civil war, were remarkable in the degree to which they addressed security sector reform. Even though radical Marxist change was a central objective of the FMLN, most of the treaty and its annexes were devoted to the problem of postwar *security*: the demobilization of the fighting forces, the reform of the army, and the establishment of new police and intelligence organizations.[5] Historically a formidable and influential player in Salvadoran politics, the main loser of the agreement was the military, which was sidelined by the political bargain struck between the government and the FMLN.

This chapter traces the historical background of the civil war in El Salvador, explaining the splits and strains in Salvadoran society and the emergence of violence. It then examines how, following twelve years of civil war, the parties managed to negotiate a settlement to that war. Finally, this chapter assesses the factors that made the settlement a success. I show that the key to the settlement's endurance was extensive SSR that downsized and professionalized the country's armed forces.

Background to the War

The basis of conflict in El Salvador was land, which divided the population between a tiny minority of landed elites and the vast majority of landless peasants who worked for them.[6] This division began in the nineteenth century with the establishment of coffee cultivation and the formation of plantations. Coffee production required intense farming of large tracts of land, and in 1881 and 1882 the government abolished communal forms of land and sold these tracts to private citizens and government officials.[7] The land-expropriation laws left the vast majority of the population landless.

By 1910 coffee represented 87 percent of Salvadoran exports, but 60 percent of the country's tax revenue came from imports, meaning that government economic policy encouraged a mono-crop, agro-export economy that concentrated great wealth into the hands of elite coffee growers.[8] A group of about sixty families controlled nearly 100 percent of the coffee trade, including the land, the means of coffee production, and the resources necessary to export the coffee. Over the years, peasant protests and agitation against the lack of equitable land distribution and the country's overarching economic policies were met with harsh and violent government responses.

The watershed event in Salvadoran politics was the massacre (*matanza*) of 1932. During the 1930s' depression there was a drop in coffee prices, which led to worker layoffs and reduced wages. In response, the workers (*campesinos*) formally organized an insurrection led by Communist leader Farabundo Martí. The government's retribution was far-reaching, with the worst effects occurring among the rural population in the western portions of El Salvador, although suspected urban leftists did not escape the wrath of violence.[9] The government identified rebels as anyone wearing "Indian" dress or those who carried machetes—basically, most rural workers. According to one account, "The government exacted reprisals in the rate of about one hundred to one.... It appears that the rebels killed about one hundred persons altogether during the uprising; [but] about ten thousand rebels may have lost their lives afterwards in the *matanza*."[10] The massacre was for all intents and purposes a slaughter of the local rural population that "effectively eliminated distinctive indigenous dress, languages, and other cultural expressions from western El Salvador."[11]

The political consequences of the massacre reverberated in Salvadoran politics for the next five decades.[12] The Salvadoran landowners viewed the rebellion as a direct consequence of misguided "anticapitalist" reforms initiated by previous presidents. Jeffery Paige writes that "the fact that El Salvador's only experience with social reform and popular mobilization ended in insurrection led by sectarian followers of the Communist International profoundly influenced popular and elite attitudes toward reform and social change."[13] The uprising and the consequent massacre cemented a relationship between the military and the landowning elite. The landed elite and conservative elements of the military came to regard any reform as a direct threat to the protection of their livelihood and the existence of the country. Military officers served as presidents and enacted policies that favored the landed elite, protecting their and the elite's interests at the expense of the broader population, who continued to live in poverty as laborers in the agricultural sector.

On February 5, 1932, the National Legislative Assembly elected General Maximiliano Hernández Martínez as the country's president. Once in office, Martínez institutionalized the military's role in all aspects of government, including managing the economy and shoring up the country's economic foundations. Martínez's government took over gold reserves, defaulted on international debt, created a central bank to print money (previously done by privately owned banks), suspended bank foreclosures on lands, and created private–public joint ventures that stabilized coffee production.[14] The Communist party was outlawed, and peasants were prohibited from organizing into rural labor unions. Martínez intertwined state and private interests and actively favored the agricultural business sectors of the economy. These policies, several of which the landed elite initially opposed, helped the coffee growers immensely and helped ensure their support for Martínez's presidency, which lasted for ten years.

One important reform under Martínez was the creation of new government economic agencies, which were then staffed by the military. Predictably, corruption became endemic.[15] In El Salvador, where social and financial mobility were nearly impossible, state corruption was a lucrative and attractive avenue through which non-elite-born Salvadorans, especially those in the military, could enrich their livelihoods.

The structure of government that Martínez institutionalized endured for the next fifty years.[16] With the blessing of landed elites, the military was allowed to lead the government; top military personnel became wealthy and took on the social status of national leaders. In return, the military ensured a strict laissez-faire, agricultural export economy. This economy augmented the wealth of the military and the elites, but it required peasants willing to work as landless laborers for pittance wages.

By the early 1950s El Salvador's coffee plantations were some of the most productive per hectare in the world.[17]

The landed elite had good reason to fear economic reform: they dominated every sector of the Salvadoran economy. According to Elisabeth Jean Wood, in 1971 the thirty-six largest landholders controlled 66 percent of the capital of the 1,429 largest Salvadoran firms. Of the twenty family groups in 1979 who controlled the largest quantity of nonagricultural investments, "only four were *not* rooted in the agro-export sector." This distribution was matched in manufacturing, with only 1 percent of the businesses controlling 69 percent of production.[18]

The country, in short, had failed to foster an independent bourgeoisie that could have demanded a voice and counterbalanced the interests of the landed elite. Instead, the banking and modest industrial sectors of El Salvador were never sufficiently independent from the landowners to advocate for a more equitable sociopolitical agenda. Therefore, there was essentially a single, private-sector voice that influenced El Salvador's military leaders, and that voice forcefully argued that no changes should be made.

For the next several decades, the military was caught in a difficult balancing act. On one hand, it was benefiting from its close relationship with the landed elite. On the other hand, the rural peasant majority was suffering, and this caused some in the military to support reforms that would benefit the peasantry.[19] The problem was that the military was indebted to the elites for its political and economic privileges and therefore could not adopt reforms that could oppose their interests. Therefore, the military lacked the capacity to develop popular support.[20] Both Enrique Baloyra and William Stanley convincingly argue that the Salvadoran military could not act as a legitimate head of state. It served at the whim of the landed elite, and whenever the landed elite felt its economic interests were sufficiently threatened, it would collaborate with hard-line elements in the military to foil any reform-minded measures. The military-led governments were thus unable to institute any truly popular reforms that could help them to maintain an independent source of political support.

Wood divides the military into three strains: (1) hard-liners who would crack down on even moderate government opposition, and who wholeheartedly supported the landed elites; (2) reformists who sought more political and economic equity, but who nonetheless wanted continued military rule (these were primarily junior officers from lower- and middle-class urban areas); and (3) democratic reformers (these were fewest in number) who were unopposed to a civilian-led government.[21] According to Stanley, the result from 1948 to 1977 was that the military high command

maintained an uncomfortable compromise between reform and repression, and between political openness and exclusion, responding, as necessary, to the most imminent threat to [its] tenure. Though presidents were vulnerable to pressures from hard-liners and reformists, neither of these tendencies could sustain power: the hard-liners lacked any basis for popular legitimacy, and the reformists were generally young, politically inexperienced, and unable to convince a majority of officers either to join with politically mobilized civilians or forgo the anticipated privileges associated with continued military rule. The resulting system was highly profitable for top echelons but fundamentally unstable in the long run and prone to considerable violence along the way.[22]

The rule of this alliance resulted in a repressive and authoritarian system. The harsh crackdowns by the government helped radicalize the opposition. For the guerrilla organizations, the government's actions swelled their ranks. In addition, the level of repression actually united the five main guerrilla opposition groups, when they might otherwise have been rivals.[23] Popular factions that went up against the government's policies, but who still did not yet embrace armed struggle, were nevertheless radicalized by the government's killings. Between 1978 and 1979 there were twenty-two kidnappings of prominent businessmen, and one guerrilla movement alone raised thirty-six million US dollars by early 1979. With the rise in guerrilla kidnappings, corrupt military officers would pose as guerrillas, kidnap wealthy citizens, and then ransom them. Wealthy Salvadorans would hire military units to protect them from kidnappings, and in some cases the wealthy citizens were kidnapped by members of the same armed services they had initially hired to protect them. In 1978 government and paramilitary death squads killed an estimated fifty-seven people per month.[24]

This regime lasted until October 1979, when a group of junior officers overthrew the government to form the Revolutionary Governing Junta. Although they did not necessarily favor civilian rule, they did oppose the repression and corruption of the existing system of government. Yet the junta was ineffectual, largely because conservative elements in the armed forces increased their death-squad killings and disappearances. During the month of October, 159 killings by death squads and government forces occurred, and in December 281 such executions took place.[25] Paramilitaries would assassinate leaders of popular organizations, and, when civilians within the junta complained, the military would assure them the killings would stop—only to allow the killings to continue: "Increased violence against civilians had a self-reinforcing quality. It became the principle topic of communications between the civilian government and the military, and every time the junta proved unable to enforce its prohibitions on violence, it lost authority in the eyes of both civilians and soldiers. Every time the security forces acted with impunity, they became more confident that they could operate freely in the future."[26]

The killings and disappearances undermined the legitimacy of the reform-minded junta and thereby strengthened the opposition to the government from both the Left and the Right. Although guerrillas representing the leftist opposition did conduct some killings during this period (they were responsible for the deaths of about 1,100 government and paramilitary forces in 1980), most of the killings were carried out by the right-wing death squads and security forces: during 1980 between 9,500 and 11,000 Salvadorans were killed by government forces and death squads, at an average of nearly 1,000 Salvadorans each month. [27] Those who were targeted included peasants, laborers, and Catholic Church organizations. These killings included the March 1980 assassination of the country's archbishop, Oscar Arnulfo Romero, a leading figure and vocal opponent of the government and the repression. Romero's assassination can be seen as the unofficial start of the civil war. If Romero was not safe from extrajudicial killings, many wondered, who was? The result was that the country became even more polarized, and opposition to the government brought forces together with the FMLN. By "May 1980 almost all of the important leftist and centrist popular organizations and political parties formed a large coalition called the Revolutionary Democratic Front (FDR), which quickly formed an alliance with the FMLN that would last throughout the war."[28]

The government was incapable of distinguishing between people who opposed its political and economic agenda, on one side, and those who opposed the state itself, on the other. By conflating the two groups, and by killing thousands of its own citizens (including prominent leaders of political and religious institutions), the government swelled the guerrillas' ranks. In doing so, it fueled the twelve-year civil war.[29]

War's End

The civil war in El Salvador exacted a large toll on the people and the economy. An estimated seventy-five thousand people lost their lives.[30] The economic impact of the war was devastating. By the end of the 1980s, the FMLN had caused more than 2 billion U.S. dollars in economic damages that included almost every sector of the economy, including "$1.1 billion in direct costs for repairs and replacement of equipment and infrastructure."[31] By 1984, 47 percent of coffee lands had been abandoned, and coffee production dropped by half between 1980 and 1990.[32] The military, for its part, drove the entrepreneurial class away when it sheltered corrupt officers who kidnapped Salvadorans. Between 1983 and 1986, eleven prominent Salvadorans were kidnapped by security forces, who then tried to blame the FMLN. The military treated such events as if they were isolated incidents carried out by renegade officers. In the end, the corruption and gross human rights violations, coupled with the military's inability to defeat the FMLN, alienated the military from private enterprise. With the government unable and unwilling to curb the violence, much less to develop an economic development program, the general population became increasingly active in calling for an end to the war.[33] By 1987, 83 percent of the population favored a negotiated peace.[34]

In May 1988 the FMLN leadership underwent a transformation in thinking following a tour of Latin American and Eastern European countries. The Latin American leaders urged the FMLN to give up their dream of a Marxist state, and after visiting the Eastern European countries, the FMLN leadership witnessed the corrosive effects of Soviet ideology and the alternatives to communism being adopted there.[35] Additionally, in 1989 the Soviet Union stopped supplying arms to the Sandinistas in Nicaragua, a country that had always been a supplier of FMLN weaponry.

In his 1989 inaugural address, the new president, Alfredo Cristiani, called for peace talks. In September of that year, FMLN leaders and representatives from Cristiani's right-wing party, Alianza Republicana Nacionalista/Nationalist Republican Alliance (ARENA), met in Mexico to discuss the outline of a peace deal. Then, in October, the two sides met again in Costa Rica. At the same time, however, the FMLN was preparing for a major offensive. In November, following the assassination of a popular labor leader by forces aligned with the government, and spurred by groups opposed to any peace deal, the FMLN—which had stockpiled tons of weapons in San Salvador—led an all-out assault against the government. The FMLN invaded San Salvador, and the military endured several days of difficult fighting to dislodge it from the poorer neighborhoods. In doing so, the military killed and injured thousands of civilians by indiscriminately firing high-explosive artillery shells and bombs from aircraft. The guerrillas then infiltrated wealthy neighborhoods. This time the government refused to use indiscriminate firepower. The FMLN occupied the wealthy neighborhoods for several days, essentially holding San Salvador's elite hostage, while the military contemplated its next move.[36]

Although ultimately a military failure for the FMLN, the rebel invasion proved to be a major political victory and a watershed event.[37] Because it revealed that the FMLN was still a formidable force, it sidelined the military from interfering with and scuttling ARENA-led peace talks. Additionally, the rebel offensive proved that the military was unable to defend the wealthy from the FMLN, and this reinforced the overall civilian distrust of the military. The failed offensive caused El Salvador's wealthy elites—now certain that the military's strategy to preserve the status quo was ineffective—to look elsewhere for forces and tactics that could secure their interests.[38]

The FMLN's offensive also affected the guerrilla leadership. After launching its invasion, the FMLN called for a massive insurrection. That uprising never came. The demise of the Soviet Union, the electoral loss of the Sandinistas in Nicaragua, the FMLN's inability to overthrow the government in a major ground offensive, and the pressure from international players—including the United States—for a negotiated peace deal forced the FMLN to consider peace negotiations seriously as their last and best chance to achieve real change in El Salvador.[39]

Negotiated Settlement

Peace negotiations and the subsequent peace accords between the FMLN and the Salvadoran government resulted from the confluence of three interlocking factors: (1) the collapse of the implicit contract between the military and the Salvadoran elite; (2) significant shifts in the international system (the end of the Cold War); and (3) the inability of the military to defeat the FMLN. In addition to these three factors, the existence and activism of the United Nations also made an important contribution.

Pressure to abrogate the traditional alliance of the Salvadoran military and the landed elite came from both of these two parties. First, the long-term devastating effects of income inequality in El Salvador created a constant supply of military officers whose families were harmed by a lack of access to education, health care, and secure living arrangements. At higher ranks, the system of rewards implicit in the long-standing contract would dampen these threats. But over the five decades from 1932 to 1982, it became increasingly difficult for each cohort of officers to make it to sufficient rank to spare their families from the debilitating effects of poverty. Second, and related to the waiting problem, was the increasing temptation to ameliorate the wait by preying upon the landed elite themselves, then blaming attacks on the FMLN. As the FMLN became more adept as a military force, life in the armed forces became increasingly dangerous. Members of the military began to question whether the benefits they waited for would ever be realized.

From the elite's perspective, two important shifts occurred. First, as the violence became more indiscriminate, the traditional landed elites questioned whether the military had the capacity to protect them. Second, the elite itself broadened to include industrialists and entrepreneurs in the urban areas. As the war continued, this broader set of elites came to realize that it did not require or want a state apparatus that was dependent on the military for ensuring the compliance of laborers. Rather, for them, order and stability were best achieved through politics and a diminished role for the military. Juhn sums up their calculations nicely:

> The longer the war went on, the less convinced the oligarchy was that war could restore its way of life. If the war went on, it was bad for business. If the left won, the oligarchy would certainly lose it privileges. If the army won, the oligarchy would probably have to acquiesce to a power-sharing arrangement with a mass-based army, economically autonomous and unvanquished in battle. To reassert its traditional position in the country, the oligarchy's best option was to win in competitive politics: victory in this arena would restore commerce, delimit the role of the military, and give the oligarchy a decisive role in shaping modern political institutions.[40]

The elite thus began to distance itself from the military and instead sought to engage in conventional politics. Without the support of the elite, the military found itself with diminished authority.

A second factor leading to a negotiated settlement was the end of the Cold War. By the late 1980s the FMLN, like communist-inspired insurgents everywhere, was forced to recognize that the world had changed: revolution and Marxism had failed in Eastern Europe, and the Sandinistas had been voted out of office in Nicaragua.[41] For its part, ARENA's now broad-based constituency wanted stable economic conditions that did not necessarily demand the repression of labor, and with the violence becoming increasingly indiscriminate and the military's apparent inability to provide stability, a peace accord with the FMLN became the only viable alternative for ARENA to satisfy its constituency.

The end of the Cold War had another important effect as well. Once the communist menace that had come to underpin U.S. calculations regarding economic aid and diplomatic support waned, the costs of U.S. support in terms of human rights abuses were thrown into increasingly sharp relief.[42] The 1989 killing of six Jesuit priests and two colleagues by members of the Salvadoran military at the Central American University in San Salvador was only the most notorious and shocking. The United States soon began making continued military aid to El Salvador contingent on an improved human rights record and movement toward peace talks.[43] By constraining the Salvadoran military from fighting a "dirty" terrorist war against the FMLN and its supporters, El Salvador's political elites believed that the United States would hamstring the Salvadoran military's ability to win the war. The military's ineffectiveness, coupled with the FMLN's persistent and devastating economic sabotage, helped facilitate the rise of ARENA, which at its inception had represented the extreme right wing. By 1988 it had become a relatively moderate political entity representing a broader constituency of a wealthy landed elite and business interests beyond agriculture. Furthermore, once ARENA began working and succeeding within the legitimate political system, the party distanced itself from the military to a degree that enabled it to explore, and later consummate, peace negotiations with the FMLN.[44]

The third primary factor leading to a negotiated settlement was the shattering of the illusion that force—extreme, and now increasingly indiscriminate—could by itself secure the interests of either group of combatants. In the decade leading up to the 1989 FMLN assault on San Salvador, El Salvador's military had been the recipient of an array of U.S. military aid, including equipment, training, and intelligence support. And yet, despite this support, the military could not adequately defend the capital—and San Salvador's wealthiest citizens—from an FMLN attack. For its part, the FMLN, like countless communist-inspired insurgencies before it, had counted on a mass uprising and mass defections of rank-and-file soldiers to its cause; but although it was able to capture and defend entire city districts for some time, this popular support (and the legitimacy that would come with it) never materialized. Thus this "failure of force" proved a watershed for both sides. The landed elites were suffering financially and individually and felt the military could no longer protect their interests. The FMLN faced the end of foreign support and a lack of domestic support beyond the vital issue of simple physical survival. Both sides thus came to see a negotiated settlement as the least of the evils they might face.

Finally, the UN's role was important in two fundamental ways. First, both sides needed the UN's help in mediating disagreements and preventing breakdowns in the peace process. It was the United Nations whose assistance the FMLN sought as it attempted to negotiate an end to the war as early as 1989. The process of negotiations required a series of agreements and took over two years, during which time the UN played the role of a trusted, neutral third party that could referee disputes. Once the accords were signed, the UN was in a position to embarrass the parties when either side failed to carry out its obligations.[45] Stemming from this, the government needed the UN's seal of approval to receive millions of dollars in international assistance. Moreover, the government—with more to gain monetarily and more compliance commitments—had more to lose if the UN disapproved of its actions.[46] For the FMLN, the UN's seal of approval for its signing and carrying out the provisions of the accords provided it with needed legitimacy, thereby facilitating its transition from an armed insurgency to a political party.

The broken contract between El Salvador's landed elite and the military, the end of the Cold War, the declining political utility of violence, and timely and skillful UN mediation and intercession all explain why the combatants chose to seek a negotiated settlement. It is the nature of that settlement, and how its provisions functioned to secure the peace, to which I now turn.

Security Sector Reform in El Salvador

The Chapultepec Accords provide a detailed blueprint for security sector reform in the aftermath of a civil war. Existing forces were rapidly disarmed and reintegrated into society; the army, police, and intelligence services were subjected to strict civilian control; the army and police were revamped and separated in function; new recruitment and training procedures were implemented to specialize these forces; and specific transitional provisions governed the processes and timetables by which these reforms were to be carried out. Most important, the Chapultepec Accords set forth a framework for the future of El Salvador's security sector that was developed and ratified by both the government and the FMLN. This early consensus on such a detailed plan for security sector reform likely played a key role in promoting national unity in El Salvador, setting it apart from so many other negotiated settlements.

There are two key issues regarding the relationship between SSR and El Salvador's enduring peace. First, there are the political conditions that gave the FMLN and government sufficient interest in designing and then implementing a negotiated settlement that emphasized SSR. Second, there are the provisions of that settlement itself. I argue that shortfalls on either count would have been sufficient to spoil a meaningful settlement and thereby undermine peace.

What is perhaps most notable about the peace treaty is that 80 percent of the document is devoted to SSR, with the first two chapters spelling out the disposition of the security forces. As to the specific provisions of the accords in relation to the security sector, five aspects stand out: (1) specialization of the armed forces; (2) disarmament, demobilization, and reintegration of combat forces; (3) establishment of civilian control over the armed forces; (4) a transition process and capacity building; and (5) an inclusive framework.

Specialization of the Armed Forces

What is so striking when reading the FLMN's overtures to peace negotiations is the group's insistence that a new police force was needed and that the military itself had to be downsized and place under civilian control. The FLMN's proposals, which were presented for negotiation in September 1989 in Mexico City and a month later in San José, Costa Rica, included explicit mention of the need for measures regarding the "self-cleansing and professionalizing of the Armed Forces," a smaller, single national army whose mission would be to defend national sovereignty, and "the dissolution of the security forces and the formation of a single security force under civilian control."[47] The San José proposal was even more explicit in demanding not only the subordination of the armed forces to democratically elected civilian authorities but also the creation of a police force that is subordinate to national civilian authority rather than the military.

Thus, although the FMLN did propose socioeconomic and political changes, including agrarian reforms, these changes were to occur within the preexisting structure of the 1983 Constitution. The farthest-reaching proposals were those surrounding reform of the security environment.

The Chapultepec Accords retained the proposals offered in the earlier agreements. The accords provide for a detailed reform of the function, recruitment, and education of the armed forces, including both the military and the newly created National Civilian Police (PNC). Furthermore, these reforms were demanded by the FMLN. According to Stanley, "the civilianization of internal security, and all of the reforms embodied in the peace accords, were *coerced* by the armed force of the FMLN."[48] The government, however, acquiesced to the FMLN's demands, making the military the biggest loser.

Whereas historically the military's primary role was internal security and control of the population, the first article mandates its mission as exclusively external, such that "the maintenance of internal peace, tranquility, order and public security lies outside the normal functions of the armed forces" (chap. 1, art. 1F). The military was to be specialized to external defense alone, while internal matters were to be the province of the police, "independent of the armed forces" (chap. 2, art. 2B), beyond which "there shall be no other armed police body with national jurisdiction" (annex 2, chap. 1). And three separate existing security agencies—the Treasury Police, rural National Guard, and urban National Police—were deemed redundant in function and dissolved altogether (chap. 1, art. 6C). By separating and professionalizing the army and police force and specializing them to external and domestic concerns, respectively, the accords sought to rationalize El Salvador's security sector, thereby rendering it more effective and serving the needs of the state and its citizens rather than preying on them.

The defining and farthest-reaching feature of the Chapultepec Accords was the creation of the PNC—"a new force, with a new organization, new officers, new education and training mechanisms and a new doctrine" (chap. 1, art. 6B). Dedicated to the "concept of public security as a service provided by the State to its citizens" (chap. 2, art. 2A), and mandated to "respect and promote human dignity [and] preserve and defend the human rights of all persons" (chap. 2, art. 2D), the PNC was hailed by the UN Secretary-General Boutros Boutros-Ghali as "one of the fundamental elements of the peace accords and perhaps the single component with the greatest hopes."[49] PNC officers were to be better educated than their predecessors and were not to engage in politics. They would be drawn from the community and would continue to be part of the community.

The treaty was also very specific about the nature of recruitment into the armed forces. According to Welch and Janowitz, recruitment processes are important determinants of civil-military relations: while universal, merit-based recruiting produces professionalized soldiers, narrow and politically motivated recruitment leads to ideologically polarized forces that are prone to repression and intervention.[50] The Chapultepec Accords made strict recruitment standards consistent with this theory. At least 60 percent of PNC officers and agents had to be civilians, and only 20 percent of the PNC could be former National Police or FMLN fighters.[51] Efforts were also made to recruit women, who were afforded "special consideration" (chap. 2, art. 7Db).

The accords provide detailed guidelines for the education of security sector forces. The military, for instance, was required to undertake "scientific and humanistic studies in order to provide an all-round education" (chap. 1, art. 2C), and soldiers would be "encouraged to take professional and postgraduate courses at the country's universities" (chap. 1, art. 2D). Explicit provisions for the makeup of the Academic Councils of the military and police were also articulated in the treaty; these served as a way to ensure not only a broad-based curriculum but civilian oversight as well (chap. 1, art. 2). In the same vein, the accords explicitly state that even after recruitment and membership into the PNC, all personnel "shall be considered civilians, regardless of origin" (chap. 2, art. 7Dj).

The extensive treatment given to the specialization, recruitment, and education of the security forces in the Chapultepec Accords was clearly aimed at specialization of function. These provisions may have played a key role in creating a stable, efficient, and legitimate security sector in El Salvador.

Disarmament, Demobilization, and Reintegration

The disarmament, demobilization, and reintegration of government and rebel forces following a war is typically the first step in security sector reform; it is also one of the most difficult. Oversized fighting forces are a common cause of instability in postconflict countries,[52] and where more than one military organization exists, as is often the case after negotiated settlements, their coexistence becomes a potential cause for the reemergence of war. DDR of armed forces is thus a critical component of postwar stability.

The Chapultepec Accords were successful at disarming and demobilizing El Salvador's various fighting forces largely because there were specific provisions for doing so. As mentioned above, the first chapter of the accords takes up the disposition of the armed forces. After detailing the mission of the military (protecting state sovereignty and territorial integrity from *external* threats) and its subordination to constitutional authorities, the accords move on to education (art. 2), vetting (labeled as "purification," art. 3), and reduction in size (art. 4). Included are provisions for the payment of one year's wage and the promotion of public works projects in support of employment (art. 13B). As part of a national reconstruction plan, the accords stipulate that "measures shall be taken to facilitate reintegration of FMLN into the country's civil, institutional and political life, including fellowship, employment and pension programs, housing programs and programs for starting up new businesses" (chap. 5, art. 9).

The reintegration of the FMLN forces into a legitimate political framework is also outlined in the accords. Chapter 7 includes a section explicitly titled "End of the structure of FMLN and the reintegration of its members, within a framework of full legality, into the civil, institutional, and political life of the country" (arts. 26–29). Meanwhile, chapter 6— "Political Participation by FMLN"—guarantees members of the FMLN their civil and political rights (art. 1). The accords also legalized the FMLN as a political party (art. 6), afforded special security protection to its leaders if needed (art. 9), and freed all political prisoners (art. 2). In terms of disarmament, the accords provide a detailed time line for the FMLN to relinquish and destroy its weapons under UN supervision (chap. 7, arts. 26–29).

While the economic reintegration program was not fully implemented,[53] El Salvador was remarkably efficient in implementing the remainder of its DDR aims. The FMLN completely disarmed as a military organization, participated in the 1994 elections, and became the country's second-largest political party. By mid-1993—ahead of the timetable set in the Chapultepec Accords—the military had cut more than 50 percent of its forces. As a result of these measures, El Salvador's security sector had been substantially reduced in size, but it still retained a critical mass of experienced, disciplined soldiers.[54] Moreover, compliance with the accords meant that this downsized military—now publicly restricted to an external security role, save in grave emergencies—and the PNC—which was specialized and trained for internal matters—had regained for the government a monopoly on the legitimate use of violence. This would be an institutional necessity for the security sector—one that most contemporary negotiated settlements fail to provide.

Civilian Control of the Military

Despite the importance of DDR, there are additional critical components of successful security sector reform. Establishing civilian control of the military is one of the crucial—and most elusive—characteristics of stable civil–military relations and an effective security sector. Yet despite the wealth of scholarship on this topic, in postwar states there is often a lack of demand for a security system that serves the citizens and protects their basic rights.[55] In Haiti and Mozambique, for example, civilian governments failed to assert effective control over the armed forces, leading to persistent instability. Subordinating the armed forces to civilian authority is especially difficulty in cases following negotiated settlements, where new governments tend to be weak, fighting forces tend to be large, and a unified political authority is in transition. The armed forces are often the only institution capable of maintaining order and administering the state functions.

The Chapultepec Accords, however, took significant steps to ensure civilian control over the new security sector. Furthermore, the accords stipulated that such forces were to perform their mission in line with democratic values and with respect for all parts of the constitution. According to chapter 1's first article, only the president of the republic and "the basic organs of government" had the authority to use the armed forces. The armed forces were to be "obedient, professional, apolitical and non-deliberative" (chap. 1, art. 1B). In the same vein, the PNC and the new intelligence services were placed explicitly under the control of civilian authorities (chap. 1, arts. 6A and 7A, and chap. 2, art. 3A) and were charged to act in the interests and protection of the citizens (chap. 2, art. 2A). Thus, generally speaking, the armed forces would no longer be immune from the law (chap. 1, art. 5).

Beyond rhetorically asserting civilian control of the security sector, the accords contain a wide variety of specific provisions to build institutional checks and balances on the autonomy of the military, police, and intelligence services. "Within the context of the objectives of this Agreement," says one provision, "the Parties recognize the need to adopt a number of measures designed to promote enhanced respect for the rules which must govern the armed forces and to prevent infringements of those rules" (chap. 1, art. 12). These rules included, among other provisions, the enactment of legislative oversight of the military, the formation of an Armed Forces General Inspectorate, the creation of independent courts to implement codes of conduct, and the establishment of a Police Disciplinary Investigation Division (chap. 1, art. 12B, and chap. 2, art. 3B). Therefore, the Chapultepec Accords not only articulated the principle of civilian control of the armed forces but also provided the specific mechanisms to bring this principle into effect.

Finally, the treaty made extensive provisions for the purging of current armed forces and the vetting of its members. "In general," writes Call, a postconflict security sector "should seek to exclude all those against whom well founded accusations of violations of international or national law exist."[56] Chapter 1, article 3, established an Ad-Hoc Commission with the mandate to evaluate all members of the military and the power to recommend that any personnel be relocated or dismissed. After some initial reluctance, by mid-1993 the government enacted the commission's recommendations, purging 102 officers from its ranks. Most of the top military leadership (including the minister and vice minister of defense) retired or were removed in the "most thorough house-cleaning ever carried out of a Latin American military not defeated in war."[57] It was the first time a Latin American military had ever submitted its officers to an external review process. The purge undoubtedly facilitated increased civilian control over the armed forces; at the same time, it allowed the Salvadoran military to regain some of its legitimacy.[58]

Capacity Building and Transitional Provisions

Many of the security sector reforms in the Chapultepec Accords discussed above were aimed at reducing the size and independence of the armed forces. But the Chapultepec Accords also contained numerous provisions to ensure that the military, police, and intelligence services had the capacity to be effective as well. Providing security in a postconflict scenario is never an easy task. When civil wars end through military victory, there is often at least some armed force that survives intact to enforce stability, but in the case of negotiated settlement, this cannot be taken for granted. El Salvador's "capacity-building" efforts thus had a crucial role to play in ensuring that the country's vicious civil war remained extinguished.

According to a RAND Corporation study, it is essential for governments to establish security during the "golden hour" after the war has ended.[59] Security sector forces must assert their authority within months— or even weeks—of conflict if they are to be effective. "Key tasks," the study argues, "include rapidly deploying international military and police forces, vetting and deploying indigenous police and other security forces, and establishing at least a temporary rule of law." Quickly establishing critical levels of security forces in this way was particularly crucial, says RAND, to peacekeeping operations in Kosovo and East Timor.[60]

It was therefore crucial that the Chapultepec Accords contained extensive transitional provisions to manage the immediate construction of an effective security sector. The treaty, for instance, required the legislature to establish the PNC within 30 days. The training of a new officer corps was to begin immediately, and the entire structure of the police was to be in place within 240 days, with territorial deployment carried out within 270 days (chap. 9, art. 3). Within two years, 5,700 new officers were to become active, and by five years out, 10,000 officers (chap. 2, art. 7Cc). Meanwhile, the Ad-Hoc Commission was given only three months to perform its internal review process, and the government was required to adopt its recommendations within an additional 60-day period (chap. 1, art. 3J). And, as mentioned above, the disarmament and demobilization of the FMLN was to take place on a similarly expeditious schedule.

As Call writes, the remarkable "level of detail and specific timelines" for security sector reform was a key to the success of the Chapultepec Accords.[61] The treaty went so far as to provide three preliminary bills in its annexes for the registration of security personnel, the establishment of the police, and the creation of a National Security Academy. As a result, SSR in El Salvador was carried out promptly and in an organized fashion. By contrast, Call explains, the treaty dealt with judicial reforms in only six vague paragraphs. As a result, through 2002, "the judicial system remained weak, inefficient, antiquated, overly partisan, and subject to corruption."[62] Explicit provisions for effective interim security and full-fledged SSR thus helped to ensure both short-term stability and future reform.

What Worked: An Inclusive Security Framework

Perhaps the most important feature of SSR in the Chapultepec Accords, however, was less the content of the accords themselves (i.e., specialization of function, DDR, checks and balances, and transitional provisions), and more the fact that both sides remained committed to a nonviolent resolution throughout the implementation process. Or, to put it another way, the content was as much a consequence as a cause of the political will to avoid a return to civil war in El Salvador.

The accords themselves contained flaws, but when a shortcoming threatened to derail the process, political elites from both factions—with help from the UN—managed to overcome the temptation to abandon the process. Almost every scholar of civil–military relations stresses that popular legitimacy is a key determinant of stable security sectors. Because they bore signatures from both the government and the FMLN, the accords had this legitimacy.

The drafters of the treaty took advantage of the rare opportunity to solidify an early and tenuous consensus among the leaders of the rival factions. By articulating SSR in such detail—down to proposed legislation in the annexes—the accords granted automatic legitimacy to even the most mundane of security sector reforms. The treaty established a common blueprint for postconflict stability and thus avoided the legal wrangling and power struggles that would have otherwise occurred later.

The elections of 1994 served as the ultimate enforcer for both sides' commitment to the accords: they pushed each party to work to gain the trust and support of undecided voters while keeping their traditional support bases intact. Compliance with the accords was the best way to appeal to the undecided voters, and yet degrees of noncompliance satisfied each side's traditional base by demonstrating a commitment to their interests and objectives.

The FMLN's traditional base was its combatants and the country's poor, particularly the rural poor. The FMLN wanted as much money and land as possible to parcel out to its constituency. Yet overall, only 10 percent of the accords dealt with economic issues, with much of the rest focused on military reforms and the creation of the new civilian police force. Even though the FMLN's struggle had endeavored for social and economic change, the focus on military reform underscored the FMLN's belief that military reform was key to its reintegration into society.[63] According to Wood:

> The principal achievement of the agreement was an agenda of reforms that would institutionalize the new—democratic—rules of the political game.... The main provisions...were reforms of the armed forces, accountability of past human rights violations, the founding of a new police force, and restrictions on the arbitrary exercise of state power.... In sharp contrast, negotiators made little effort to finalize the details of the socio-economic agreement.... [A]s a result it was one of the weakest sections of the Chapultepec Accords.[64]

The FMLN had come to accept that only minor constitutional changes would be enough to secure its political and economic interests, so long as the armed forces were downsized, transformed, and sidelined from politics. Furthermore, because the accords laid out an implementation process overseen by the United Nations, the FMLN felt secure enough to demobilize. For instance, the accords mandated that National Guard and Treasury Police be disbanded. However, the government simply renamed them and integrated them into the army. The FMLN challenged the government's action. The United Nations Observer Mission in El Salvador

(ONUSAL) mediated talks between the government and the FMLN, resulting in an agreement that led to the dissolution of the two security forces.[65] In addition, the accords provided a detailed calendar for the demobilization of the different forces. Although the calendar did not require an explicit staging, such that one side completed its disarmament and demobilization or transformation before the other, the process was staggered enough to guarantee security. Thus, for example, the first 20 percent of the FMLN was to disband only after the National Guard and Treasury Police were dissolved.[66] Merely a fraction of the FMLN was required to demobilize; further, this would take place only on the condition of the demobilization of government forces. The sequencing thus afforded the parties some security guarantees as they moved forward.

The National Guard/Treasury Police episode reveals that the government, too, was forced to worry that compliance with the accords would cause a reaction whereby the military would disrupt the peace—or even reignite the war. The military had much to lose from the accords. However, because the government under ARENA rightly perceived that it no longer needed the military to stay in power, it felt as if it could accede to the main demands of the FMLN, even though those demands directly opposed those of the military.[67] Furthermore, because much of the funding for postwar economic reform was coming from international sources, the government feared that its noncompliance would reduce that funding.[68] Once the FMLN disarmed, there was less of a chance that the former combatants could restart the war easily; the military, however, was another story. Because the government feared alienating the military, it wanted as much money as it could obtain to reintegrate its decommissioned soldiers (by 1993, 54 percent of the armed forces had been decommissioned).[69] Because funds flowing from foreign donors were to provide two-thirds of the financing for the peace process, the government had more incentive to comply with the accords so as to keep open the flow of foreign aid.[70]

A good deal of credit for the achievement of consensus in the Chapultepec Accords belongs to the efforts of the United Nations, which mediated the peace process from 1989 onward. However, it was the parties to the agreement that made it a possibility and a success. As David Holiday and William Stanley point out, "Both the greatest setbacks and most significant breakthroughs of the process can be traced to the domestic political interests of the actors."[71] Other scholars credit the role of national exhaustion and strategic stalemate for driving the parties toward a compromise of necessity.[72] But whatever the reason, the final product of the negotiation between the government of El Salvador and the FMLN was characterized by a high degree of creativity, detail, and progressive reforms that were ultimately ratified by both sides. At points, the accords read more like domestic legislation than an agreement between warring parties. This characteristic must have exercised a profound effect on the ability of both sides to establish a national security framework in a unified fashion.

What Did Not Work

For all the potential good news about the negotiated settlement that brought the civil war to an end, however, the effective defeat of the FMLN on socioeconomic issues does not bode well for El Salvador's future, either economically or in terms of political liberalization. Two factors explain the lack of socioeconomic change. The first was unanticipated advantages that the government accrued as a result of key provisions of the accords themselves. The second was the lack of major structural economic reform that could have alleviated the high levels of poverty and inequality that helped fuel support for the war in the first place.[73]

In terms of advantages for the government, the accords, for example, stipulated the creation of a National Commission for the Consolidation of Peace (COPAZ), which was intended as a way to give the FMLN an active role in implementing the peace accords *after* it had disarmed but *before* the 1994 elections, when presumably it would have elected representatives in the Legislative Assembly. The FMLN disarmed—almost entirely—by December 1992, albeit two months behind schedule.[74] At the same time, COPAZ, with its structural symmetry of representation, was ineffective. The equal number of representatives on each side uniformly opposed each other, and when stalemate occurred, disputes had to be taken up directly by government and FMLN leaders. The two sides would then negotiate a settlement between themselves, often with the ONUSAL as mediator.[75]

For its part, ONUSAL's most effective leverage was its moral authority. Publicizing noncompliance had a significant impact on both sides because of the publicity's effect on foreign donors and on the undecided voters among the electorate. However, because of its multifaceted role in the verification process, ONUSAL could not always seek to use its publicity and moral authority to gain leverage. If it constantly criticized the government—which had more duties to carry out under the accords—ONUSAL could appear overly biased, and this could threaten the overall peace accords if the government and the military felt inundated with criticism. As a result, ONUSAL had to pick and choose when to throw its weight around. The downside to this strategy was that there were times when the government, often with support from the FMLN (whom the government bought off in certain situations) would shirk its responsibilities under the accords. And when ONUSAL failed to sound an alarm, breaches of the peace accords would go unpunished.[76]

Additionally, while the accords were specific in some areas, particularly with regard to the restructuring of the armed forces, they were unspecific in others, such as plans for economic reconstruction. As a result of the nonspecificity in how postwar spending was to occur, the government was able to put forward and control a reconstruction plan with little input from the FMLN.[77] While international NGOs funded many programs beneficial to the FMLN, the government's reconstruction plan was implemented relatively unilaterally. The government had the power to allocate its resources in ways that directly benefited the portion of the population expected to support ARENA in the 1994 elections, including urban dwellers and the wealthy. This power of the purse gave an unfair advantage to the government that was unforeseen by supporters of the peace agreement, making it clear that the government preferred instituting its economic program over implementing the terms of the agreement. According to Wood, "although the FMLN's recommendations and requests would be 'taken into account' [by the government], its role was clearly secondary," and therefore its economic interests were not served and many of the provisions of the accords were delayed or not implemented as mandated.[78]

In hindsight, the process of SSR in El Salvador was far from comprehensive, either in conception or implementation. Important civil-military reforms were not carried out completely, and the autonomy of the armed forces remained higher than that which was demanded in original negotiations. Following the implementation of the accords, the army continued to carry out certain internal functions, such as policing highways and patrolling coffee harvests. For its part, the new police force (PNC) was subject to training and deployment delays, which were largely political. The original police force (PN) refused to demobilize and hand over equipment, and the civilian authorities did not press them to do so. Only in late 1994, following a serious increase in the crime rate and evidence of the involvement of PN officers in organized crime, was the government compelled to dissolve the old force.[79] Money then flowed, which allowed the PNC to arm, educate, and train, turning its members into a professional force.[80]

Nevertheless, El Salvador did manage to demobilize a substantial proportion of its fighting forces, while leaving a critical mass of experienced soldiers in place. Civilian control significantly curtailed the political influence of the military and the police.[81] The new security forces were widely perceived as legitimate, especially after the 1993 purges of the military had been carried out and the police received proper training and equipment. Above all, the new security sector achieved its primary objective: both sides argued, struggled, and fought, but civil war did not begin again in El Salvador. In order for future negotiated settlements to achieve similar success, they would do well to study the examples of security sector reform set forth in the Chapultepec Accords.

The Postsettlement Environment

If success is defined narrowly as a conclusive end to civil war, then El Salvador must count as one of the few cases of a successful negotiated settlement. Moreover, the end of this civil war and its lack of recurrence are not the result of third-party guarantees, but of extensive internal reforms that brought about significant changes to the security sector. According to Mark Peceny and William Stanley, "the UN focused on a thorough reformation of the central coercive institutions of the state to guarantee that the army and the police would be professional apolitical institutions clearly subordinated to civilian control."[82]

The changes in the security sector have resulted in the end of the Salvadoran armed forces' characterization as autonomous repressive institutions with broad powers, and in the establishment of their new role as more professionalized services that are subordinate to civilian authorities. The military underwent purges of the highest ranks, which sent a message to those who remain that the military's power and status have been diminished. Furthermore, the military downsized rapidly, and at a faster rate than prescribed by the settlement.[83] As discussed above, the constitution stipulates that armed forces are to be excluded from internal security matters, except in emergency situations.

As to the PNC, Stanley points out that although the FMLN did not fulfill its 20 percent quota, the PNC has become a force with much more civilian character than anticipated. The force quickly expanded "to a size that exceeded the actual complement of the armed forces, with virtually all of the additional recruits drawn from civilian life." Stanley adds that although the force has not conducted itself perfectly, it is nevertheless "far more efficient, responsive, transparent and accountable than the old police."[84]

Crime remains a significant problem in El Salvador. In fact, during the mid-1990s the levels of violence due to criminal activity exceeded those during the civil war. However, those rates have since declined, in part because the police have become more effective. Between 1993 and 2000, victimization rates among El Salvador's population dropped by half.[85] And perhaps more important, the violence is not due to the police or the armed forces, but to criminal activity that the government and the broader population have committed themselves to fighting.[86]

The political system has experienced successive electoral cycles without significant violence or fraud, with the government ARENA party and the FMLN as the main contenders for power.

Most recently the FMLN party's candidate, Mauricio Funes, won the presidency for the first time since the end of the war, some 17 years later in March 2009, with 51 percent of the vote against ARENA's 49 percent. Such a political victory bodes well for continued peace in El Salvador. Although major changes to the economic system were only a small part of the agreement, El Salvador's economy has largely recovered from the ravages of the civil war: its GDP increased from 3.8 billion U.S. dollars in 1986 to 18.7 billion in 2006.[87] However, some deep-seated issues remain, including continued economic inequality and high levels of poverty. The most recent Gini index of 52.5 indicates a moderate level of inequality in El Salvador; since the first peace talks began in 1989, the Gini index has risen from 49, demonstrating ineffectiveness of the accords in addressing economic inequality.[88] Even more discouraging is the ratio of the richest 20 percent of Salvadorans to the poorest 20 percent: since 2001 the gap between the two groups has increased from 14.8 to 20.9, while the equivalent ratio for the richest and poorest 10 percent of the population has increased from 28.5 to 57.5.[89] Most significantly for our purposes here is that land tenure and reform were not fully handled as a result of the war and the accords, raising the question of whether El Salvador remains at risk of another agrarian revolution. Despite high levels of poverty in the rural areas, the consensus among scholars seems to be that migration and urbanization have lessened the importance and severity of land reform in El Salvador.[90] It is important to point out that the FMLN did not insist on deep structural economic changes to the economy, including a more thorough redistribution of the land as part of the settlement.[91] Had it done so, it is unlikely that the accords would have been signed.[92] Despite the unresolved socioeconomic issues and the high levels of inequality and poverty that still plague El Salvador, civil war does not loom on the horizon.

SSR and Negotiated Settlements: Lessons Learned

El Salvador's successful negotiated settlement counts as a tough case for my peace through security argument because it appears to have resulted in enduring peace. Yet careful analysis of the political environment in which the settlement was negotiated, along with the content of the settlement itself, reveals key insights into both why it worked and why so many other negotiated settlements fail. There are three key points.

First, in order for a settlement to work, combatants must possess an inherent and direct stake in the nonviolent resolution of their conflict. This is rare because often the process of negotiation itself disrupts one side's chances of winning outright. Thus, depending on the stage of the conflict at the time of third-party intervention, there is almost always at least one actor who believes it can still win everything it wants by force of arms on the battlefield. In the case of El Salvador, this accurately characterized the relationship of the combatants to each other and to potential mediators until the FMLN's all-out assault of 1989. It did not succeed in defeating the government and military, but it did succeed in convincing key elites in both groups that so long as they relied on force of arms alone to secure their interests, neither they as individuals nor their collective economic interests could be made safe. For its part, the ideological disappointment of the FMLN's more conservative elements must have been considerable. Not only had they failed to defeat the corrupt Salvadoran military, but the relied-upon popular uprising never materialized. In short, both sides fairly instantly developed a keen and direct interest in an alternative to civil war and extrajudicial killings as a means to reach their political objectives.

This overarching craving for security did not only affect the content of the Chapultepec Accords themselves; the share devoted to security overwhelms that devoted to all other issues combined, and the level of detail regarding security provisions is also striking. It also explains why, when inconsistencies, cheating, and bitter-enders threatened to derail the plan, skillful intervention by UN mediators was able to persuade both sides to continue the process toward nonviolent conflict.

Second, the fact that the document focused overwhelmingly on security issues accounts in large measure for the success of the settlement. Had the document been less detailed and devoted less space to security and police reform, it is highly doubtful El Salvador would have remained free of civil war. The high rate of violent crime in El Salvador—intolerable in the long term virtually anywhere else—not only indicates a failure of the accords to deal adequately with economic reforms but further highlights just how desperate both sides were to escape civil war as a modus vivendi. In El Salvador, high levels of property theft and even violent crime still seem acceptable as compared to life at the height of the civil war.

Third, the quality of the peace that has emerged in El Salvador following its successful negotiated settlement should stand as a warning that even this type of settlement might not result in outcomes that provide much benefit to former combatants. El Salvador's economy is doing better now, but how much better might it have done had the government not won the peace as a result of structural advantages and FMLN concessions on key economic reforms? El Salvador is still a country with extreme income inequalities—the very inequalities that advanced the original demand for reform that over time escalated into all-out civil war. Yet civil war in the near to medium term at least seems unlikely.

Chapter 6

Uganda: Rebel Victory Begets Stability

UGANDA'S CIVIL WAR, which lasted from February 1981 to January 1986, represented the culmination of more than two turbulent decades following independence from British colonial rule in 1962. The combined experiences of Idi Amin's brutal reign and the destructive civil war left Uganda's economy, civic life, and infrastructure in ruins. Quite remarkable, however, is the fact that in the postwar period Uganda became one of only a handful of Africa's success stories of stabilization and growth. Despite a persistent insurgency in northern Uganda, led by the Lord's Resistance Army (LRA), and widespread concern today that Uganda's strides toward democratization have slowed or even backtracked, the country continues to be relatively stable, and economic growth is strong. Particularly when juxtaposed with the instability of its neighbors (it borders Sudan, the Democratic Republic of the Congo, Rwanda, Tanzania, and Kenya), the fact that Uganda's civil war has not recurred is striking.

The relative success that Uganda has enjoyed since its civil war ended in 1986 illustrates a pattern that has been largely overlooked in the statistical literature on civil war: the tendency for military victories by rebel groups to usher in stability and greater political openness. Chapters 1 and 4 established this relationship, showing that civil war recurrence is less likely following rebel victory than it is following all other civil war termination outcomes, including negotiated settlements and victories by governments. While scholars have increasingly focused attention on the strategies and sources of support for rebel movements, the question of how victorious rebels behave in the aftermath of war has not yet been rigorously examined. This chapter addresses that gap, arguing that the strategies employed by victorious rebel groups during and in the aftermath of war often allow for inclusive, participatory government institutions, buttressed by a robust security sector.

The victorious rebel group in Uganda's civil war, the National Resistance Movement (NRM), led the country in a direction that confirms the logic of many of the aspects of the ideal postwar environment outlined out in chapter 3. Civil wars ended by rebel victories tend not to recur and appear to be associated with the subsequent opening of political space. That is, rebellions often take place in authoritarian settings, and in cases in which the government is able to suppress rebellion, it stands to reason that the government would be wary of democratization. On the other

Figure 6.1. Location Map of Uganda

hand, rebels are more likely to enjoy support from civilians and to have a need for international legitimacy, support, and aid; thus, when rebels win, they may be more likely to encourage, or at least tolerate, an increased degree of political competition. For similar reasons, security sector reform meets fewer obstacles. This framework fits the Ugandan case well: Yoweri Museveni, a former rebel who has served as president in the postwar period since 1986, made great efforts to form an inclusive government and military, adopting a strategy of openness as he aggressively pursued liberal economic reforms. The World Bank praised Uganda's postwar recovery as a "major turnaround" characterized by "astonishing efficacy" in aspects of government behavior.[1] While myriad structural and proximate factors contributed to this success, the capacity and legitimacy of the victorious National Resistance Army (NRA) rebel group and that of its political wing, the NRM, were pivotal.

This chapter describes Uganda's postcolonial history, focusing on the 1980-1986 civil war and its aftermath. It chronicles Uganda's remarkable recovery from that war, investigating how the victory of the rebels over the government and other rival factions paved the way for much of the post-war reconstruction success that has been achieved. While Uganda remains deeply flawed by most standards of democratic consolidation and prosperity, the country has made considerable progress in both dimensions since the end of major conflict in the mid-1980s, when it was devastated by decades of violence and neglect. With the exception of the tragic humanitarian situation caused by the violent LRA insurgency, concentrated in the far north of Uganda, the country has enjoyed considerable stability.

Overview

Uganda's civil war broke out against a backdrop of political turmoil and economic decline. The war came on the heels of almost two decades of turbulence that followed independence from British colonial administration. Uganda obtained its independence from the United Kingdom in 1962, underwent an antidemocratic concentration of power in the executive branch under Milton Obote from independence through 1971, and then endured repressive and violent rule under Idi Amin from 1971 to 1979. From 1980 to 1985, civil war raged following the contested return of Obote to the presidency. In general, this postindependence period was marked by government collapse, poverty, and chaos. The primary rebel group, the NRM, was thus formed in the midst of a power vacuum caused by a government that was weak in both credibility and administrative capacity. In total, roughly 800,000 people were killed during the political violence between Amin's coup in 1971 and the end of the civil war in 1985.[2]

The war was triggered by a combination of structural and proximate factors, but most scholars primarily credit ethnic and regional rivalries and inequalities that were exacerbated by colonial policies under the British. Conflicts in the postcolonial period lacked democratic institutions to mediate between opposing factions. As in many postcolonial African countries, this institutional vacuum lent itself to ethnic favoritism, patronage politics, and the flagrant use of the national security forces to intimidate opposition. The rebellion that initiated Uganda's civil war thus arose out of a context in which the state often preyed upon its people and lacked the capacity and the desire to provide security and basic services to most of its population.

Uganda's Postcolonial History

When Uganda obtained independence from the United Kingdom without struggle or violence in 1962, few would have predicted the tragic violence that would follow: almost one million people would be killed in politically oriented violence over the next twenty-three years.[3] Particularly as compared to neighboring Kenya, with its destructive Mau Mau rebellion recently suppressed, Uganda's prospects for prosperity and stability appeared to be high.[4] Unlike Kenya, for example, Uganda lacked a privileged, widely resented white settler class, and independent Uganda inherited a healthy economy, a sizable middle class, high literacy rates, a prestigious national university, and fairly strong health and transportation infrastructures. Rich soil enabled thriving cotton and coffee industries.

However, growing tension between the southern and northern regions of Uganda soon came to dominate the country's contentious postindependence politics. Immediately following independence, the outlying regions of the country feared domination by the Kingdom of Buganda, which lay in the south of the modern state of Uganda on the shore of Lake Victoria.[5] The Kingdom of Buganda had been the heart of Britain's colonial administration, with the British using the Baganda capital, Mengo, as their communications center. By the time the British reached this region of Africa, the Kingdom of Buganda was the largest and most prosperous kingdom in the area.[6] Following the success of Christian missionaries in converting Baganda elites, Britain first annexed the Kingdom of Buganda in the late nineteenth century. After annexing Buganda, Britain occupied land to its north and east, largely to secure Buganda from external threats, including that of French colonial expansion.[7] Buganda, along with the occupied land surrounding it, later became Uganda.

British favoritism toward Buganda led other Ugandan groups to resent the Baganda people. In contrast to those of neighboring tribes, Buganda's centralized governance systems closely resembled the hierarchical administrative structure Britain had put into place; consequently, Britain used the Baganda people's system as a model that it extended across the colony.[8] Southern Uganda's favorable climate, with two rainy seasons per year, made it the agricultural and economic center of the country. However, the British encouraged migrant laborers from the North to travel to work on farms as a source of cheap labor for the South. Economic inequality between the North and South ensued. While Buganda had one-third of the country's total population at the time of independence, in 1958, the Statistics Department of the colonial government reported that roughly 80 percent of the country's gross income was concentrated in Buganda and the Eastern Province. The British favored Baganda for civil service positions; however, they sought to balance Baganda power in the government by filling the ranks of the military with northerners.

After gaining independence from Britain, Uganda was ruled by northerners until the end of the civil war in 1985. Milton Obote, a political organizer from Lango (just north of Buganda) who founded the Uganda People's Congress (UPC) party, led Uganda as part of an early power-sharing agreement with the Baganda from independence until 1971, and again from 1980 to 1985. Between those periods, Uganda was under the dictatorial rule of Idi Amin, who took power from Obote in a military coup. Amin had been an army officer from the West Nile region in the far north of the country, bordering Sudan.

The regimes of both Obote and Amin were fraught with political abuses and fragmentation along ethno-regional lines. Early in Obote's first period in office, which he began in the role of prime minister, Uganda's political climate was relatively calm. But following allegations in 1965 that he profited from covert smuggling deals with rebels associated with Patrice Lumumba, the murdered prime minister of the Democratic Republic of Congo (then Zaire), Obote consolidated power in the executive branch. He abolished the constitution, which had enshrined basic human rights and articulated semifederal relationships between the central government and outlying kingdoms. Obote also abolished the ceremonial presidency of the Baganda king, the *kabaka*; suspended the powers of the leaders of Uganda's tribal kingdoms; and declared himself executive president in March 1966. A power-sharing agreement that had been a compromise between Obote's UPC and the Baganda party of the *kabaka* thus ended. The *kabaka* was forced into exile in 1969, and bitterness between the Baganda and the UPC continued in the lead-up to the civil war.

Obote used the military for personal gain, projecting his power to the periphery of the country by building military bases in each district.[9] He continued the colonial policy of weighing the military in favor of the North. By 1969 the Baganda represented 16 percent of the population, but only 5 percent of the army. In contrast, northerners were 19 percent of the population but constituted 61 percent of the army ranks.[10] Obote also favored northern ethnic groups in filling the ranks of the civil service, reversing the trend of Baganda domination of government employment, yet also exacerbating his government's poor relations with Buganda. While Obote gave the military an increasingly influential role, this strategy backfired when Amin, who had been rising in the military's ranks throughout Obote's reign, seized power in a military coup in January 1971. Obote and Amin had been allies—Amin was implicated alongside Obote in the smuggling scandal—and Obote had been largely responsible for Amin's rise through the military ranks. However, Obote became threatened by Amin's growing power in the military, and a rift emerged when Amin learned that Obote sought to oust him.

Amin's coup was at first cheered by Ugandans and the international community, who hoped he would provide a welcome contrast to Obote's corruption. However, Amin quickly became internationally notorious for his megalomania and irrationality. For example, Amin declared his title to be "His Excellency President for Life, Field Marshal Al Hadji Doctor Idi Amin, Victoria Cross (VC), Distinguished Service Officer (DSO), Military Cross (MC)." According to the author of *The Last King of Scotland*, Giles Foden, to that title Amin also added "Lord of All the Beasts of the Earth and Fishes of the Sea, and Conqueror of the British Empire in Africa in General and Uganda in Particular." During the Watergate crisis in the United States, he wrote in a telegram to President Richard Nixon: "If your country does not understand you, come to Papa Amin who loves you. A kiss on both your cheeks.... When the stability of a nation is in danger, the only solution is, unfortunately, to imprison the leaders of the opposition."[11]

In addition to Amin's peculiar antics, under Amin Uganda was ruled with utter brutality (Uganda's polity score during Amin's rule was −7, designating an extreme autocracy[12]), and the country's political and economic infrastructure deteriorated. Violence was employed prodigiously to intimidate the opposition: among the 50,000 to 300,000 politically motivated murders that occurred at Amin's behest were that of the chief justice, the vice chancellor of prestigious Makerere University, the governor of the Bank of Uganda, and the Anglican archbishop.[13] By some estimates, one million people were displaced from their homes and farms at the hands of government coercion, and most skilled laborers left the country, especially after Amin expelled the Asian population in 1972 and Britain cut off diplomatic relations with Uganda in 1976. Between 1970 and 1980, Uganda's gross domestic product declined by 25 percent, and exports declined by 60 percent.[14] To finance his government amidst this economic collapse, Amin printed his own money, causing extreme inflation.

Amin's rule finally ended when he was forced into exile by an alliance of Tanzanian forces (who were angered by Amin's invasion of Tanzanian territory in 1978), Obote's troops, and a new group led by Yoweri Museveni, who would later lead the rebellion against Obote and remains president of Uganda at the time of writing. Much of the abuse and mismanagement that became commonplace under Amin continued under Obote's second presidency from 1980 to 1985, which coincided with Uganda's civil war. The war marked another devastating episode in the country's postindependence years, with estimates of war-related death tolls ranging from 100,000 to 300,000.[15]

The Factions and Fighting of War

Scholars typically trace the outbreak of Uganda's civil war to interethnic competition for political control of the state—a state that had little capacity to monitor or control its outlying regions. Due to a lack of democratic institutions to mediate conflict, control over the military and private forms of coercion became the means to power, resulting in a power struggle between ethnic groups. Bias against the Baganda and the western

Banyankole, the groups that formed the basis of the resistance army, "had been enshrined by a succession of political leaders from northern ethnic groups, each of whom resented the favoritism experienced by southern groups under the colonial regime of the British." Furthermore, Uganda's state had been crippled by the violence and pillaging carried out by Amin, which came to a head when he was forcibly removed from office. GDP declined throughout the 1970s, with the exception of the coffee boom in 1976 and 1977, and in 1979 GDP fell by almost 12 percent.[16]

In addition to these structural factors, the proximate event that provoked war was the 1980 election, which had been intended to restore the country to stability and democracy. Amidst complaints of widespread electoral corruption, Obote's UPC party was declared the winner. Allegations held that UPC members dominated the electoral commission, giving the party effective control over districting, voter registration, and the selection of monitors. Furthermore, after voting was completed, the acting head of government, Paulo Mwanga, demanded that all electoral returns be submitted directly to him. Despite observers' claims that the opposition Democratic party received the plurality of votes, Mwanga announced that Obote had won, making him president of Uganda for the second time. Obote then appointed Mwanga as his vice president and minister of defense. Museveni later explained that while the injustice of this electoral outcome sparked the war, the rebellion sought to do more than to simply rectify these election results; it sought to redress the structural inequalities faced by Ugandan society.

The corrupted elections prompted Museveni, a member of the Banyankole ethnic group who was born in southwestern Uganda, to form the Popular Resistance Army and later the National Resistance Army, as well as its political wing, the National Resistance Movement, and to initiate a rebellion against Obote's government army, the United National Liberation Army (UNLA). Museveni received military training in Mozambique from the anticolonial revolutionary Liberation Front of Mozambique (FRELIMO) movement and was educated in Tanzania, where he fled when Amin seized power. In Tanzania, Museveni emerged as a political leader, recruiting thousands of troops to join the coalition that sought to topple Amin.

The rebellion was initially based in western Uganda, Museveni's home, but it soon expanded operations to the Luwero Triangle, a region of roughly 10,000 square miles in size north of Kampala. As Jeremy Weinstein notes, the early years of the war represented a classic case of asymmetric warfare, and the early NRM was a vulnerable organization. Museveni used the tight social networks of his Banyankole ethnic group to identify his earliest recruits, some of whom were men who attended church with him. The predominately Banyankole early NRM also found allies in the Baganda people, who had not forgiven Obote for dethroning their king in 1965 and had voted overwhelmingly against Obote in the 1980 election. The war was fought largely in Baganda territory, so recruiting Baganda and gaining the support of civilian Baganda was essential. The alliance was not seamless: complaints were widespread that Baganda were insufficiently represented in the NRM leadership, threatening the Bayankole–Baganda alliance. In 1983 several Baganda were promoted to commanders, largely resolving the tension.[17]

By late 1981 Museveni's rebels had taken administrative control over the Luwero Triangle, and while they encountered some resistance there, it became the center of the NRM's human and logistical support in the early years of war. Museveni and his leaders formed a National Resistance Council (NRC), which served as the decision-making body of the NRM, and the council organized civilian support for the rebellion in the form of food, clothing, and medicine. As Weinstein argues, because this nascent rebellion had no external source of support or funds, civilian support was crucial to its success, and its campaign was characterized by "political mobilization, local organization, and discipline."[18] From this early stage, the rebels formed participatory local organizations known as Resistance Councils to educate and coordinate civilians.

After a setback in January 1983 known as Obote's Grand Offensive, the NRA lost its dominance in the Luwero Triangle and retreated to Singo, on the outskirts of the Luwero Triangle. Obote's UNLA, however, was notoriously poorly trained and undisciplined, engaging in looting and humanitarian atrocities against civilians. Obote's military launched extensive military campaigns in the area, looting, raping, or killing civilians in their path. Some civilians were forcibly placed in government "relief centers," characterized by conditions reported to be similar to Nazi concentration camps.[19] In contrast, the NRA committed just 17 percent of the total incidents of violence against civilians during the war.[20] Civilians in the Luwero Triangle thus increasingly looked to the NRA for protection, and when the NRA retreated in defeat during the Grand Offensive, 1.5 million civilians reportedly followed them.[21] Meanwhile, various smaller rebellions took place on other fronts, overstretching the UNLA's capabilities. For example, remnants of Amin's defeated army fought Obote's troops from Amin's home region of West Nile, and Obote's UNLA terrorized civilians there who were suspected of sympathizing with Amin.[22] This rebel group in the North coordinated their activities with the NRM only to a small degree because of the geographic remoteness of their fight and because they resented Museveni for his involvement in ousting Amin's regime.

Gradually, the NRA reconstituted its forces, and by April 1985 it had regained territory and prepared to take over the capital. This plan was delayed when two army officials overthrew Obote in a coup, and Museveni participated in peace negotiations between the army and the many rebel movements. However, once it became clear that the military coup leaders did not seek genuine reform, the NRA left the talks. The NRA attacked Kampala, ousting the UNLA easily—in just twelve hours, according to one account.[23] Shortly thereafter, in January 1986, Museveni became president of Uganda. The NRM declared a four-year transition period in which it would rule, leading up to democratic elections.

The NRM thus laid the foundation for its success in governing postwar Uganda through its strategy of relying on—and gaining—civilian support for its rebellion. Museveni recognized early in the war that civilian support was crucial. As a result, he viewed educating the masses about the justification for resistance, and training and organizing them in support of this cause, as a fundamental part of the NRM's strategy. The relatively broad-based support that the NRM achieved through this policy also served it well as Museveni embarked on an ambitious strategy to reconstruct the country.

Theorizing Postwar Uganda

The toll of the war deteriorated the Ugandan economy and infrastructure to an even more miserable state than it had been at the end of Amin's rule. Taken together, the Amin dictatorship and the war had brought the country to the brink of collapse. A.B.K. Kasozi writes: "By the time Obote fell in 1985, Uganda could no longer be described as a state. No one military or political organization commanded the legitimate use of violence in the country. . . . Violence, dishonesty, corruption, and moral degeneration permeated the whole social system."[24] The war had also taken a dramatic toll on the economy: infrastructure was woefully neglected, annual inflation was at 120 percent, and income per capita was at just 59 percent of its 1971 level.[25] Economic development had been reversing for almost two decades; whereas in 1970 there was one motor vehicle to every 178.5 people, by 1987 there was just one motor vehicle to every 511.07 people.[26] Cash-crop farms that had once been expected to serve as the basis of an export economy had turned to subsistence farms, and infrastructure had deteriorated such that the twenty-six-kilometer trip from Entebbe Airport to the capital of Kampala took hours.[27]

Today Uganda stands as a success story in many respects. In particular, the results the country has achieved in building effective governance and military institutions, alleviating poverty, and fighting HIV/AIDS have been extraordinary. Most observers consider 1986 as a turning point for the country. While refugees in the North continue to pose deep humanitarian problems, and democratic competition in Uganda is far from perfect, a recent World Bank report states that "Uganda is widely characterized as a country that went from 'basket case' to 'success story.' Since 1986, Uganda has transformed from a nearly failed state as a result of various brutal dictatorships, to a country that has achieved consistently high economic growth rates, significant reductions in poverty, and steady improvements in health and education status."[28]

What accounts, then, for the reversal in Uganda's fortunes since the end of the civil war? The stewardship of Museveni's regime deserves much of the credit, having formalized in the Ugandan government the institutions that the NRM had put in place in the midst of war. The following section describes how the organizational structure and culture of the NRM during the war lent itself to successful SSR in the postwar period. It argues that the domestic support that the NRM gained in the course of the war, which was a crucial factor in its victory and was based on principles of relative deference to the collective good, enabled Museveni to open the political space in the years following the war. This opening of the public space, along with an intense focus on rebuilding Uganda's reputation abroad, enabled Museveni's postwar government to regain the international community's confidence and to usher in a period of sustained growth and relative stability in Uganda.

Conduct of the NRA and Security Sector Reform

The professionalism and inclusiveness that were the cornerstones of the NRA as it fought the war formed the foundation for the national army that was created in the late 1980s under Museveni. The loose alliance of forces that the NRA easily defeated in Kampala was incoherent and incapable. When the NRA entered Kampala, most of its opponents—some of whom were allied with Obote and others within the new military regime that had toppled Obote in 1985—either surrendered to and joined the victorious NRA or fled to northern Uganda. Many of those who fled remain in northern Uganda and southern Sudan today. They would go on in 1987 to form the Lord's Resistance Army, which has since fought an insurgency against Museveni's government and has committed grave atrocities against civilians to prevent them from aiding the NRA. Because the forces opposing the NRA at the end of the civil war were inept, and because most forces had either sought to join the NRA or fled, Museveni replaced Uganda's old national army with the NRA troops and institutions in which he had invested so much during the war. These were instated along with new, former enemy troops that the NRA had absorbed. After the war ended, the national army was one of the few government institutions to be disbanded and reconstituted. The police and intelligence services remained largely in place, and little has been written about their trajectory following the war.

There is little doubt that the discipline and respect for civilians that pervaded the NRA's organizational culture formed a strong basis for postconflict military reform and national stability. In essence, a great deal of SSR, as it is conceived of in scholarly works on postconflict, occurred in the midst of the war: the NRA built a formal framework for behavior during war that ensured the army would gather a broad base of domestic support. This laid the organizational groundwork for a restrained, professionalized army that would be well suited for civilian control at the end of the war. As noted above, ethnic rivalries within the NRA were not prevalent, and soldiers maintained an impressive degree of discipline. One senior officer in the NRA who was from northern Uganda recounted: "Regardless of one's social background or level of education, all recruits were subjected to the same conditions of basic training and promotion to positions of leadership depended solely on one's capability, commitment, and contribution to the struggle. The result was a cohesive army."[29]

Museveni's army grew from 27 armed rebels in their first attack in February 1981 to 4,000 by 1983 and 10,000 by 1985,[30] and the NRA leadership put great care into designing an organizational structure whereby new fighters would be educated about the resistance and lack of discipline would be punished.[31] In part because of its success on the battlefield, the NRA attracted increasing numbers of recruits as the war progressed, including UNLA deserters.[32] The war had also produced a high degree of cohesion within the NRM leadership that was apparent in the postwar years.[33]

Using extensive interview data from ex-combatants, Weinstein chronicles how the NRA indoctrinated new recruits into an organization that valued the opinions and contributions of noncombatants and respected their lives and property. A former commander told Weinstein: "The main issue was teaching respect for the local population. An army is meant to be controlled by the people, the ones who pay the taxes to feed and clothe it, not to rape and loot from the people."[34] The NRA remained selective in its choice of recruits, seeking discipline and a shared long-term vision for the country, rather than seeking to swell the sheer quantity of its fighters. Throughout the war and in its aftermath, promotions and rewards within the NRA were granted on merit, with little ethnic favoritism. Recruits were required to attend courses and training that were taught first by Museveni himself—and later by other NRA leaders—about Uganda's history and political economy, how to fight a revolution, and how to treat civilians properly. Troops were expected to act as diplomats on behalf of the resistance movement to local communities, and they honed their ability to explain the goals of the rebellion to civilians. Even in the face of

near defeat in 1983, NRA leaders invested the movement's limited resources in their army and in services for the civilian population, rather
than stealing those resources for personal gain.

Museveni also put in place processes and norms within the NRA that
have continued to guide Uganda's current national army, the Ugandan
People's Defence Force.[35] In particular, a Code of Conduct articulated
how troops should treat one another, their leaders, and civilians. It established formal guidelines, including steps to make the NRA a democratic
institution whereby troops could freely criticize leaders. It also laid out a
framework for punishing those who did not follow the code, and indeed,
both commanders and combatants were put on trial for violations. Civilians came to trust the NRA, in part because they knew that crimes committed against civilians would not go unpunished. While abuses did occur
during the war, and have continued and possibly worsened in recent years
during the counterinsurgency against the LRA in northern Uganda, public punishment of officers in military tribunals continued after the war,
lending a great deal of public credibility to the military.[36]

Throughout the war, the NRA absorbed surrendering soldiers from
other armies, including that of Obote, into its ranks. NRA leadership made
instituting policies to guide this integration process an immediate priority.[37] While this absorption of former enemies was controversial because
many civilians preferred to bring them to justice, these new troops were
sent to undergo intensive education and training before being deployed,
in order to socialize them to the NRA. The policy appeared to be quite
successful in building a cohesive force, particularly around Kampala.
While the capital city had been wracked with looting and violence before
the end of the war, "the most distinguishing feature of the NRA's capture
of power was the fact that it was not accompanied or followed by looting."[38] While isolated incidents of NRA soldier indiscipline took place,
the transgressors were caught and punished.[39] At the end of the war, after
the NRA captured Kampala, the government financially compensated
many of its soldiers for their efforts, along with civilians who had contributed to the movement.

After the war, the NRA successfully continued to absorb many soldiers
from what had been opposing armies during the war, including the ex-
government's military. This strategy enabled the NRA to learn technolo-
gies and strategies of the former opposition, which was important as the
NRA continued to seek stabilization in remote regions of the country for
years after 1986. Even with surrendered troops from the insurgents that
continued to rebel from northern Uganda, the approach of integration
into the national army has continued to some extent. After 1986 the new
national army also recruited from all Ugandan ethnic groups, increasing
the size of the military.[40] This broad-based and expanding army also took

on social tasks during postwar reconstruction, including growing food for the population.[41] Ex-combatants from the NRA were also recruited into government administrative positions.

For ex-combatants who were not absorbed into the national army, or for those who remained in the army only in the immediate aftermath of war, demobilization was also relatively successful. Out of fear that former soldiers would turn to violent crime if demobilization occurred too quickly, the process was delayed in the years immediately following the war.[42] When roughly thirty thousand soldiers were eventually demobilized in 1993 and 1994, they were taken to their home villages and provided with financial assistance. International community donations enabled Uganda to offer a severance package of a thousand U.S. dollars to each soldier, which included medical care and iron roofing sheets for home building.[43] This approach appears to have worked, given that crime rates did not increase in the first year of demobilization in the villages to which demobilized soldiers returned.

The Lord's Resistance Army

The security situation in Uganda since 1986 has remained far from perfect. Conflict with the LRA has sputtered on, with the living conditions of civilians in northern Uganda worsening while the rest of the country has achieved growth. Founded in 1987 by Joseph Kony, the LRA traces its activities back to the previous year, when Alice Auma "Lakwena" established the Holy Spirit Movement (HSM) in the wake of a coup carried out by President Museveni.[44] In the years following its creation, differing reports have estimated that the number of persons displaced by LRA violence is between 500,000 and two million, with up to 100,000 killed.[45]

The high numbers of displaced persons are largely due to the organization's tactic of abducting children in the middle of the night. As of 2006 approximately thirty thousand children had been abducted by the LRA and compelled to act as soldiers.[46] Payam Akhavan notes: "The socioeconomic impact of this massive dislocation and the resulting need to provide humanitarian aid has been catastrophic for northern Uganda."[47] With a majority of LRA forces consisting of abducted children, the LRA is often reported to have little to no base of popular support,[48] which is perhaps well demonstrated by the frequent suggestion that the group is being sustained, to some extent, by arms contributions coming from Sudan. This comes despite the 1999 agreement between Sudan and Uganda to terminate any support being transferred from Sudan to Uganda.[49]

Making the situation of the LRA insurgency more complex, it has been reported that its political aims are somewhat unclear. Indeed, for the Ugandan Army, the LRA at present represents little more than a terrorist group.[50] In the late 1990s the LRA worked toward a clearer political goal, seeking explicitly "to overthrow the Ugandan Government and inflict brutal violence on the population in northern Uganda."[51] Nonetheless, for many the ultimate aims and strategies of the LRA remain ambiguous.[52]

In 2004, although the Ugandan military reported making progress against LRA forces, it also stated that an increase in monetary and strategic support would make its efforts more effective. Critics, however, note that the military's already high budget (150 million U.S. dollars in 2003) could be used more efficiently in bringing stability to all of Uganda; as they report, "cuts of 23 percent have been made from the budgets of other ministries to boost military spending with little to show for it in terms of increased security for the northern Ugandan population."[53]

The government of Uganda has attempted continuously to stop LRA activities, whether through military efforts or via peace talks. Despite those efforts, and notwithstanding some advances made by the Ugandan military through 2004, attempts of the Ugandan military to defeat the LRA were obstructed by continued and intensified LRA attacks. Negotiations between Uganda and the LRA, beginning with the Cessation of Hostilities agreement reached through August 26, 2006, have been drawn out, due in part to the somewhat dubious commitment of both parties to the peace process and to other complications such as the International Criminal Court's indictment of LRA leaders.[54] In February 2008 leaders of the LRA appeared to be ready to sit down with the Ugandan government to agree to a final permanent cease-fire.[55] Further stumbling blocks over the next few months, however, led Kony to refuse to sign another peace agreement. As of writing in mid-2009, the LRA continued to operate in Uganda.

Other low-intensity violent conflicts have continued to plague Uganda in recent years. Although the violence carried out by the LRA might seem threaten the stability achieved in postwar Uganda, the broader dynamics of the country have been more strongly affected by the successful transition brought on by rebel victory. Despite the above setbacks, Uganda's lack of recurring large-scale civil war remains an important example of relative postwar stability.

Postwar Reconstruction under Museveni

After taking control of Uganda in 1986, while he faced large obstacles in bringing stability to the country, Museveni and his administration took decisive steps to open the government to a range of perspectives. For example, shortly after taking power in 1986, the government gave up control over the radio and television media. Such steps were doubtless enabled by the strong public support that the NRM had cultivated throughout the war, as well as a desire to attract foreign investment and aid.[56] However, the NRM inherited a highly polarized country, and convincing citizens that the NRM would not institute a dictatorship was not easy. To do so, the Museveni administration announced that it would be an interim government, lasting just four years until elections would take place.[57] Local-level elections were held in 1989, and "all sorts of sociopolitical forces, representing a mosaic of political opinions, took part."[58] These elections presented a critical step forward for democracy because they gave individuals at the grassroots level an avenue of direct political participation that was unprecedented in Ugandan politics.[59]

Early on, Museveni's rhetoric was highly conciliatory and focused on development. He said at his swearing-in address on January 29, 1986:

> Past regimes have used sectarianism to use and divide people along religious and tribal lines. But why should religion be considered a political matter? Religious matters are between you and your god. Politics is about the provision of roads, water, drugs in hospitals and schools for children.... How do you become divided on the basis of religion or tribe if your interests, problems and aspirations are similar? Don't you see that the people who divide you are only using you for their own interests?[60]

Museveni largely put this rhetoric into action. The inclusiveness of the new government's institutions extended beyond the NRM's allies, although many representatives from groups not originally allied with the NRM are said to have been selected by Museveni. The NRM took an inclusive stance toward its former rivals, offering top government posts to leaders from other political parties in order to broaden its political base.[61]

Similar to the case of military reform, Museveni's NRM had developed participatory institutions during the course of the war that served it well when it took over the government in the postwar years. For example, the centerpiece of the NRM's agenda was a promise of political reform, articulated through its Ten-Point Programme. The program promised to establish democracy, security, and economic growth. Furthermore, point 3 of the program was "consolidation of national unity and elimination of all forms of sectarianism." It also promised to curb abuse of government power. This document became the written promise of the NRM to the people of Uganda about the vision of the country that would be pursued if the NRM was victorious.

In the immediate aftermath of the war, the movement drew on institutions that the NRM had developed for war-making such as the National Resistance Council and its supporting structure, including its network of political mobilizers, its political and diplomatic committee, and its finance and supply committee. After Museveni's ascension to the presidency in

January 1986, the NRM-led government expanded these committees. The 38-person National Resistance Council, composed largely of early members of the NRM, was entrusted with running the government. In early 1989 this council was expanded, with 220 new members, including 1 representative from each county, 1 female district representative, 10 representatives from the army, and 20 presidential nominees.[62]

Representative government was also expanded in 1987, when the Resistance Council Statute legalized the Resistance Council system that the NRM had designed during the war.[63] During the war, Resistance Councils existed at the village, parish, subcounty, county, and district levels where the NRM controlled territory, but Museveni's government extended this system throughout the entire country after the war. The initial purpose of the committees was to serve as a mechanism of communication between localities and the NRM leadership, and to hold officials and military officers accountable in cases of corruption or mismanagement. Additionally, during the war, a primary aim of the Resistance Councils was to provide food and logistical support to rebels, and to allow for joint NRA–civilian governance of the NRA-controlled territories.[64] After the war, the councils also had responsibility for assisting the police and chiefs in maintaining order, law, and security.[65] These councils served to promote the legitimacy of the new government and to foster political participation from a fairly broad range of social groups.[66] All adults were automatically members of their village Resistance Council, which managed local affairs, such as development projects. According to one scholar, while the councils were plagued by corruption, they also provided crucial institutions through which the national government could hold elections for the legislature, and through which it could reach areas on the periphery of its control.[67]

In its early years of governance, the NRM also enjoyed a good deal of popular support, despite the limits of its democratic reforms. Part of this support appears to have carried over from its domestic support during the fighting, when local communities had supplied the NRA with food, shelter, and information about the opposition.[68] Because the NRM had publicly decried state-inflicted violence during the war, it committed to democratic reform in a persuasive way.

There were limits, however, to Museveni's willingness to open the political space. For example, the five-year extension of the interim government that Museveni's National Resistance Council instituted in 1990 was not well received by the opposition parties, which were not permitted to hold rallies or establish local party branches.[69] Museveni had a philosophy of "no-party" or "movement" democracy, which in practice meant that parties could exist but could not campaign or nominate candidates to election. This approach found some support in an African intellectual tradition that Museveni adhered to, which posited that multipartyism suited the class conflicts of Western capitalism but was ultimately unfit for African societies.[70] The NRM also argued that multipartyism would undermine national unity and destabilize the polarized country. This experiment with "no-partyism," however, ended in 2005 with a constitutional referendum.

In more recent years, Museveni has also come under heavy attack for blocking democratic consolidation. While international observers declared that the 2006 elections themselves proceeded fairly, the lead-up to the elections generated a great deal of controversy, deteriorating Museveni's image in the international community.[71] For example, the opposition leader Kizza Besigye was arrested in November 2005 after being accused of rape and involvement with anti-Museveni rebels. These accusations led to protests, riots, and clashes with the police. Besigye lost the election in February 2006 to Museveni, and he filed a petition alleging electoral fraud, which was defeated in court. The election had been Uganda's first multiparty voting since the contested election in 1980 that triggered the civil war. In addition to these lapses in democratic consolidation, observers have registered concern over Museveni's ten-thousand-strong Presidential Guard Brigade, and the perceived increasing power of the military.[72] Museveni continues to block efforts to impose term limits on his presidency. Some argue that Uganda's lack of genuine democratic competition has reached the point of a "legitimacy crisis."[73]

Despite these growing problems with democratization, the extent of reforms that did take place after 1986 was quite significant. This restored the international community's confidence in Uganda, with the World Bank declaring it a "star pupil."[74] While the country's reputation was in shambles after Amin's rule and the civil war, and while the international community was initially skeptical of Museveni, given his past Marxist tendencies, by 1989 the donor community's confidence in Uganda had been restored.[75] Museveni made considerable efforts to reach out to the international community, casting himself as a champion of international principles. For example, in an October 1987 address to the General Assembly of the United Nations, he said:

> It is our profound conviction that the survival of mankind and the fulfillment of our dreams as individuals or nations must be in direct proportion to the extent to which we adhere to the ideas and values articulated in the UN Charter, and all other international treaties and declarations. Mr. President, notwithstanding our limitations, my country stands tall in the endeavours to uphold the great purpose of this organization. The Uganda Government under the National Resistance movement begins, first and foremost, with an unwavering commitment to the respect of human rights and to the sanctity of human life. We waged a protracted war against tyranny on a platform of restoring

personal freedoms and the amelioration of the socio-economic conditions of our people.[76]

Museveni's courting of the international community was effective, and by 1987 Uganda had undertaken an aggressive program of structural adjustment under the advice of international financial institutions. Donor aid began pouring in. Museveni soon emerged as a favorite of the international financial community because of his deep commitment to economic liberalization and financial discipline. While he had first opposed structural adjustment programs, he became persuaded that they would bring needed development to Uganda.[77] In the late 1980s and throughout the 1990s, the NRM made economic reconstruction a high priority, arguing that it was crucial for stabilizing country. This approach differs markedly from Obote's strong embrace of socialism, and Amin's policies of arbitrary economic rule ostensibly based on nationalism and whim. The Economic Recovery Program that Uganda began under Museveni aimed at lowering inflation, stabilizing currency, and stimulating growth. Currency was substantially devalued, and government borrowing was strictly limited.

Foreign aid, along with this economic reform program, played a crucial role in the country's recovery. Uganda received hundreds of millions of dollars in the late 1980s, along with debt rescheduling agreements. By 1991 the international community's confidence in Uganda was fully restored, as evidenced by the 1.1 billion U.S. dollars in multilateral economic assistance that Uganda received in the early 1990s, following the 1991 African Caribbean Pacific/EEC joint assembly meeting in Kampala.[78] According to the BBC, by 2005 half of the Ugandan government's budget was funded by international donors.[79]

While the immediate results of the structural adjustment program were mixed, overall the NRM's relative successes in democratic reforms were matched, and probably surpassed, by these economic reforms. At the end of the war, just 300 km of Uganda's 2,000 km of roads were in good condition; however, 1,562 km had been restored by 1994.[80] When the war ended in 1986, Uganda's per capita GDP was just 58 percent of what it had been at independence, but this improved to 69 percent by 1994 and 80 percent by 1997.[81] Uganda became Africa's largest coffee producer, and the industrial sector enjoyed 12 percent annual real output growth throughout the 1990s.[82] GDP growth in Uganda between 2000 and 2007 ranged between 4.3 and 6.8 percent, on a par with other strong African economies such as Ghana and Kenya.[83] These economic strides, however, have not been evenly distributed throughout the country, as poverty rates remained high in northern and eastern Uganda.[84]

Museveni also received international acclaim for his aggressive stance toward addressing HIV/AIDS when he embarked on an ambitious program of education and openness that achieved remarkable results relative to other African countries. In 2007 national HIV rates were roughly 6 percent, down from over 20 percent in the late 1980s.[85] The ability of the Ugandan government to tackle such a formidable public health challenge is a testament to the high level of organizational capacity and responsiveness that its institutions have attained.

While Uganda's post-1986 history has been remarkably stable in contrast to that which preceded this recovery, its security and democratic credentials have been far from perfect. As discussed above, the country has been forced to deal with an ongoing insurgency from the Lord's Resistance Army in the North, and the central government has stymied crucial democratic reforms. However, Uganda has made remarkable strides toward democracy and prosperity, and the point is not that rebel victory is a panacea. Rather, it is that rebel victory can bring forth considerable reform, and that it outperforms negotiated settlement, the international community's preferred means of managing civil wars. These findings warrant careful consideration, particularly when the international community considers the costs and benefits of negotiated settlement.

Conclusion and Implications

The case of Uganda's civil war and its postwar recovery demonstrates the positive outcomes that can be associated with outright military victory by a rebel group. In effect, the provision of harm and benefit that must feature in negotiated settlements, if they are to prevent war recurrence, was built into the end game of the civil war. As a result of this domestic support base, and also because of a need to gain support from the international donor community, the NRM had strong incentives to provide stability, voice, and services to its citizens, and to avoid preying upon them. These factors, along with the sheer military capacity that the NRM developed over the course of the war, resulted in a robust security sector in the aftermath of war.

The factors that propelled the NRM to victory—namely, a strong domestic support base and a professionalized, competent military—also enabled the NRM to achieve a stable peace. Unlike numerous African countries, such as Angola, Burundi, Congo-Brazzaville, Rwanda, and Sudan, Uganda has avoided the tragic return to large-scale conflict. Given the absence of external patrons for the NRM, the movement relied on civilians for logistical support and a base for recruitment. The NRM painstakingly developed this domestic support base over the course of the war through careful adherence to the NRA Code of Conduct and use of participatory local institutions, such as the Resistance Councils. The discipline of the NRA troops, which the Code of Conduct fostered, formed the basis for a military that was well equipped, from an organizational standpoint, to take on the task of stabilizing the country at the end of the war. While stability in Uganda has been imperfect, it stands as an exemplar of how rebel victory can diminish the likelihood of war recurrence, enhancing the chances not only for peace but also for democracy.

Chapter 7

The Republic of Sudan: A Collapsed Negotiated Settlement

THE ADDIS ABABA AGREEMENT of 1972, which ended a seventeen-year war between Sudan's northern region and its southern-based Anya-Nya rebels, endured for just over a decade. It collapsed in 1983. Although some scholars consider this decade of peace a remarkable achievement and more than a "mere interlude in war," in this chapter I focus on the reasons why the agreement failed to secure a lasting peace.[1]

Sudan's history has been marked by hundreds of years of violence and conflict, from Arab invasions in the sixth century, to the Mahdist resistance to colonial rule in the nineteenth century, right up to the present-day troubles in the Darfur region. While little of this conflict could be characterized as civil war, today Sudan is a striking case in that it possesses *all* of the elements that scholars believe are the root causes of civil wars.[2] It has vast economic, educational, and political inequities between its center elites and its periphery. As if that were not enough, it has acutely divided ethnic and religious loyalties, geographical and environmental challenges, external actor interference, elite manipulation and bargaining, religious outbidding,[3] and resource greed. These factors are almost insurmountable hurdles for achieving peace agreements, much less for sustaining them. Because conflict seems overdetermined in Sudan, it constitutes a tough case for my theory of benefit and harm as key determinants of enduring peace.

Sudan is also a good candidate for comparative analysis for another reason: its second civil war, an even longer North–South civil war of twenty-one years (1983–2005), was also concluded by means of a negotiated settlement—the Naivasha Agreement of January 2005.[4] This allows us two separate tests of competing explanations of enduring peace within a single historical case.[5] Both of these wars ended with negotiated settlements arguably after the wars had reached mutually hurting stalemates between the government troops and the rebels—the Anya-Nya in the first war and Sudan People's Liberation Army (SPLA) in the second. The war that ended in 1972 was political and economic, and it held the prospect of the breakup of the state into two separate entities. The 1983-2005 war also held the prospect of the breakup of the state. The Naivasha Agreement was complicated by the fact that although it essentially ended the North–South conflict, a conflict *within* the North's region of Darfur esca-

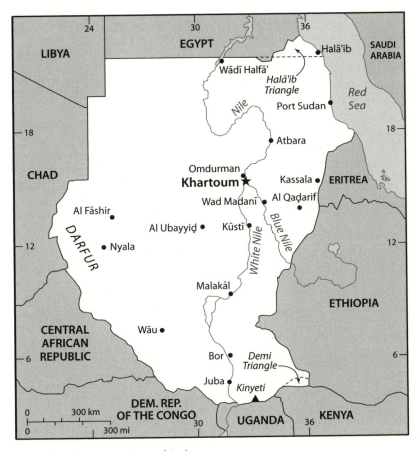

Figure 7.1. Location Map of Sudan

lated (in 2003) before the 2005 North–South Comprehensive Peace Agreement (CPA) was signed.

What was it about the Addis Ababa Agreement that brought peace for eleven years yet did not endure? What might the 2005 CPA portend in terms of success or similar failure?

One explanation of the breakdown of the Addis Ababa Agreement might be unilateral action on the part of the northern-dominated government headed by Jaafar Muhammad al-Nimieri to rescind key elements of the agreement. On the other hand, the agreement itself contained no institutional provisions for "punishment" of noncompliance or selective abrogation. In Sudan's lengthy wars, no side has been able to gain dominance; each side—through either outside support or internal resources—maintains its ability to threaten and harm the other. It is therefore not clear what the best means of achieving lasting peace might be, since Sudan has been at civil war for all but eleven of its fifty-plus years of independence.[6]

Negotiated settlements have broken down, yet even with outside support for warring factions, none has managed to obtain a military victory.

Since no single group has managed a military victory, no group—including the government itself—has been able to dominate in enforcing the peace and maintaining stability. Whereas the Addis Ababa Agreement might have provided political and economic benefits in the longer run, the agreement did not give the South any means other than a return to war to punish Northern noncompliance or defection.

Whereas the peace treaty that ended the Salvadoran civil war (which has so far held for seventeen years) contained detailed annexes on demobilization, reformation of the army, and new police and intelligence organization, the Addis Ababa Agreement only restructured the army in the South to contain half northern and half southern officers and soldiers. The rest of the agreement lacked a security setup for protection of the South and for enforcement of good behavior in the North. There is almost no mention of police, intelligence, or other security forces. Conversely, and reflecting the southerners' experience with the lack of detail in the 1972 agreement, the Naivasha Agreement contains details on the restructuring of the armed forces, its time frame, and the governing bodies as well as their monitors. "Joint Integrated Units" are specified along with the exact areas of deployment, command and control structures, and provision for other armed groups to join the army, police, prison guard, and wildlife resource forces. To establish civilian oversight of the military, the second treaty places police and national security forces under the joint government. In terms of my overall argument that credible promises of both harm and benefit must be contained in any negotiated settlement with a chance to last, the Naivasha Agreement therefore appears to mark a clear improvement over its Addis Ababa predecessor. Unfortunately, the rebel uprising in Darfur (2003–present) endangered the Naivasha Agreement before the ink was dry on the paper.

In this chapter, I review the history leading to Sudan's "first" civil war, the nature of the Addis Ababa Agreement, and the causes of its collapse. Then, in chapter 8, I recount the "second" civil war and the nature of the Naivasha Agreement that has, so far, led to the greatest hope for an end to civil war in Sudan. I conclude the case study of Sudan by analyzing the conflict and settlements in terms of my larger argument, testing the evidence for the mutual harm, mutual gain sustainability matrix proposed here.

Overview

The three civil wars in Sudan since 1955 cost more than two and a half million lives and displaced almost half a *billion* people. The first two major wars (1955–1972 and 1983–2005) were fought between the government, whose authority and military control were centered in the northern area of the country, and rebel groups in the southern part of Sudan. The third war, between the government and rebel groups in the North's own western region of Darfur, began in 2003 and is still ongoing. Although it not addressed here directly, I do deal with it as it impacts the North–South conflict.

Sudan is the largest country in Africa, and with an area of approximately 2.5 million square kilometers it is more than a quarter of the size of the United States. The Darfur region alone is almost a half million square kilometers and is larger than Iraq. Sudan is surrounded by nine mostly underdeveloped states (only two of which have a GDP per capita of greater than 2,000 US dollars per year), connected to Sudan by 7,687 kilometers of weakly controlled borders.[7] Until the Naivasha Agreement in 2005, Sudan's southern regions did not have much infrastructure at all, and little of the North was developed outside the capital, Khartoum. The country's wide variations in climate, its size, and its geopolitical placement alone make it difficult to govern even in the absence of the other extenuating circumstances.

The current *CIA World Factbook* estimates major ethnic divisions to be 52 percent black African and 39 percent Arab, and the religious divisions to be 70 percent Muslim, 5 percent Christian, and 25 percent indigenous religions. Different sources place the number of tribes higher than four hundred and sometimes as high as six hundred, and the number of distinct ethnic groups as high as fifty.[8] Estimates of the total population vary from thirty-six to forty-one million people in 2006, creating a fairly large margin of error that is not particularly surprising in a country almost perpetually at war. Though Arabic is the main language in the North and the official national language, English is the unifying language in the South, and more than 130 languages divide the tribes.[9] The mean Gini index for Sudan is 45, indicating extreme inequality (scores range from 28 to 55, with 55 being the most unequal), and a measure of education inequality gives Sudan a mean score of 79 (scores range from 8 to 99, with 99 being the most unequal).[10] A nation divided so distinctly by region, race, religion, income, and education, and with few binding factors, makes the task of unification a difficult one.

Background to Civil War in Sudan

According to Francis Deng, a preeminent scholar of Sudan and a former Sudanese ambassador to the United States, Canada, and Scandinavia, Sudan's civil war "culminates a long history in which the North has tried to spread its religion and language to the South, which has resisted these efforts."[11] Deng adds, however, that viewing the civil wars through narrow lenses of North versus South, Muslim versus Christian, or Arab versus African would be far too simplistic. Sudan's cultural diversity is immense, and heterogeneous religious, racial, cultural, tribal, and lingual compositions characterize both regions. Deng writes that many northern ethnic groups

> are clearly non-Arab, have retained their indigenous languages, practice a paganised version of liberal Islam, and are as economically backward as the South. Many peoples of the South have adopted racial, cultural, and religious elements from the North over a long history of interaction, but have adapted them to their local conditions and assimilated them to such a degree that they are viewed as authentically indigenous.[12]

The North is full of people from the sub-Saharan region who have brought their Dinka, Nuer, Shilluk, and Zande tribal traditions with them. In recent years, a two-million-strong concentration of southern Christians has migrated to the capital city of Khartoum, further complicating any simple North/South, Muslim/Christian divide.

Still, one useful way to reduce Sudan's prima facie complexity is to understand how the large divide between the North and the South is affected by religion. Religion is complicated by geography, demography, and colonization and is a pivotal and contentious factor when imposed. Deng describes the northern two-thirds of the country's territory and population, though ethnically mixed, as "an inseparable amalgamation" of Islam and the Arabic language. Christian influence and a Western orientation, by contrast, dominate the principally indigenous African South. The history and conquests of the previous millennium helped to shape these factors.[13]

For close to a thousand years, Christianity prevailed in the ancient northern Sudanese kingdoms of Nubia, Magarra, and Alwa. Christianity predated Islam's arrival in North Africa and remained the region's dominant religion from the fifth and sixth centuries CE until the sixteenth century. Arab Muslims had advanced as far as Egypt at the conquest of Alexandria in 642 CE but did not succeed in advancing up the Nile River into Sudan.[14] They conquered westward to the Maghreb and were apparently discouraged by the southern territory's inaccessibility and poverty. However, the arrival of Islam in North Africa did lead to a gradual decline of Christian influence in Sudan.[15] Arab merchants and holy men infiltrated the region over the centuries, introducing the Arabic language and teachings from their holy book, the Qur'an, and intermarrying with the inhabitants. The holy men were mostly Sufis, followers of Islam who advanced a more personal, spiritual, and emotional relationship with God than their orthodox counterparts, and who emphasized the love of God rather than the fear of God that dominated orthodox Islamic thought.[16] "It was these holy men," writes Milton Viorst, "that, over several generations, Arabized Sudan."[17] This Arab influence culminated when an alliance of Arabs and the Muslim kingdom of Funj invaded and overthrew the Christian kingdoms in 1504.[18] The Funj kingdom was eventually brought down by an Egyptian-Ottoman invasion in the early nineteenth century. With Islam established in the North, Muslim Arabs tried to assert control over the South.[19]

Southern Sudanese resisted the Arab/Muslim incursions from the North. The swamps and tropical humidity in the South further deterred the Northern Arabs, causing their incursions to be neither deep nor permanent. Consequently, the successful Arabization and Islamization that occurred in the North failed to take root in the South.[20] It was, however, deliberate policy stemming from British colonial rule that helped create the economic and religious chasms.

While the final successful Arab/Muslim invasion at the beginning of the sixteenth century cemented Islam's domination of the North, the South became increasingly Christian. Missionaries, particularly during the British colonial era of the nineteenth century, spread their influence and fomented fierce antislavery campaigns both in Africa and in Britain. The southern Sudanese unified against Arab traders, who had been raiding the South for slaves as ivory became scarce. The missionaries brought education, development, and social services along with the Christian gospel, resulting in the conversion of many Southerners.

In the late nineteenth century a boat builder's son from the Dongola region of the Nile River began a messianic revival of Islam and rose up against the Turko-Egyptian and English colonizers. Muhammad Ahmad bin Abdallah proclaimed himself the Mahdi (the expected one): the second prophet and restorer of the Islamic faith. He raised an army of "Ansar" followers between 1881 and 1884.[21] The British general Charles "Chinese" Gordon, a devout Christian, had been appointed Ottoman governor general in Khartoum in the 1870s and had vigorously overseen several antislavery campaigns. He was tasked with resisting the Mahdi's army, but without adequate forces he was surrounded and captured in Khartoum by the Ansar. In 1885 he was famously beheaded.[22] Following the Mahdi's death from typhus, his deputy, the Khalifa Abd'allah, ruled until 1898. That year, in a punitive expedition, Lord Kitchener's British and Egyptian forces destroyed the Mahdist regime and subsequently established the Anglo-Egyptian condominium rule.[23] Islamic governance was allowed to continue, and the Mahdi's great grandson, Sadiq el-Mahdi, is part of Sudan's current political elite.

The British dominated the Anglo-Egyptian condominium rule. They left the North nominally under Arab/Egyptian rule, but they replaced the

Arab bureaucratic officials in the South with black Africans and prevented northerners from entering the South.[24] Publicly, the separation of the regions was said to be aimed at preventing imposition of the Arab Muslim influence in the South, but in reality the British were hoping that the South would be completely separated and then integrated into British East Africa.[25] The British encouraged use of the English language in the South, and while African traditional religions became revitalized, the missionaries vigorously advanced conversion to Christianity.[26] However, the British neglected the South's economic development and failed to create an effective administrative infrastructure, a strategy that crippled the South well into the twentieth century. The southern administration remained under the traditional control of the chiefs and sheikhs of the villages, thus hampering the cohesion of the region.[27]

By contrast, the British advanced the North's economic and social development and groomed an educated Sudanese elite. At the same time, Egypt encouraged Islamic values and beliefs in the North, and the cumulative effect was the administrative, cultural, economic, and religious division of North and South.

Following increased signs of Sudanese nationalism in the North and awareness of the inevitability of a Sudanese bid for independence, the British united the separately ruled zones in 1947. Later that year at a conference in Juba, the main southern city, the southern chiefs cooperated with the northern nationalists to pursue independence from colonial rule. As had occurred following Britain's departure from India—where Muslim Pakistan and Bengal had been used by the British as a counterweight to Hindu nationalism in India proper—Britain's paternalistic colonial policy had created such a sharp separation between the sides of Sudan that not even the shared desire for an end to colonial rule was sufficient to build trust between the regions.[28] Most of the industry was concentrated in the North, and group suspicions and antagonisms had been exacerbated by a low level of integration during the colonial period. Interaction with the North had often been by means of the invasion of slave traders and through ancient disputes between the regions, both of which had created bad memories for the southerners. The southerners were weak, lacked education and cohesion, and were thus unprepared to represent themselves on an equal footing with the North.[29]

As the British troops began to withdraw in preparation for independence, the southerners perceived themselves to be unfairly disadvantaged. Most administrative posts were already filled by better-educated northerners. Southerners were at an additional disadvantage because few of them spoke Arabic, which had already become the de facto official language of the North. Thus, in the South, "Sudanization" became tantamount to "northernization." According to Deng, for southerners, "independence was to prove merely a change of outside masters, with the northerners taking over from the British and defining the nation in accordance with the symbols of their Arab-Islamic identity."[30]

Sudan's First Civil War, 1955–1972

By the mid-1950s the divisions between northern and southern Sudan had taken on a multilayered complexity. Differences of geography, race, language, education, and economic development—in addition to differences in religion—made conflict between the two regions appear overdetermined.

On August 18, 1955, several months before Sudan's scheduled independence, violent conflict broke out when soldiers of the army's Southern Corps mutinied after hearing rumors they were to be disarmed and taken northward. Led by Lt. Reynaldo Loyela, a group of southern soldiers at Torit refused to comply with orders and attacked its officers. On the same day, another 190 southern soldiers mutinied in the districts of Juba, Yei, Yambio, and Maridi. The government at Khartoum declared a state of emergency, and on August 21 Royal Air Force transport aircraft airlifted some eight thousand Sudanese army troops into the South.[31] Sudan's civil war had begun.

In 1956 Sudan was ruled by a democratically elected prime minister, Ismail al-Azhari. His leadership proved short-lived—apparently due to his inability to deliver on his promises of Ansar independence, unity for the Khatmiyyah, and federation for the southerners. He was replaced by Prime Minister Abdalla Khalil, who was also toppled after a short reign. Led by General Ibrahim Abboud, in November 1958 the military seized power, quickly suppressing the opposition and attempting to accelerate the Islamization of the South through aggressive proselytizing.[32] Abboud's coup against Khalil ushered in a long period of fluctuation between civilian and military rule. Abboud's military campaign forced thousands of southerners into exile in neighboring countries, where they soon formed more militant opposition organizations. The remnants of the mutiny of 1955, for example, formed the most violent among southern Sudanese opposition groups: the Anya-Nya ("snake poison"), with Joseph Lagu as its founder and leader. The Anya-Nya enjoyed widespread support in the South. For this reason, General Abboud's full-scale military campaign tended to target southern Sudanese civilians and Anya-Nya combatants indiscriminately. His campaign against the Anya-Nya and other southern opposition movements generated some 500,000 refugees.[33]

By all accounts, the underlying cause of the 1955 mutiny had been southern frustration over the systematic denial of civil service posts in the state government (including the army). In fact, six years after General Abboud's so-called Islamization campaign, southern resistance groups continued to focus their demands on a need for economic development, which they believed could be secured only through increased autonomy—preferably full political independence. The priority of southern grievances is reflected in a memorandum sent to the Organization for African Unity (OAU), in which the Sudan African National Union (SANU) complained that the North had denied southerners participation in the administration, stunted southern economic development, and hampered educational progress.

After Abboud's ouster, the next prime minister, Sayed Sir el-Khatim el-Khalifa, attempted to address the southern problem by engaging southerners' grievances rather than simply trying to coerce them into unity. He arranged a Round Table Conference in which for the first time the North considered extending representation to the Southerners. Overall, el-Khalifa represented a faction of northern leadership who favored a more conciliatory approach to the South. When Sadiq el-Mahdi took over in 1966 for his first term as leader of Sudan, he was much more intent on the revival of Islam and urged the adoption of an Islamic constitution.[34] War continued through the el-Mahdi and Mohamed Ahmad Mahgoub regimes until 1969.

On May 25, 1969, following student demonstrations and a revolution, a military junta headed by Jaafar Muhammad al-Nimeiri overthrew a civilian caretaker government that had ruled since October 1964. Nimeiri strengthened the relationship between Sudanese government and the Soviet Union, already the main financial and military backer of Khartoum. He also increased his country's support of and identification with Arab states in their conflict with Israel.[35]

In July 1971 a failed communist coup attempt led to the termination of Soviet support. Bereft of its strongest military supporter and facing an increasingly skilled, destructive, and well-led resistance, Nimeiri made peace overtures to the Southern rebels. After the failed coup, Nimeiri had a number of the more radical Southern leaders working in Khartoum or abroad arrested and executed, including Joseph Garang. He replaced them with moderates, such as Abel Alier.

One of the major problems in both wars was identifying leaders to approach for negotiations. The leadership on both sides often changed, particularly among the rebels. Several other factors, such as agreements between Nimeiri and President Idi Amin of Uganda, and between Nimeiri and Emperor Haile Selassie of Ethiopia, stopped the arms flows to the rebels and stopped cross-border support to the North. Neutral church organizations served as unofficial mediators in the negotiations, and Haile Selassie lent his support. Despite these obstacles, in March 1972

Nimeiri's government signed the Addis Ababa Agreement. It granted the South partial political and economic autonomy and marked an end to Sudan's first, seventeen-year-long civil war.[36]

The Addis Ababa Agreement: A Failed Settlement?

We already know that the Addis Ababa Agreement "failed" to secure a lasting peace in Sudan. After seventeen years of war, however, an eleven-year respite is no mean accomplishment. There must therefore be something in the agreement itself, and in the constellation of other forces surrounding the agreement (including relations with bordering states, the ebb and flow of superpower fortunes in the Cold War, and the Arab-Israeli dispute), that were conducive to peace. In this section, I analyze the key components of the Addis Ababa Agreement and then show that a lack of attention to security sector reform proved a major shortcoming.

As noted above, two factors led the warring sides to advance from the early work on reconciliation begun in 1965 to a true cease-fire and a negotiated political settlement: (1) the painful military stalemate, which had not changed since the mid-1960s; and (2) the consolidation of leadership in the North and South that resulted from the failure to find a military solution to the problems of either side, along with shifts in each side's access to external support from regional and distant allies.

The first factor that led both sides to the bargaining table was the hurtful military stalemate that had already developed by the time of Abboud's ouster in 1964. As El Obeid puts it: "Above all, there was a rooted conviction, held by both southerners and northerners, that the conflict had become, to all intents and purposes, unending. The Anya-Nya had made the south virtually ungovernable, but an internationally recognized secession was as far away as ever."[37] But peace did not break out as a result of these early efforts to engineer a negotiated settlement to the civil war. A second factor was necessary, and that proved to be the consolidation of leadership in both the North and the South.

One of the most interesting features of Sudanese politics in the 1960s was the tendency of national policy to be guided more by instrumental political expediency in elite competition for the presidency and less by practical connections between the strategies pursued and their impact on the conflict itself.[38] The attempt by Abboud to engineer national unity by means of Islamization, for example, had the opposite of its intended effect.[39] It strengthened and unified southern resistance, and no amount of coercion appeared sufficient to overcome that resistance—especially since much of it was based in surrounding states that had been alienated by Abboud's policies and brutality in the South. This left Abboud vulnerable, and his opponents began basing their claim of a need or right to succeed him on possession of an opposite, more conciliatory strategy in the South. Thus, the "reconciliation" strategy was less about ending the civil war (which many in Khartoum at that time felt they could live with), and more about one faction opposing another faction's rule. As a result, a change of leadership *often* implied a change of strategy. Thus, Abboud's resignation following student protests in 1964 created a window of opportunity, and his successor, Sayed Sir el-Khatim el-Khalifa, extended an olive branch to the South, wrongly assuming that the chief cause of southern resistance was opposition to Abboud's regime rather than a genuine bid for secession.

In both the North and the South, this process of competition for leadership eventually resulted in two political figures who exercised relatively unified control over their respective constituencies.[40] In the North, the Nimeiri coup transferred power to a military dictator who was supported by the Soviet Union and who did not have to pander to public opinion in order to promote a preferred strategy. In the South, leadership of the fractious southern resistance movements eventually came under the control of Joseph Lagu, founder of the military resistance movement, Anya-Nya. The two factors—a military stalemate exacerbated after 1971 by the termination of Soviet support for Nimeiri's regime and the consolidation of leadership on both sides—led to the completion of the process that began half a decade earlier and would result in the Addis Ababa Agreement in 1972.

Key Provisions of the Addis Ababa Agreement

My thesis leads us to expect that the distribution of issues within an agreement will reflect the true interests of the parties who will contract an obligation under that agreement. Agreements that are dominated by cease-fire provisions but contain few annexes on power sharing or compliance oversight, for example, tend to indicate that one or both of the parties are actually interested in an opportunity to rearm rather than in lasting peace. It therefore makes sense to look at the contents of the Addis Ababa Agreement in an effort to deduce the major concerns of the contracting parties, as well as to compare its provisions with outcomes, both in Sudan and across cases.

The Addis Ababa Agreement, known in Sudan as the Southern Province Regional Self-Government Act of 1972, is generally short. It contains only six sections, as follows:

1. The Basic Law Organizing Regional Autonomy
2. Amnesty Bill

3. Administrative Measures Organizing the Transitional Period for the Southern Region
4. Cease Fire
5. Temporary Measures Concerning the Armed Forces
6. Rehabilitation of the Refugees

Overall, the bulk of the twenty-page agreement focuses on the division of sovereignty between North and South, while less of the document addresses economic reforms and refugee repatriation. Its two most striking features are (1) the relatively slight attention paid to SSR beyond that necessary for a simple cease-fire, and (2) the weak provisions for oversight of implementation and procedures for resolution of conflicting interpretations of the agreement's spirit and mandates.

Why the Addis Ababa Agreement Failed

Before the question of the agreement's failure can be addressed, we must dispense with the important argument that, given the overdetermined likelihood of conflict throughout Sudan's history, the agreement is not a failure but a success.

No one who has studied Sudan's troubled history will deny that the Addis Ababa Agreement and the eleven years of relative peace that followed its ratification in 1972 count as a major accomplishment. But a closer look at the agreement itself and at the attempts to implement it in the years following its ratification make clear that it in fact failed to address the key political issue that lay at the root of the conflict it ended: the question of southern autonomy.

An analysis of the agreement reveals two issues that precluded its success in achieving a lasting peace in Sudan. First, the agreement was successful at achieving a cease-fire because it effectively institutionalized southern political autonomy (de facto) within a framework that appeared to guarantee Sudanese unity (de jure). In other words, while not formally recognizing southern demands for secession, it effectively promised the South a general and indefinite respite from traditional northern efforts at religious and cultural assimilation.

Second, the agreement did not address SSR. Instead, it effectively left *two* armed forces with responsibility for securing southern Sudan. True, it called for integration of national and regional militaries, but it left the means, and in particular the *timetable*, for achieving this integration unspecified. After the cease-fire came into effect, for example, the question of integration and recruitment for the southern contingent was to be the work of a Joint Technical Military Commission (JTMC) composed of six officers—three from the old northern forces and three from the absorbed southern forces. The commission's key mandate was to ensure integration in a way that ensures "an atmosphere of peace and confidence" in the South.[41] The JTMC was to oversee a general downsizing of troops in the South to a maximum of twelve thousand officers and men. Yet the JTMC was also strongly cautioned against moves that might reignite war, such as physically integrating southern Sudanese troops with troops drawn from the North and elsewhere. As a result, the troops tended to stay in the areas they controlled at the time of the cease-fire, and no effective integration took place.[42]

An additional barrier to integration was the unforeseen number of former southern soldiers who wanted to keep their ranks (and jobs) within the combined armed forces. Two problems emerged. First, there was simply not enough money to pay them. And because these soldiers were armed and experienced at guerrilla warfare, neither northern nor southern commanders were willing to simply let them go, for fear they would turn to banditry. Second, integration also required education in a different type of soldiering than that to which most southern soldiers had become accustomed. Barracks duties, sophisticated weapons training, and state defense missions were all alien to them. Thus, beyond the problem of finding sufficient cash to pay these troops, the JTMC struggled to find ways to retrain officers for more traditional duties.

Still, the political problems ran deeper. Within a year, southern regional officials began to complain that Khartoum had not only neglected to draw down its forces in the South but had repositioned them so as to be able to control southern towns.[43] Southern armed forces were thus doubly disadvantaged, and southern insecurity and resentment deepened.

Finally, the agreement did not contain adequate provisions for the resolution of ambiguities or contradictions—both of which were rife in the document itself. Paradoxically, in the context of Sudanese politics, this feature of the agreement—the problem that policy effectiveness was systematically discounted as compared to its utility in acquiring offices—probably explains the duration of the cease-fire better than any other single factor. This arises because leaders in the North and South spent so much time and effort attempting to clarify what the agreement committed them to that reflection on their deeper political disagreements was delayed. In addition, early in the war, both sides had become convinced that their respective military efforts had reached their limits in terms of political effectiveness. But this effect was bound to wear off over time, as leaders on both sides began to imagine that some new constellation of support might tilt the military balance decisively in their favor in a future engagement.

As it became clear that the South would never yield to integration with the North by means of assimilation to a conservative interpretation of Islam (represented most clearly in southern calculations by the question of Sharia law), and that the North would not or could not undertake southern economic development, war appeared to be the best option for both sides.

In sum, either of the first two factors would have been sufficient to doom the agreement on its own, but in combination with the third factor, we arrive at an explanation both for the duration of the cease-fire and for its eventual collapse. The next chapter will trace the sequence of events during the eleven years of peace that ultimately led to the reignition of the Sudanese civil war.

Chapter 8

The Republic of Sudan: Prospects for Peace

THE PREVIOUS CHAPTER detailed the history of Sudan, from the ancient origins of North–South tensions to the "first" civil war. It also examined the content of the Addis Ababa Agreement, which resulted in eleven years of peace, and analyzed how the agreement failed to address southern autonomy, provide for security sector reform, and resolve the ambiguities and contradictions inherent in the treaty. In this chapter, I describe how these factors led to the breakdown of the Addis Ababa Agreement and to the renewal of civil war—Sudan's "second" civil war (1983–2005). I then evaluate the Naivasha Accords, which ended the second civil war, in terms of their potential to address the failures of previous treaties and to ensure a lasting peace in Sudan.

The prospect of social, religious, and economic autonomy for the South contributed to the negotiated end of Sudan's first civil war. So long as the prospect of that autonomy lasted, the incentives for the South to fight were low as compared to the costs of returning to war.

The Road to a Second Civil War

Despite the potential costs of returning to war, neither Sudan nor most of the rest of North Africa and the Middle East could escape the outside world or its pressures. In March 1973 Nimeiri was forced to deal with a terrorist attack, which instantly became an international incident. Eight members of the Palestinian Black September Organization (BSO) assaulted the Saudi embassy in Khartoum, taking a number of diplomats and guests hostage. The BSO terrorists demanded the release of a number of Palestinian prisoners in return for sparing their hostages. After sixty hours of tough bargaining, which resulted in the execution of both the U.S. ambassador and the Belgian chargé d'affaires, the terrorists surrendered. Outraged, Nimeiri accused Yassir Arafat of complicity and insisted the BSO terrorists be tried and punished. His security forces later found a record of the entire operational plan for the attack when they raided the offices of the Palestinian Liberation Organization (PLO) in Khartoum. But in most of the Middle East, the BSO were seen as heroes and as a bulwark against Zionism. Nimeiri was warned not to try the eight captive terrorists, but he moved forward anyway. In July 1974 all eight pleaded guilty and were sentenced to life imprisonment. Nimeiri later commuted their sentences to seven years. He then ordered them handed over to the PLO to serve the remainder of their sentences, and they disappeared. The United States immediately recalled its ambassador from Khartoum in protest.

This incident highlights the difficulties of Sudanese leadership in the 1970s and was a clear prequel to continued challenges between the East and the West up to today. If they leaned too far in support of pan-Arabism, they would alienate the West and risk civil war in the South. If they leaned too far in support of southern autonomy, they risked being called an enemy of Islam and of the Arab struggle against Zionism. Nimeiri's reaction to the BSO embassy assault ended up hurting him personally. He made enemies on all sides and no new friends.

After 1973 and the defeat of yet another Arab coalition at the hands of Israel, it became clear that no Arab coalition would be able to defeat Israel militarily. Islamic leaders throughout the region—including Sudan—engaged in fierce rhetoric against Israel (and Israel's supporters) and advocated an increasingly conservative brand of Islam.[1] A number of the region's leaders took to supporting terrorism against Israel and repressing non-Muslim minorities within their own countries. In Sudan, Nimeiri came under increasing pressure to abrogate the Addis Ababa Agreement and begin the work of securing all of Sudan for "God."

In March 1975 Nimeiri quelled an army mutiny in the South, which his political adversaries had launched from Ethiopia. The incident was kept quiet, but the Akabo Mutiny, as it became known, proved to be a major military operation and resulted in thousands of refugees and hundreds of casualties.[2] More ominously, it revealed how deeply southerners resented the Addis Ababa Agreement and how willing they were to abandon it.

Several months later, in September 1975, Nimeiri survived a coup attempt by a conservative army colonel, who was supported by Sudan's communists and the Muslim Brotherhood. The Osman Rebellion, as it was called, ended when troops loyal to Nimeiri captured Colonel Osman and his men surrendered. He was tried and executed by firing squad in January 1976.

In July 1976 Nimeiri was forced to respond to yet another plot to remove him from office by force. This time, the plan came from Libya with the support of the Muslim Brotherhood and at the behest of Nimeiri's longtime antagonist and rival, Sadiq el-Mahdi (then living in Paris). The movement was foiled, according to testimony from one of its captured leaders, by "the absence of promised reinforcements from Libya; the absence of any public support from the Sudanese masses, which somehow the plotters had expected; and the failure of the plotters to identify them-selves to the public, as the radio broadcasting staff at Omdurman had fled before any rebel broadcasts could be made."[3]

The process of revolution and infighting in neighboring Ethiopia re-sulted in February 1977 in the accession to leadership of Colonel Men-gistu Haile Meriam. Ethiopia became a client state of the Soviet Union and, after Nimeiri's successful election to a second six-year presidential term in April, he voiced Sudan's support for Eritrea's independence from Ethiopia. In May of the same year, the Soviets were ejected from Sudan. (They had been deliberately delaying the shipment of spare parts for So-viet military equipment, which had become increasingly useless to Sudan as a result.)

Nimeiri weathered an average of two major challenges to his leader-ship during each year of his tenure. After the discovery in southern Sudan of more significant petroleum deposits in 1980, the pressure on Nimeiri to abrogate the agreement reached a new level of intensity.[4] Nimeiri or-dered the division of the southern region into three "autonomous" re-gions and simultaneously redrew boundaries so as to place the newly discovered oil deposits into northern Sudan. In 1981 Nimeiri approved the formation of the White Nile Petroleum Corporation—a joint venture with Chevron. No southerners were on the board.

In January 1983, in an act of defiance similar in nature and effect to the mutiny of August 1955, southern troops of the 105th Battalion refused orders to disarm and be transferred to the North. After several months of negotiations, Nimeiri in May ordered an attack on the rebels. Members of the unit fled to neighboring Ethiopia, where they formed the Sudanese People's Liberation Movement/Army (SPLM/A)—the main southern rebel faction, led by John Garang, who had fled to Ethiopia under Nimeiri.[5]

The Addis Ababa Agreement was officially abrogated in June 1983, when Nimeiri issued Presidential Decree No. 1, which formally returned regional powers to the central government, ended the autonomy of the South, and divided the southern region into three separate and powerless administrative provinces (Upper Nile, Bahr al-Ghazal, and Equatoria).[6] The financial responsibilities of the South were transferred to Khartoum, and Arabic was declared the country's official language. In addition, the central government seized control of the armed forces of the South.[7] Since the Addis Ababa Agreement had never risen much beyond the status of a tentative cease-fire, by deliberately repealing the agreement, Presidential Decree No. 1 effectively returned Sudan to civil war.

In September 1983 Nimeiri went further than mere retraction of the agreement. He promulgated the so-called September Laws, which im-posed Islamic religious law (Sharia) on Sudanese people and sanctioned the use of *hudud* (physical punishment such as flogging, amputations, and cross-amputations,[8] stoning, and execution for various crimes). Southerners labeled the imposition of the harsh laws a "rising tide of Muslim fundamentalism," which "threatened to unsettle the spirit of tolerance characteristic of the Addis Ababa decade."[9] The SPLM/A, now unified behind Garang, declared that it would fight until the September Laws were revoked. Similar to Nimeiri's attempt to assimilate Sudan into a homogenous Arab-Islamic state, the South promulgated a position that moved beyond southern autonomy; it included calls to transform Sudan into a multiracial, multireligious, and multiethnic democratic state.[10]

Fighting around Sudan's oil fields intensified in 1984. Three expatriate Chevron workers were kidnapped near Bentiu in March and later murdered by the SPLM/A. Chevron responded by suspending operations.

After difficult months in which SPLM/A forces proved impossible to destroy, Nimeiri announced in March 1985 a unilateral ceasefire in the South and renewed his offer of amnesty to opposition forces.[11] His government was under increasing pressure from the economic depression it had suffered since 1984, exacerbated by Nimeiri's introduction of Islamic taxation and banking systems. Making this situation worse, a regional drought and famine were producing increasing numbers of refugees that flowed into Sudan. The effects of the drought in Sudan had also been magnified because most of the best land had been farmed in an unsustainable way, for pure profit, by Sudanese political and military elites. As crops failed, the quest for more land led to fights with tribesmen, who depended on range land for their cattle. Edgar O'Ballance describes the results: "Due to the death of cattle in the drought, many tribesmen suddenly had no income at all, and as an attempt to channel them into agricultural work on the major schemes proved unsuccessful, they had to be put into camps and fed by the government. By mid-1985 there were over 100,000 poverty-stricken tribesmen in almost 50 temporary camps, the government not quite knowing what to do with them."[12]

Thus, a combination of military setbacks followed by a peace overture and then an escalating series of economic crises led to the downfall of Nimeiri. On the evening of April 6, 1985, while Nimeiri was in the United States, he was overthrown and replaced by a transitional military council, which promised to surrender power to a civilian leadership after elections a year later. Nimeiri was refused reentry into the country.

In April 1986, as promised, general elections were held in Sudan, and the transitional military council was replaced in May by a supreme council headed by Nimeiri's longtime rival, Sadiq el-Mahdi. But despite some efforts on his part to end the civil war by negotiations in a constitutional conference, the war escalated and continued to go badly for the North.

El-Mahdi, as head of the Umma party, refused to consider abolishing the September Laws. As this was the key political demand of the SPLM/A, peace talks failed to develop much momentum.

In 1987 and 1988 the el-Mahdi government did what it could to balance threats from within Sudan and from without. In 1987 el-Mahdi dissolved and rebuilt the government in the hopes of eliminating political stalemates and moving toward a cease-fire with the South, but nothing came of it. In May 1988 el-Mahdi formed a new National Unity government, which took up the thorny issue of the September Laws, and whether as a price of peace they might be modified or suspended. Again, negotiations broke down on a refusal of the North to abandon the laws and a refusal of the South to proceed until the laws were abandoned.

SPLM/A leader Garang announced a unilateral one-month cease-fire in May 1989, which he extended due to U.S. influence even though the North again refused to consider abandoning its insistence on Sharia law throughout Sudan.

El-Mahdi stood as a democratically elected prime minister of Sudan until 1989. His regime pushed for an Islamic constitution, and he carried out some of the most intense and brutal attacks in the South through his armed Arab militias, known as the Murahalin.[13] El-Mahdi later responded to increased SPLM/A successes in the field by attempting to negotiate another peace. As had happened nearly every time beforehand, peace overtures to the South led to a coup.

On June 30, 1989, General Omar Hassan al-Bashir seized power in a bloodless coup, toppling el-Mahdi's government. President Bashir, born in 1944 about 150 miles south of Khartoum, was a devout Muslim, having been a career soldier and a member of the National Islamic Front (NIF), an Islamist movement with its origins in the Muslim Brotherhood. He had fought in the 1967 and 1973 Arab-Israeli wars as well as in Sudan's first civil war.

Although the two sides had undertaken serious negotiations and had even met preconditions for a constitutional conference, Bashir's new regime immediately canceled all agreements reached between the el-Mahdi government and the SPLM/A.[14] The reason for this was that Bashir's authority derived in part from his alliance with the NIF, led by Hassan el Turabi.[15] The NIF advanced a radical Islamic vision and was determined to transform all of Sudan into an Islamic religious society.[16]

The Bashir regime quickly moved to preempt all political opposition by abolishing parliament, banning political parties, and imprisoning all party leaders. It imposed a state of emergency and created the Revolutionary Command Council, which served as a cabinet and was chaired by President Bashir. The new regime also closed down the newspapers. Leaders of student groups, unions, professional associations, and political parties were arrested and disappeared in "ghost houses" and prisons where they were tortured or murdered.[17] Undeterred by recent successes of the SPLM/A, which had in part prompted the el-Mahdi government's more conciliatory stance, the Bashir regime intensified the civil war.

Bashir refused to consider revoking Sharia law and, with NIF support and guidance, intensified efforts to force Islam on all Sudanese.[18] As in the previous civil war, religion was only one of many issues of contention between North and South. But increasingly, the Bashir regime described the war as a jihad, and the northern Muslim fighters as martyrs.[19]

Bashir's intensification of the war (still costing an estimated 1 billion US dollars per day), combined with Sudan's support of Iraq after that country's invasion of Kuwait, proved an economic disaster for Sudan. Aid from the United States and most Arab countries dried up, as did vital remittances of Sudanese workers in Kuwait and other Gulf states. By 1991 the entirety of Sudan's per capita income—100 U.S. dollars—came from international aid.

Yet Bashir persisted, and on the military front, the combination of SPLM/A fragmentation (the group split into Torit [Dinka] and Nasir [Nuer] factions), Iranian military and financial support, and the loss of Ethiopian sanctuaries led to a series of crushing military defeats by government forces in February and March 1992. Yet the separate factions rallied and then began again to inflict defeats on advancing government forces. In October the Nasir group, led by Riek Machar, captured Malakal, a major government base well stocked with weapons and ammunition.

In March 1993 the combination of food and fuel riots, along with an escalating dispute with Bashir's longtime ally Turabi, led to the declaration of a general cease-fire and peace negotiations. The negotiations never got under way, however, and within a month three of the splintered SPLM/A groups had united to form SPLA-United. Soon after, Torit (Garang's group) signed a cease-fire with SPLA-United; in August, however, the government launched a major offensive against Garang's Torit group. This fighting proved inconclusive but clearly showed that "the Torit group still retained considerable firepower."[20]

As the year closed, Bashir dissolved the Revolutionary Command Council and transferred its powers to a "civilian" government led by himself. He declared his intention to hold presidential elections the next year, and a general election in 1995. But his government was under tremendous economic pressure, and riots over shortages were prevented only with difficulty and constant vigilance on the government's part.

In January 1994 SPLA-United and Garang's Torit faction met in Kenya for cease-fire talks with the government; but clear evidence of an imminent attack by the government caused the talks to founder. In February Bashir launched an all-out offensive against all factions of the SPLM/A in the hopes of destroying them once and for all. The fighting again proved inconclusive, but it generated as many as 100,000 refugees, most of whom fled to Uganda.

In July 1994 another round of peace talks between Bashir and the SPLM/A factions began in Kenya. This third round of talks resulted in a cease-fire, but a fourth round of talks in September collapsed over the problem of Sharia law.

On the international stage, Bashir's government had been stung by its inclusion on the list of states supporting terrorism. The effect of this U.S. declaration had been to isolate Sudan from much-needed foreign assistance, and in an attempt to ease the pressure on his government, Bashir took part in a scheme headed by Turabi to extradite one of the world's most famous terrorists—Carlos the Jackal—to France. The move did not remove Sudan from the list.

In January 1995 Bashir "called for a jihad against unbelievers in Sudan, meaning the mainly Christian SPLA."[21] Bashir's rhetorical escalation led to a renewed effort by Garang to unify resistance to Bashir's rule personally, as well as domination by the North. SPLA-United split, as Machar created the Southern Sudan Independence Movement (SSIM), based in London. But the newly divided opposition groups met in Eritrea in June (without the SSIM), where they agreed that "religion should be separated from politics in Sudan, and in due course a referendum on secession from the republic should be held in the south."[22]

In April Uganda severed diplomatic relations with Sudan over accusations of Sudanese support for Ugandan rebels. In June Sudan was widely implicated in an attempted assassination of Egypt's president Hosni Mubarak. Bashir denied any knowledge of the plan but reshuffled his cabinet afterward. In September Garang led a new offensive against government forces on the White Nile. Bashir's government claimed that Garang had direct support from Uganda, including tanks, but Uganda denied this.

Unanimously, the UN Security Council in 1996 adopted a resolution that named Sudan as responsible for the assassination attempt on Mubarak and demanded the extradition of three Egyptian terrorists being sheltered by Sudan. Bashir went ahead with presidential and general elections while waiting to see what sanctions the United Nations would impose. In presidential elections held in March, Bashir was elected president by 75 percent of the votes, with voter turnout claimed at 70 percent. Hassan Turabi was named speaker of the Assembly on April 1. UN sanctions were imposed on April 26, and, though mild, "they nonetheless angered the Sudanese."[23]

On April 10, Bashir signed a peace deal with the two smaller main factions of the former SPLM/A: the SSIM and SPLA-United. The deal had been closed when the latter two groups agreed to give up their demand for full independence in return for allowing southerners the "right of special legislation with regard to the implementation of Sharia law."[24] Garang, claiming that the language of the agreement was much too vague, would have none of it.

In August the UN Security Council escalated its sanctions against Sudan for noncompliance with its extradition demand, and in September widespread bread riots broke out in northern cities, particularly Khartoum.

The actual fighting between northern and southern armed forces reached its highest intensity yet in January and February 1997, with great gains being claimed by Garang and subsequently denied by Bashir. In March and April it was still difficult to tell who was doing better, but things seemed to be favoring the southerners. In April intense fighting broke out in the East, where Garang's units received direct support from Eritrean and Ugandan units. According to O'Ballance, however, nothing ultimately came of what might have been a severe challenge to Bashir: "Various reasons were put forward for this [lack of a real attack], mostly political. The real reason was that the attacking forces were highly diverse, completely uncoordinated and logistically incapable of anything more than a skirmish. Meanwhile the government sat back and waited for the military opposition's unity of purpose to shatter, which it soon did."[25]

Thus, while the southern military resistance repeatedly failed to prove decisive, its impact on Bashir (along with his recurring economic and diplomatic troubles) was having a cumulative effect. Bashir suddenly agreed, in late April 1997, to a deal with the smaller surviving factions of the old SPLM/A that guaranteed them amnesty, Southern self-determination, and the suspension of Sharia law (i.e., a return to ante bellum conditions). But in May Garang's forces continued to assault government positions, with typically mixed results.

By July 1997 Bashir had agreed to a peace deal that would include both southern self-determination and the separation of religion and state, but Garang refused to take it seriously so long as these "principles" were not binding on Bashir's government. Fighting continued in August, and the peace talks in Nairobi were abandoned in November. Bashir claimed that his offer of autonomy would be limited to confederation, not full statehood, and he accused the United States of torpedoing negotiations by imposing harsh sanctions on Sudan—sanctions whose timing and nature were specifically intended to lead to his ouster as Sudan's president.

Little changed in 1998 and 1999. Both sides agreed to periodic ceasefires in order to stave off widespread famine, and once the immediate danger had passed, each side began anew the attempt to overcome the other by force. Sudan inaugurated a new constitution in June 1998, and Bashir promised to share power with exiled opposition politicians (Nimeiri returned from exile in Cairo in May 1999).

In September 1999 Sudan resumed exporting crude oil, producing an estimated 20,000 barrels per day;[26] and in November, after a number of attempts to reconcile their differences, the National Democratic Alliance (an umbrella opposition group) split over el-Mahdi's signing of a "Call of the Homeland" declaration with President Bashir. In December Bashir imposed a state of emergency and dissolved the National Assembly.

While Bashir was reelected president in December 2000, little changed in the civil war over the subsequent two years. In 2001 Bashir's increasing oil revenues (oil production had increased tenfold from 1999 to 200,000 barrels per day) resulted in a doubling of the North's military spending, which was subsequently used in a series of new offensives against rebel strongholds in the South that failed to achieve lasting military effect.[27] The impact of oil exploration concessions and development on southern civilians, however, has been devastating and well documented. Essentially, the North funds, supplies, and supports militia raids into oil concession areas in order "to drive civilians from the . . . area, to allow oil exploration to proceed unimpeded . . . the offensive also aims to move out relief agencies who might report the atrocities."[28] The process is circular: oil revenues are used to pay militiamen a stipend and compensation for lost horses or camels (the real pay for militiamen allied to Bashir's government comes in the form of loot and slaves). The raids depopulate areas suitable for exploration or road building, which results in additional oil revenue, and the progression continues. Under normal circumstances, the militia run risks of counterattacks by the SPLM/A, but in 2001 the SPLM/A was largely ineffective at mounting counterattacks due to factional infighting.[29]

The year 2001 proved to be a boon for Bashir's NIF-dominated government in another way: the attacks of September 11 made it possible for the government to condemn terrorism rhetorically and to supply limited but valuable intelligence to U.S. counterterrorism officials, while at the same time opening new oil exploration or development contracts with Western companies. Sudan invested 400 million U.S. dollars in oil revenue in new MiGs, which were then used against southern rebels—in particular those concentrated near oil exploration or production areas.[30] In short, Bashir's government, though closely aligned with the very conservative brand of Islam being mobilized against the United States, Israel, and Europe, managed to expand economic contacts with those very same target states and deflect international condemnation as a supporter of terrorism. As *Africa Confidential* notes: "Competition for oil-related contracts is intense and raises questions about commerce driving diplomacy. It means governments have no sticks to balance their much vaunted carrots; indeed, the NIF holds out the carrots."[31]

In January 2002 U.S. special envoy John Danforth brokered a cease-fire between the government and SPLM/A rebels in the Nuba mountains. Danforth hoped that this break in fighting could be expanded into an overall cease-fire, but within six months it became clear that the government had used the armistice to redeploy its troops and aircraft to the oil-rich Western Upper Nile, where fighting and attacks against noncombatants escalated as a result. The agreement was supposed to have guaranteed both the delivery of aid to civilians living in SPLA-controlled areas and the monitoring of violations, but neither in fact occurred.[32] Although the Bashir government undermined the cease-fire, Garang's SPLM/A forces nevertheless proved superior on the battlefield, and government forces were forced to retreat. Despite the prowess of the rebel soldiers, however, famine and an outbreak of meningitis threatened to undo the gains made by Garang and his southern allies and rivals against the government.

Finally, in July 2002, the two sides, in need of a respite from constant fighting, began the hard work of coming to agreement on a negotiated resolution to their dispute. The first version of what would in January 2005 become the Naivasha Accords or Comprehensive Peace Agreement was the Machakos Protocol, in which the government and SPLM/A agreed on a basic framework of (1) southern self-determination (a formal referendum following a six-year transitional period); and (2) the exemption of the South from the application of Sharia law. Both sides apparently believed they could still win on the battlefield and, according to *Africa Confidential*, Bashir's NIF-dominated government would never accept an independent South nor one in which Sharia law was not enforced. Instead, Bashir's government skillfully used peace rhetoric to gain time to further develop its oil wealth—and consolidate support from Egypt and other Arab states—in preparation for a renewed assault on the South: "The government clearly has no intention of losing control of the oil reserves, almost all in the south, and sees the south as its future breadbasket and Islamist springboard into Africa."[33]

Thus, the protocol was never intended by either side as a genuine peace agreement, but rather was a means of lessening U.S. and British pressure while simultaneously holding out the prospect of a chance to regroup resources for another fight. The ambiguity of its key points was intended not only to convince the United States and Britain that they had achieved the basis for a lasting peace in a unified, secular Sudan, but also to allow Bashir, Garang, and their respective allies to claim that they had not abandoned their core causes.

In 2003 Bashir's government was poised to take advantage of the U.S. focus on Iraq, and especially to aid the Bush administration in its attempt to overcome a complete lack of evidence and to discover a link between

Saddam Hussein's secularist Ba'ath Party and Al-Qaeda.[34] It continued to build new roads into oil-rich southern areas and then used the roads to transport heavy weapons for use against Garang's SPLM/A.

In the West, the Bashir government escalated attacks against isolated civilians in Darfur. These attacks followed a similar pattern. First, helicopter gunships or fighter bombers would attack a village in early morning, routing inhabitants who then attempted to flee. Most would be subsequently killed by Arab militia troops on camel or horseback, who would rape and murder any females they could catch and then set any remaining structures alight after looting them. Males and children were simply murdered out of hand. Often, the Arab militias received direct support from uniformed Sudanese troops.[35]

A year later, as anti-Americanism in Europe and the Middle East increased due to U.S. troubles in Iraq, Sudan was once again able to block reinstatement of a special rapporteur. As violence continued to escalate in Darfur, Western nations proved unable (the United States) or unwilling (Europe) to risk derailing the North–South peace process by pressuring Bashir's NIF-dominated government to cease attacks.[36] This led to the odd but successful strategy of the NIF using peace talks in Kenya as a way to deflect serious reaction and action on Darfur.[37]

In May 2004 in Naivasha, Kenya, the SPLM/A and Bashir's NIF-dominated government signed the first draft of a comprehensive peace agreement. This early agreement had three main sections or protocols: (1) power-sharing; (2) resolution of the conflict in Abyei; and (3) resolution of the conflict in the Southern Kordofan, Nubia Mountains, and Blue Nile states. In keeping with the basic tenets of the earlier Machakos Protocol, core issues included a referendum for southern political status within Sudan to be held in six and a half years, the sharing of oil revenue, and the restriction of Sharia law to the North (with the exception of Khartoum, where it is to apply only to Muslims). Implementation details and contradictions were to be hammered out over the next several months.

On January 9, 2005, Khartoum—represented by its vice president, Ali Osman Taha—and the SPLM/A—represented by John Garang—finally signed the Comprehensive Peace Agreement formally ending the North–South civil war. The two had become the principal negotiators of the agreement from September 2003.

The Second War's End: A Negotiated Settlement

As the story of Sudan's second civil war makes clear, the politics of war and peace in Sudan are as complicated as they come. All of the terms we use to attempt to understand war and peace in Sudan, or how and whether they apply, are themselves contested: "Arab," "militia," "tribe," "animist," "Muslim," "democratic," "rebel," and so on. Douglas Johnson, perhaps the best representative of careful and recent scholarship on Sudan, suggests that the main axis of conflict (and, by extension, the main place to focus peace efforts) has to do with the confluence of Sudan's long history—in which a strong pattern of asymmetric economic development emerges. This, coupled with Sudan's geography, has made it physically difficult, even when Northern political elites were willing, to unify Sudan's many different peoples into a cohesive political entity.

In short, Johnson argues that the most common way of understanding Sudan's divisions—North–South, Arab–African, and Muslim–Christian/Animist—are all misleading at best. Instead, he proposes that the root cause of Sudan's many conflicts (and two civil wars) lies in an ancient pattern of exploitation of the South and Southwest by the North. By extension, any long-term solution to Sudan's conflicts demands rationalization and redistribution of Sudan's development resources.

Before moving on to an analysis of the strengths and weaknesses of the Naivasha Accords (the Comprehensive Peace Agreement) and its all-important impact on the likelihood of an enduring peace in Sudan, it makes sense to highlight the key features of that agreement as it was signed.

The Comprehensive Peace Agreement, 2005

The CPA grew directly from the Machakos Protocol into a document with the same basic political features, with more specific sharing and oversight mechanisms added. Specifically, it included a guarantee of a southern referendum on independence to be held in six and a half years (June 2011), and an agreement to suspend the imposition of Sudan's conservative version of Sharia law on the South and on non-Muslims living in Khartoum.

In addition to these basic political compromises, and unlike previous versions, the CPA contained numerous power, military, and economic sharing provisions (most of which remain strikingly similar to those of the previous Addis Ababa Agreement), as well as a number of detailed implementation oversight and timetable provisions.

Key Provisions of the Comprehensive Peace Agreement

The CPA contains six key provisions:

1. An interim national constitution. Northern and southern representatives were expected to prepare a new state constitution that incorporated the CPA within six weeks of the agreement's signing. This interim constitution established an Office of the Presidency, National Assembly,

and Government of Southern Sudan (GOSS). Northerners were to get 70 percent of the review commission's seats, and the NIF was guaranteed an overall majority of 52 percent.

2. Office of the Presidency. The new executive branch was to be divided between a president (Bashir) and two vice presidents (Garang, first vice president, and Ali Osman Taha, vice president). All three would be members of the Presidential Council, Council of Ministers, and National Security Council. Interestingly, however, in the event of a presidential vacancy in pre- and postelection periods, it is the vice president (Taha, a man with no military experience) who becomes commander-in-chief of the Sudan Armed Forces, rather than First Vice President Garang (a general).

The first vice president's other powers are not trivial, however. He must approve appointments to key councils and commissions, including the Councils of Ministers and State Governors, as well as a Special Commission to ensure the rights of non-Muslims in Khartoum, and a Human Rights Commission.[38] Garang's approval was also necessary for the appointments of judges and other important officials, such as chairman of the National Land Commission. The CPA specified Garang's (i.e., the first vice president's) responsibilities and authorities in detail but said next to nothing about Osman's (i.e., those of the vice president). Paradoxically, this meant that Osman had more power than Garang, since the president (Bashir) was free to give him responsibilities and authorities as he saw fit so long as they did not conflict with those formally given to Garang.[39]

3. National Assembly and elections. A state legislature of 450 members was to be appointed within two weeks of the adoption of an interim national constitution. As noted above, 70 percent of this body would be reserved for the North and 30 percent for the South. In addition, "although other Northern parties overwhelmingly outnumbered it in the elected parliament which the NIF overthrew in 1989, the [National Congress Party/NIF] keeps its inbuilt majority."[40]

4. The Government of Southern Sudan. Garang was given a free hand in appointing ministers, judges, and state governors. The NCP/NIF also gained representation in the South: 15 percent of the 170 seats in the Sudan Southern Assembly were reserved for them (far greater representation than they could have achieved in elections). The CPA thus gave the SPLM "a majority even in parts of the South it does not control."[41]

5. Armed forces. Sudan's defense ministry was to have no jurisdiction over the SPLM/A, which was required to withdraw its forces from eastern Sudan. Northern forces in the South were not required to withdraw for two and a half years (or until July 9, 2007). With the exception of Joint Integrated Forces (JIF), the two armies were to remain separate until the referendum. Northern troops were to redeploy to the North,

and southern forces in the North were to redeploy to the South. Command and control of the JIF was to be the responsibility of a Joint Defense Board, comprising officers from both sides. The Joint Defense Board was also charged with coordinating the activities (or lack thereof) of the two separate forces. All other nonstatutory armed groups were to be disarmed, and none would be allowed to operate outside the North or South armed forces or joint forces. Provisions were made for the other armed groups to be incorporated into the police, the ranks of prison guards, or army or wildlife protection forces. Other such groups could be integrated into civil service institutions.

6. Wealth-sharing. Customary law will govern land distribution. The first vice president was entitled to appoint the chairperson of the National Land Commission. Petroleum revenues were to be shared under the supervision of a National Petroleum Commission, which for the first time gave the SPLM/A access to petroleum production data and contracts.

Overall, and on paper, the CPA's implementation and monitoring instruments were more robust than those of the Addis Ababa Agreement, which ended the first civil war. The World Bank and the Government of Sudan's Constitutional Committee, for example, were two of the bodies responsible for keeping track of the intricate timetables for implementation of the treaty's provisions, including division of the oil revenues. The funding of the armed forces was specified, the domestic security duties were outlined, and SSR was carefully covered.

Analysis: The CPA, SSR, and Enduring Peace in Sudan

Perhaps the two biggest differences between the first and second civil wars in Sudan are the roles of petroleum and religion in the second civil war. Before the advent of significant oil revenues in the mid-1990s, northern political elites made increasing use of religious appeals, both to gain the resources they desperately needed to keep control of the South and to delegitimize rivals with less radical or conservative interpretations of Islamic law and faithful practice. The more conservative appeals were most effective at gaining financial and diplomatic support from regional Islamic states (e.g., Saudi Arabia). Thus, what clearly began as a resource in a power struggle among northern political elites soon came to affect the peace (i.e., the Addis Ababa Agreement) and, later, the nature of the second war—including who was targeted or ignored, as well as regional and interstate politics.[42]

The CPA reflects the escalating role of religion in its incorporation of a series of agreements, beginning with the Machakos Protocol of 2002. To outsiders, the agreement by the North to allow the South freedom from the imposition of Sharia law appeared to be a victory. Yet it was actually a retreat from previous practice, in which separation of church and state (secularism) was recognized as a foundational principle of legitimacy in Sudan's constitution. After Machakos, it became increasingly common for actors on all sides to ignore this key difference, and the lack of serious challenge from the South on this issue has proven equally revealing: Garang and his closest allies were focusing less on compromise and accommodation with the North, and more on an internationally supported path to full sovereign independence.

Security Sector Reform

The evidence suggests that most contemporary negotiated settlements go wrong by promising benefits without sufficient attention to the threat of harm, should one or both sides defect. Security arrangements are therefore a good place to look for evidence that defectors will be harmed.

In the CPA, security provisions were minimal. Essentially, the agreement ratified a status quo in which the security of the South would be the responsibility of the SPLM/A and the government of Southern Sudan (GOSS), and that of the North would be the responsibility of the Government of Sudan (GOS). Sudan would therefore be effectively partitioned into two states, each with its own military and police.

Two additional factors complicate this simple but fairly accurate picture. First, the CPA (as had the Addis Ababa Agreement before it) called for the formation of Joint Integrated Units and provided fairly detailed instructions as to how these were to be formed and who was responsible for integration, training, doctrine, and so on. Interestingly, the CPA more broadly promised a referendum on southern independence, while at the same time mandating the creation of a force it referred to as constituting the "nucleus of a post referendum army of Sudan, should the result of the referendum confirm unity, otherwise they would be dissolved and the component parts integrated into their respective forces."[43] Second, while the SPLM/A was expected to immediately withdraw its forces from East Sudan, the GOS received a two-and-a-half-year grace period before being required to remove its forces from the "South"; where South is specifically designated as the boundary of January 1, 1956.[44] (Recall that in 1980 Nimeiri unilaterally declared a new state, "Unity," as part of northern Sudan, just after large oil reserves were discovered in the South.) This means that once both sides have fully complied and the grace period expires, the GOSS would gain physical control of the oil production facilities in Unity.

The inclusion of the January 1, 1956, boundary in the CPA also high-lights the importance of this definition of "South" for future negotiations between Khartoum and the SPLM/A (now GOSS): should the "South" vote for independence from the North, it would stand to gain control of Sudan's current and considerable petroleum reserves, infrastructure, con-tracts, and revenues. Thus, even in the text of the agreement itself, the GOS committed itself to a profoundly implausible position, and this alone should cast doubt on the extent to which the North was negotiat-ing in good faith for lasting peace, or simply buying time in order to re-initiate hostilities under conditions more favorable to it.

As noted above, the Joint Integrated Forces were to form the core of security sector reform as outlined in the CPA. Once operational, the JIF were to be expanded as needed to secure a unified Sudan from external threats. The CPA and interim national constitution both mandated the formation and expansion of local, regional, and national police forces to take over the task of providing the Sudanese people with sufficient secu-rity to go about making a living.

Police forces were to first supplement and then eventually supplant the informal networks of tribal law enforcement mechanisms in place throughout Sudan. Besides a lack of tradition in statutory law enforce-ment and a lack of resources (both of which can be remedied, or at least ameliorated, by United Nations assistance as mandated in UN Security Council Resolution 1590), however, another major problem complicates Sudan's efforts to separate law enforcement and national security respon-sibilities, and that is the nature of the judicial system that supports law enforcement. Will police be arresting Sudanese people for religious crimes or not? If so, which religion's crimes will be grounds for arrest, detention, and trial?

What ultimately emerges from an analysis of the CPA is a picture of two parties desperate for a cease-fire but committed to achieving their ex ante political objectives. For the North, these included the establishment of Sharia law as a foundational principle of law and legitimacy through-out Sudan[45] or, failing to accomplish this at an acceptable price, the hiv-ing off of southern Sudan ("southern" as defined by Khartoum) into a separate state, while the North maintained complete control over Sudan's oil resources and wealth. For the South, increasingly certain that the North would not yield on Sharia law or treat the South with respect (or seriously devote development resources to it), these objectives were re-duced to full independence from the North, along with control over most of Sudan's oil resources.

The text of the CPA could become either a tool for true reconciliation and national unity, or a rhetorical cover for tactical regrouping. In any case, each side would be able to use key provisions of the CPA as a litmus test of the other's true intentions.

Implementation of Security Sector Reform in the CPA

Peace agreements, like any agreements, may be more difficult to achieve in reality than signatories believe, even when signed in good faith. That said, the history since January 9, 2005, of the implementation of the CPA in Sudan makes key differences between the two signatories increasingly transparent, and it casts doubt on the future stability of the peace itself.

By the end of 2007, two and a half years after the CPA's signing, the Joint Integrated Forces exist mainly on paper, and in reality the personnel designated for it remain under separate chains of command.[46] This shortcoming is as devastating to the prospects for long-term peace as it is revealing of the true valuation each side has given the CPA. In addition, the July 9, 2007, deadline for the North to remove its forces from southern Sudan has come and gone, but the North still maintains upwards of 3,600 troops in and around oil production facilities south of the January 1, 1956, border. (A commission mandated by the CPA to establish the precise location of this border has only just been formed and was scheduled to offer its report to Bashir in June 2008). Bashir's government claims that the 3,600 troops (the governor of Unity province, south of the 1956 border, claims a much larger number) "are required to protect the oilfields pending full deployment of Joint Integrated Units."[47] Additionally, a February 2009 report released by the Center for American Progress highlights the lack of progress in transforming the SPLA into a professionalized and modernized army and warns that stability will be impossible until this objective is attained.[48] Secretary-General Ban Ki-moon concluded in a report to the UN Security Council on the situation of the Sudan from October 20, 2008, to January 18, 2009, that demobilization had stalled and that, overall, the CPA was not being implemented.[49]

In terms of real security, since early 2005 the United Nations Mission in the Sudan (UNMIS) has reported an overall increase in "militia" activity threatening to the peace and eventually shifted from referring to this problem as "about to be resolved" to referring to it as "using militias as proxy forces."[50] In its final report (S/2007/500, August 20, 2007), UNMIS highlights progress on most fronts, but key security-related shortcomings remain. Aside from the status of militias, delays in integration of GOSS and GOS forces (the JIF), and delays in the redeployment of GOS troops north of the 1956 boundary line (all serious security problems in themselves), each of these delayed or abridged processes is closely linked with the formation of political oversight institutions. Such groups, as the UNMIS report makes clear, are finally coming into being but are not receiving adequate financing.[51] In violation of the requirements of the CPA, control of most of Sudan's wealth still resides almost entirely with the GOS. Oil wealth and arms purchases notwithstanding, the GOS often demurs from dispersing much-needed funding for CPA oversight bodies and claims that tending to its foreign debt prevents it from obtaining sufficient funds to do so.

Moreover, all parties recognize that the only alternative to renewed violence is elections, yet as the UNMIS report highlights, the difficult work of ensuring free and fair elections—a process that must be expected to take years—is now far behind schedule. The lack of priority given to elections may indicate that both sides understand the outcome as being settled, or it may indicate that neither side has any real intention of going forward with elections. Given the expense (which has already been considerable, even with foreign help) and the importance of other pressing issues, it now seems increasingly unlikely that a referendum for southern independence will take place in 2011, as mandated in the CPA.

In sum, SSR—including selecting and training security personnel, and the creation of a system of laws and courts governing their conduct—is now far behind schedule. This is partly because of the fact that although both sides experienced more difficulties than anticipated in the selecting and training of domestic security personnel, the real disagreement is over *what kind of laws will be enforced.* Will it be Sharia law, customary law, or some amalgam? And in which areas of Sudan will which sort of law be enforced?

Conclusions

The CPA is in danger of failing. With considerable effort, both sides have managed compromise on marginal issues, but core issues have yet to be even broached: (1) Will the NIF share power? (2) Will the North equitably share oil revenues and undertake real development of the South? (3) Will a moderate or an extreme version of Sharia law be enforced, and where? (4) Will the South be allowed to secede and become an independent state? The CPA says less about Sudan's form of government largely because, while alive, Garang appears to have believed that if the NIF did not compromise on power sharing (as well as Sharia and oil revenues), the South would simply secede with the full (and perhaps even military) support of the international community.

The CPA mandates the sharing of oil revenues, but two factors have already undermined this process. First, much of the data on oil production and distribution remains in control of the North, which shares data only selectively. Thus, it is at present impossible to know whether the

North is sharing 50 percent of total oil revenues or 50 percent of the revenues it has made public. Most Sudan watchers argue the latter. Second, the North has continued to station troops in key oil production areas south of the 1956 boundary (which has yet to be definitively established), in direct violation of its obligations under the CPA, while the South has complied with its redeployment requirements.

On the issue of Sharia law, the North agreed in the CPA to allow non-Muslims in Khartoum to be exempt from Sharia law enforcement. It is unclear, however, whether this refers to the city itself or the city and its surroundings; the question of who has the authority to decide this is also left unanswered. The North agreed to establish a joint commission with the South and with opposition parties to monitor compliance, but that commission has yet to be formed.

Benefit and Harm

The CPA is further weakened by the fact that each side is affected by foreign support to a different degree. Unlike the North, which has been able to use its oil wealth to deflect international criticism and to insulate itself to a large extent from the threat of economic sanctions, the South has become almost entirely beholden to foreign aid for its operations. The North has therefore been frequently observed breaking portions of agreements it previously signed, and systematically hindering the work of foreign organizations, governments, and nongovernmental organizations with which it had previously agreed to cooperate. The South, by contrast, has yielded on many core issues, with the theory that to be seen going against the CPA would result in a loss of international support. Thus, the North is benefiting more from the current lull in the violence than the South is.

In terms of a threat of harm from defection from the CPA, both North and South are keenly aware that the likelihood of foreign military intervention is low. That said, the threshold for military coercion may be lower in Sudan than many believe. *Africa Confidential*, for example, argues that the 1998 cruise missile strike against the Shifra pharmaceutical facility still reverberates in elite politics in Khartoum.[52] The credible threat of a similar attack might therefore be sufficient to encourage Bashir's government to accede to its treaty obligations for fear of losing power to rivals. On the other hand, sharing power and giving up radical Sharia law, total control of oil revenues, and southern independence are four core issues over which the North's current leaders have shown themselves consistently unwilling to compromise. If they are to lose power either way, it might be rational for them to continue to flaunt their treaty and human rights obligations in the hopes of dividing the international community as it contemplates a military option, however circumscribed, against Khartoum.

Overall, on the basis of my theory, I predict renewed civil war in Sudan. The CPA does not promise sufficient benefit to both sides. Even if it succeeded in this respect, the settlement still fails to promise sufficient harm to either side in the event of defection. A likely scenario as the referendum for southern independence nears, the North will make peace with surviving rebel groups in Darfur and then claim some violation of the CPA by the South. Having established a pretext for abrogating the treaty, it will unleash its increasing store of heavy weapons—tanks, combat helicopters, and fighter-bombers (the latter two being relatively difficult for the South to counter)—first to reestablish complete control of the oil infrastructure, and then to depopulate areas of southern resistance. The South, which continues to build up its independent army, will resist, inflicting heavy losses on the North but ultimately retreating across international boundaries to form a government in exile and await serious international intervention. The North will then attack civilians, trying to force as many to flee as possible before establishing garrisons in major southern towns. Finally, the North will set about building better communications between central and southern Sudan so as to facilitate its control.

The war in Sudan is not yet over, as the implementation of the Accords continues in starts and fits.

Chapter 9

Conclusion

IF ONE REVIEWS the long history of civil wars and then records how each came to an end, a pattern begins to emerge: wars ended by military victory tend to stay ended longer than wars ended by negotiated settlement and, in many cases, stay ended in what most would consider a constructive way. Identifying that pattern must stand as one of this book's core contributions.

But my aim was not only to establish a significant correspondence between the nature of a civil war's termination and long-term political, social, and economic outcomes. Rather, I sought also to introduce a general *explanation* for that pattern, which might inform better policy and, by extension, reduce the frequency or intensity of civil war recurrence.

Summary of Key Arguments and Theory

This analysis began with an empirical survey of civil war termination and asked how, over the course of time, most civil wars end. I divided the universe of termination possibilities into three (mutually exclusive) types: (1) military victory (in which one side admits defeat and ceases attacking the other); (2) stalemate or cease-fire (in which both sides agree to halt organized violence but offer no resolution to the underlying conflict issues); and (3) negotiated settlement (in which two or more warring parties contract to halt organized violence and redress outstanding political, social, and/or economic grievances). Historically, the distribution of civil war termination types has not been even but has strongly favored military victories.

This fact is interesting in itself for two reasons. First, in the absence of my survey, a review of the academic literature (and this is increasingly true as we move from the end of the Cold War to the present day) would lead one to the opposite conclusion: that negotiated settlements were the most common type of civil war termination. This is because while well over half of civil wars end with an outright military victory by rebels or incumbents, over 90 percent of the academic literature is focused on the minority of cases in which a civil war was ended by a negotiated settlement.

Second, my survey shows that civil wars ended by military victory had a strong tendency to stay ended, as compared to negotiated settlements, which appeared more likely to end in renewed violence. This is crucial because it suggests that one of the most important expected benefits of negotiated settlements—a diminution in death and destruction—might not in fact be realized because negotiated settlements so often break down and, when they do, frequently result in additional or even much more intense destruction. Because advocating a general policy of supporting outright military victory seemed untenable, this led naturally to the question of whether there was something in the nature of negotiated settlements that caused them to reignite more often than military victories—or, conversely, what in the nature of military victories made them so stable as compared to negotiated settlements.

At this point, it made sense to highlight the logic of each policy option, as well as its pros and cons, before comparing actors' expectations of a given option's utility and actual historical outcomes. On the plus side, negotiated settlements promise to help end violence definitively in a way that is itself nonviolent (though not necessarily noncoercive). As is often done by actors working to end violence, when compared to the alternative of allowing combatants to go on killing each other, negotiated settlements also promise the general benefit of lower cost in terms of lives lost and property (often in addition to precious cultural artifacts) destroyed. Finally, negotiated settlements can be organized and prosecuted by very few foreign nationals as compared to more militarized forms of intervention and thus do not carry as high a likelihood of sparking unanticipated nationalist resistance in the way a foreign military intervention (and occupation) might. In short, for those well-intended third parties often initiating or facilitating negotiated settlements, their advantage is that they promise a general and tangible short-term benefit to all sides (i.e., the cessation of violence), while risking mainly money rather than lives. Thus, negotiated settlements promise benefits to all parties, with some being relatively direct and targeted, and others relatively indirect and diffuse.

The negative side to negotiated settlements, however, is that the promised benefits are often overwhelmed by the desire of each side to have the expected benefits of peace for itself, but also to continue to inflict pain on the other side. Because the cause of the fight is so important in motivating sacrifices and justifying risks of violence, the promised benefit of a short-term halt to violence is often not sufficient to consolidate peace. Moreover, participants are aware that although they must sustain very real costs if they defect from the contract, these will be primarily economic or opportunity costs. This implies that punishment for defection will be indirect, and it is therefore much more likely to be discounted as compared to more direct and physical threats, such as death, destruction of materially or culturally valued property, torture, and imprisonment. This leaves negotiated settlements vulnerable to the problem of false intentions, in which one or both parties use the good offices of third parties and the process of negotiation simply as a tactical pause in which to rearm for a future confrontation. Finally, negotiated settlements leave each side believing its cause was just and, as such, deserving of special consideration in the distribution of postconflict values, such as offices and economic or cultural benefits. Since the actual physical capacity of either side to obtain its political, social, or economic objectives remains clouded by third-party intervention, this leaves negotiated settlements vulnerable to a particular problem: each side feels passionately that, because it could have won, it deserves a greater share of postconflict values than the other side is likely to grant. Therefore, once the initial delight in a respite from constant violence has worn off even slightly, one or both parties might take to the battlefield again in order to try to win through violence what it was not granted through settlement. In short, negotiated settlements are weak in the promise of direct and physical harm to defectors.

Military victories, as I observed in previous chapters, appear by and large to have the opposite effects as negotiated settlements do. They promise the losing side direct and physical costs should violence continue, and unlike negotiated settlements, they leave little doubt about who had the physical capacity to win and thus who should have the most say (or the only say) in the postconflict distribution of values. True, "defeated" actors can almost always continue to impose costs on winners, but because those costs are increasingly indirect and diminished, they come to be perceived by winners as marginal. This makes the sharing of values by winners appear generous rather than coerced. Losers may therefore feel lucky to have offices or to share in postconflict reconstruction or other aid. Yet winners may find it difficult to act generously toward losers, even when they calculate that positive or negative retribution may compromise other key goals, such as reconstruction and economic development. This is due partly to the problem that all sides share grief and anger over losing loved ones, personal property, or treasured cultural monuments. But it also matters whether the victor was an incumbent government threatened with a loss of authority (and legitimacy) or a rebel group seeking fundamental change. Given that the initial distribution of legitimacy and conflict resources tends to favor established governments, rebels tend to win *only* when they gather sufficient social support to overcome those government advantages. This, in turn, implies that they will be more necessarily beholden to a broader social segment than incumbent governments and, all other things being equal, that victorious rebels will be in a position to be more generous in victory than incumbent governments. Military victories are weakest, therefore, at the credible promise of benefits to losers. In short, military victors have an advantage in directly threatening losers with harm, but a disadvantage at promising benefits as a result of compliance.

This analysis of the logical strengths and weaknesses of both negotiated settlement and military victory led me to propose not the axiomatic support of military victory by incumbents or rebels, but a new form of negotiated settlement that made use of the strengths and minimized the weaknesses of either type of settlement. My theory is that ending civil wars and keeping them constructively ended demands settlements capable of credibly threatening harm and credibly promising benefits. Oddly, this theory mainly challenges contemporary conventional wisdom. As my research makes clear, post–World War II international relations scholars understood well the crucial role that the threat of violence played in post-war reconstruction and peace.

In the context of contemporary scholarship on civil wars, however, this theory of benefit and harm, as I call it, appears almost radical. This is the case particularly because the theory suggests two things: both that non-violent means may not be the best way to achieve nonviolent ends, and its corollary, that in order to achieve lasting peace, contracting parties to a negotiated settlement must be threatened with harm at the same time as they are promised direct and indirect benefits from compliance.

After an initial testing of my theory and the logic of competing arguments (in particular, the argument that negotiated settlements axiomatically result in lower costs to war-torn societies) against an expanded data set and finding it strongly supported, I operationalized the concept of "promise of harm" in security sector reform. At its root, SSR aims to give survivors of civil wars the tools they need to threaten potential rebels and/or organized criminals with direct and physical harm, should they threaten or undertake violence. I then examined three historical cases of negotiated settlement success and failure, along with a case of military victory by rebels. Each case fulfilled a specific set of criteria: first, it contained useful variation of dependent (i.e., quality and duration of peace) and independent (i.e., nature of settlement) variables; and second, each challenged my central thesis, which is that securing the peace demands a careful mix of benefit and harm in order to succeed.

The results of my case study analysis are summarized in table 9.1. As the table shows, the case study analysis, like the large-n statistical analysis, supports the argument that while the promise of both benefit and harm is necessary to achieve lasting peace, neither aspect of this promise by itself is sufficient. In case 1 (the Salvadoran civil war), eleven years of brutal violence were brought to a close with a negotiated settlement. If negotiated settlements were themselves the problem, we would expect another failure. Yet as I argued, it is not negotiated settlements *in general*

TABLE 9.1
Summary of Theoretical Expectations and Research Findings from Cases

Cases	Termination type	Theory of benefit/harm explain case?	SSR? Democratization?	Was outcome expected?
Case 1 El Salvador 1979–1993	Negotiated settlement	Yes	Yes Yes	Yes
Case 2 Uganda 1981–1986	Rebel victory	Yes	Yes Yes	Yes
Case 3 Sudan 1956–1972	Negotiated settlement	Yes	No No	Yes
Case 4 Sudan 1983–2005	Negotiated settlement	Instability predicted	Too soon to tell	Too soon to tell

that are the problem, but only those that do not threaten defectors credibly with direct harm. In the Salvadoran case, the Chapultepec Accords contained detailed SSR provisions. (These in fact dominate the document, even though the material grievances of both sides, but especially of the FMLN, were focused on economic issues.) I argue that this obsessive focus on SSR, including the professionalization of security personnel other than the army and the support of a nascent impartial judicial system, proved sufficient to ensure a lasting peace. However, in the Salvadoran case, the peace has not resulted in justice. Conflict and crime still rage in El Salvador, but the likelihood that either will escalate to civil war levels remains low—a considerable achievement, given El Salvador's long and tragic history of violence and oppression. My theory would have predicted enduring peace and an expanded political space, and although not ideal by most standards, this is what we see.

In case 2 (Uganda), a civil war ended when rebels overthrew a corrupt and oppressive incumbent government. This rebel victory left essentially a single actor in charge of the redistribution of political, social, and economic values. The rebels having won by tireless devotion to respect for noncombatants and equitable social organization, the new government set about attempting to reform the security sector while at the same time attracting foreign aid and diplomatic support. Again, my theory predicts enduring peace and an open political space, and this is by and large what we find in Uganda. Moreover, Uganda's economy has dramatically improved since the end of the civil war.

In case 3 (Sudan's first civil war), for example, a negotiated settlement ended nearly twenty years of civil war. Yet the Addis Ababa Agreement did not contain the necessary SSR, and it lacked oversight mechanisms. Both sides soon came to feel that they could achieve their political objectives more effectively on the battlefield, and the final years of peace were spent preparing for war rather than attempting to solidify the peace. My theory would have predicted failure, and the only puzzle not entirely explained by my theory is why it took as long as it did for conflict to reignite in Sudan in 1983.

In case 4 (Sudan's second civil war), twenty-two years of war were ended by another negotiated settlement. Unlike the Addis Ababa Agreement, the Naivasha Accords engaged core political disagreements and contained much more robust monitoring and verification instruments (e.g., SSR). Although SSR was taken quite seriously in these Accords, implementation has undergone difficulties. The Joint Forces are nonexistent, and while the South now has an autonomous army built with the assistance of international actors (i.e., the U.S.), the North, too, has been building up its own forces. The Accords thus left two de facto states within Sudan, with independent armies but enduring grievances. Political instability is likely to continue, and with the 2011 referendum looming in the near future, key considerations at this stage are whether the southern Sudanese force will be capable of deterring the North from further military action and whether the South recognizes that it might benefit in union with the North. Generally speaking, it is still unclear whether the mechanisms of mutual benefit and mutual harm are in place now, or are likely to be put in place for securing the peace in Sudan.

Before offering final conclusions on the theoretical and policy implications of my analysis, it is worthwhile applying my theory briefly to the ongoing war in Iraq (2003–present) to see how it fares at explaining that war and what insights it might hold for pragmatic policy there.

The Iraqi Civil War, 2003–Present

In an important sense, although it did not meet the six criteria for a civil war set out in chapter 1 until 2004, we may think of Iraq as being in civil war since the First Persian Gulf War (1990–1991). At that time, what had been a tense equilibrium between the three main peoples of Iraq—Sunni Arabs in the Center, Kurds in the North, and Shi'a Arabs in the South—began to unravel following the efforts of the United States to incite the Kurds and Shi'a to revolt and topple Saddam Hussein's Ba'ath party dictatorship. Following the cease-fire in 1991, Hussein's armed forces sought to do what states have traditionally done in reaction to rebellion: to put it down thoroughly, brutally, even genocidally. However, given that the United States and its Coalition allies had been responsible for goading the Shi'a and Kurds into rebellions in the first place, the same armed forces Hussein wanted to destroy, the United States initiated two no-fly zones as a way of minimizing the damage Hussein's air-mobile forces could do in the North and South. Consequently, the central government was prevented from reestablishing full control over either area, Iraq was divided de facto into three groups (each of which then had fresh and intense grievances against the others), and the central authority was somewhat hobbled by internationally patrolled no-fly zones and ever-present weapons inspection teams.

It is important to note at this point that tensions and fresh resentment notwithstanding, disputes between Sunnis, Kurds, and Shi'a in Iraq need not have escalated to violence.[1] The reorganization of identities in Iraq—that is, the disintegration of the state into three "Iraqs"—was instead the unintended consequence of a number of *choices* made by the United States following its decision to use armed force to overthrow Saddam Hussein's Ba'ath party dictatorship.[2] As is now widely recognized, the George W. Bush administration maintained a rather simple view of the world, choosing to see issues of national security in black-and-white terms and then acting accordingly.[3] Consistent also with long tradition in American history, the Bush administration held that the Iraqi people were good—innocent victims of a brutal dictator—and it was only the country's leadership that was bad. Thus, removing that leadership would necessarily result in a good outcome in and of itself. Once freed from their dictator, the Iraqi people would—with relatively little difficulty—elect a new leadership democratically and take charge of their own affairs; including security. Oil revenues could be used to reconstruct Iraq after the United States left, and democracy in Iraq would set an example for nearby Iran, where political moderates would be emboldened and Iran's radical conservatives would be further marginalized.

Unfortunately, the Bush administration's worldview was too simplistic. U.S. and British armed forces began their assault on March 20, 2003, and quickly overwhelmed Saddam Hussein's military. Some intelligence analysts believed Iraq possessed "weapons of mass destruction," and in particular chemical and biological weapons. The Bush administration, knowing that Hussein bore the United States and its allies no good will, and in possession of evidence that Iraq had worked to frustrate the efforts of international weapons inspectors since 1991, assumed that not only did Hussein's Iraq possess a usable chemical and biological arsenal, but that Iraq was close to obtaining a radiological or even nuclear weapons capability. In addition, the Bush administration appears to have assumed that because Hussein was ruthless with his own citizens (living a life of luxury under international economic sanctions, he oppressed, murdered, and tortured them, and denied them food, medical aid, and other necessities), it must follow that Iraq would be a dangerous neighbor and that Hussein himself could not be deterred.[4] The two ideas, along with the positive goal of creating a viable, stable, oil-rich, and advanced-industrial democracy next to Iran and Syria, led the Bush administration to favor a military campaign overwhelmingly, but it also led that same administration to neglect postwar planning.

Since it has now become clear that the Bush administration believed the problem with Iraq was Saddam Hussein and the Ba'ath party, it followed that there would be little need for postwar contingency planning once Hussein was removed from power.[5] This is despite the fact that the U.S. State Department had been investigating a postwar situation in Iraq since October 2001, issuing warnings that occupying and administering Iraq would demand a serious and sustained effort.[6] In April 2003, after the war had begun, the U.S. Office of Reconstruction and Humanitarian Assistance (OHRA) produced a draft plan for the postwar administration of Iraq, but that draft was never completed. Tellingly, section 1.6 of the *Unified Mission Plan for Post Hostilities Iraq* notes:

> The potential for instability, likely to exist for some time after the war is over. The most probable threat will come from residual pockets of fanatics, secessionist groups, terrorists and those would seek to exploit ethnic, religious, and tribal fault lines for personal gain. The threat from these groups would manifest itself in high impact tactics such as car or suicide bombings, sniping, and "hit and run" raids. A high level of such attacks will have an adverse impact on the creation of stability, a prerequisite for self-sustaining peace.[7]

Almost from the instant Saddam's military collapsed, Iraqi civilians in Baghdad began to loot Iraqi businesses, military and weapons facilities, homes, and national treasures. Ba'ath party bitter-enders initially led pin-prick assaults on Coalition forces, but as it became clear to Iraqis that the United States had no real plan and did not have sufficient forces in country to provide even basic physical security, euphoria over freedom from tyranny turned to bitterness about "occupation." Now increasingly forced by circumstances to identify as Sunni, Shi'a, or Kurd, Iraqis began to target U.S. forces and one another more frequently and more effectively. Sunnis were especially implicated in attacks on Iraqi Shi'a civilians, and the growing internecine violence escalated to full civil war by February 2006. Following the near-demolition of one of Shi'a Islam's holiest shrines in Samarra, Shi'a and Sunni fighting reached new intensities (the Kurds, trusted allies of Coalition forces in Iraq, kept out of most of the Shi'a-Sunni fighting and remain mostly isolated from civil war violence to this day), resulting in the immediate death of 1,300 people, most of whom were Sunnis killed in retaliation.[8]

The first postwar administration of Iraq began in April 2003 with an experienced U.S. soldier at the helm: retired Army Lt. General Jay Garner.[9] Yet within six weeks the Bush administration replaced him with L. Paul Bremer III—a man whose chief qualification (besides being a Republican and the right-hand man of former U.S. secretary of state Henry Kissinger) was that he knew next to nothing about the Middle East, its history, or its politics.[10] Bremer took over from Garner on May 11, 2003, ten days after President Bush's famous "mission accomplished" speech aboard the USS *Abraham Lincoln*. Bremer's first two actions as head of the Coalition Provisional Authority (CPA) remain controversial to this day. On May 16, 2003, he issued CPA order number 1, entitled "De-Ba'athification of Iraqi Society," and a week later (May 23) followed this with CPA order number 2, "Dissolution of Entities." In a situation in which a relative handful of U.S. and Coalition *soldiers* were nominally responsible for the domestic and interstate security of twenty-five million Iraqis, in two strokes of the pen Bremer eliminated all Iraqi human political capital from the state's administration, and then followed this by dissolving Iraq's only functioning security institution: its military.[11] As in many places in the developing world (and especially in authoritarian states), there was little distinction in Iraq between military and law enforcement personnel, and so dissolving one effectively dissolves the other. In addition, however, Bremer had instantaneously created 300,000 unemployed men, all armed, and with no certainty of a future paycheck with which to support their families.[12]

Taken together with a lack of positive political planning following the defeat of Hussein's armed forces, this mass firing of skilled and security personnel proved to be the exact opposite of SSR. Now few Iraqis had any certainty about either their physical security or their economic security, and these same people dwarfed, by numbers, the few soldiers sent to "protect" them.

The point is not that things would have gone smoothly had Bremer avoided CPA orders 1 and 2, but rather that the *quality* and *effectiveness* of the violence that followed Hussein's defeat and capture—an insurgency and then civil war—were not inevitable. Rather, these were the unintended consequences of a postwar occupation policy that was not informed by historical experience, sound theory, or effective political leadership.[13] The U.S. effort also demonstrated an appalling lack of appreciation for both the utility and limitations of armed force. The Bush administration appears to have assumed that military and political victories amounted to the same thing, or, to put it differently, that winning a war against a dictator axiomatically meant winning the peace.

In sum, the fractures and cleavages that existed within Iraq were real, but they remained dormant or contained throughout most of Saddam Hussein's long rule. The aftermath of the First Persian Gulf War left Hussein's government marginally weakened in terms of capability and concurrently led to the creation of real grievances among Iraq's Kurds and Shi'a. Such sentiments were felt against the United States, who effectively incited these Iraqis to revolt *as* Kurds and Shi'a and then left them to Hussein's reprisals once Kuwait had been liberated, while also giving them reason to resent each other. This resentment was directed in particular toward Iraqi Sunnis, who, though a minority of Iraq's population, dominated its military and civilian elite and effectively oppressed the majority Shi'a and Kurd populations. Even this state of affairs need not necessarily have resulted in a civil war. But repeated U.S. political blunders and insufficient Coalition forces to provide for basic security led to an escalation in violence within Iraq. As one might imagine, a lack of security would lead to a corollary deficit in reconstruction. Likewise, this absence of reconstruction would lead to a dearth of security.[14] The ensuing violence forced people wont to identify as "Iraqi" or "Arab" (or Iraqi Kurd) to shift their identity and think of themselves as "Shi'a," "Kurd," or "Sunni" in Iraq.[15] Iraq today *is* in civil war, but as of the writing of this book that war has been suspended at least temporarily.[16]

There is little mystery about why this is so. Two factors explain the current lull in violence in Iraq. First, the fighting from 2004 to 2007 resulted in significant population transfers, effectively segregating ethnoreligious groups. Iraq is now demographically three states rather than one. Within each mini-state, once ad hoc militias are taking on the trappings and capabilities of more formal security forces, and even differentiating to some extent into police and community security forces. This is the main cause of the cessation of violence widely reported in November 2007.[17] Second, the United States has altered its counterinsurgency strategy to match the historical "state of the art." This means that the U.S. military is using specially trained, well-led, and overwhelming forces in a "hearts and minds" strategy to stabilize limited territories (mainly core urban areas possessing important national infrastructure).[18] Third, while some former insurgents have joined the political arena, others have not, presumably waiting to see what the United States will do next before choosing an ideal strategy to pursue their political objectives (and these vary a great deal across insurgent groups).[19] Whether this means they are girding themselves for an offensive assault in the near future is less important than the underlying fact that we still do not know whether

Iraq's peace will be self-sustaining and whether Iraq itself will survive as a multinational state.[20]

Securing the peace in Iraq demanded a transitional security sector aimed at law enforcement capability (not Iraqi combat units), followed closely by a well-led and fully implemented reconstruction effort.[21] Failure on the first count aggravated failure on the second count, and each failure tended to accelerate the other. The 2008 "Surge," along with the U.S.-supported "Sunni Awakening," combined to finally bring a measure of security to Iraq's largest population centers; thus, among the questions that remain are: (1) will the United States be able to manage a stable withdrawal of coalition combat forces; and (2) will Iraqis be able to maintain a unified state following that withdrawal?[22] The answer to this last question depends on the capability of Iraq's security forces to keep down the violence and to do so in a way that serves the broader Iraqi population, not sectarian interests.[23]

Conclusion

To again paraphrase one of the most famous contemporaries of both types of war, life during civil or religious war is perhaps best characterized as "nasty, brutish, and short."[24] In the last few decades, many civil wars ended in a military victory and remained ended. Yet negotiated settlements to civil wars have become more popular, even as they appear to be less effective at keeping wars ended.

In this book I have argued and shown that what is good about military victory is that winners can promise great harm to losers who continue to threaten violence, but what is bad about military victory is that winners often have difficulty giving losers a positive stake in a future of peaceful cooperation (or at least coexistence). By contrast, negotiated settlements promise many benefits, but without a threat of direct injury as a consequence of defection, they tend to break down and fail.

Having identified the strong and weak points of each termination type, I proposed a hybrid settlement design capable of leveraging the strengths of each termination type while avoiding its weaknesses. But hovering over this ideal civil war termination policy is a dark shadow.

Since World War II, another important trend explains both the popularity of negotiated settlements as a termination strategy for well-meaning third parties and the difficulty of achieving a "benefit–harm" settlement. Put simply, the same advanced-industrial states and coalitions of states who pioneered a method to win wars against one another have found that over time, their war-winning capabilities have become less potent against insurgents in the vehicle-impassible terrain and harsher climates of much of the developing world. In these types of asymmetric conflict, the record of wins and losses since World War II places the advanced-industrial states in the loss column. France in Indochina and Algeria, the United States in Vietnam, the Soviet Union in Afghanistan, and Britain in India all exemplify this trend. The trend itself and the logic behind it—a perfect storm of national self-determination as a motivation and revolutionary guerrilla warfare as a military strategy—have been well canvassed elsewhere.[25] But in "Hard Choices and Tragic Dilemmas," Richard Falk appears to have been right: "Non-intervention is intolerable, but intervention remains impossible."[26] So long as the Cold War raged, and bloc leaders (the United States and Soviet Union) could imagine that the outcome of conflicts in distant (from them) reaches of the world would materially affect their rivalry, each side maintained an understandable interest in *military* intervention in civil wars. The result was a string of unexpected defeats and unanticipated long-term consequences. For our purposes, the most important result was a debate within each bloc leader's military over the utility of intervention. In the United States, the "no more military interventions" faction came to be represented by Caspar Weinberger and, following overwhelming U.S. success in the First Persian Gulf War, Colin Powell.[27] Although the Bush administration made a concerted effort to banish this apparent limitation on the utility of armed force in two major regional efforts—Afghanistan (2001–present) and Iraq (2003–present)—in neither case did the armed forces supremely capable of achieving a military outcome prove, ipso facto, capable of achieving a desired political outcome. Both Afghanistan and Iraq have, as a result, become military and political quagmires, and U.S. armed forces continue to struggle brilliantly and die incrementally with little guarantee of achieving a positive political gain.[28]

In short, with the continued challenges in Afghanistan and Iraq and a power shift within the U.S. Department of Defense away from former secretary of defense Donald Rumsfeld's "five high-tech guys are enough to win any war" school of thought, the likelihood of U.S. or UN diplomats being able to threaten harm credibly as a component of a negotiated settlement to a destructive civil war has diminished greatly. U.S. and allied publics are also unlikely to support future military interventions *even in cases of gross humanitarian need*, such as the ongoing genocide in Sudan's Darfur region and the continued violence, brutality, and suffering in the Democratic Republic of Congo.

The bad news does not end here. If it is true that only benefit–harm negotiated settlements, with their emphasis on SSR, have a chance of securing the peace and benefiting everyone, and that third parties intent on facilitating that type of settlement have diminishing credibility in the provision of the harm side of the settlement, it follows that the promise of direct military support of incumbents or rebels in a civil war (with an aim toward facilitating military victory) will also be less credible.

In sum, securing the peace demands (perhaps paradoxically) making sticks as credible as carrots, and then balancing them on a case-by-case basis in negotiated settlements or, failing that, in support of outright military victories. The alternative is continuing to make promises that are progressively less credible to both domestic and target audiences, and accepting civil wars that never end. That in itself is something the developed world—where civil wars are rare—can no longer afford to ignore as a matter of *interest*, if not moral principle.

We in the advanced-industrial world have always had the power to change these outcomes; however, the once well-understood knowledge of how best to use that power has been largely forgotten or deliberately overlooked. It is my hope that the analysis, theory, and policy recommendations in this book will change that, making it as possible as it is clearly desirable to secure the peace once civil wars end.

Appendix 1

Civil War Data, 1940–2003 Key Variables, Summary Statistics, and Cases

Summary Statistics

Variable[a]	Observation	Mean	Standard Deviation	Min	Max
Warterm	117	1.008547	1.029695	0	3
Recur	117	0.1623932	0.3703974	0	1
Identity	117	0.3675214	0.4842038	0	1
Terrwar	117	0.4615385	0.5006627	0	1
Total deaths	116	127680.1	305365.2	1,000	2,097,705
Battle deaths	106	72579.58	196262.8	25	1,321,442
SSRI	117	0.0854701	0.2807825	0	1
TPG	94	0.1702128	0.3778347	0	1

Cases

State	War	War term		Recur	Identity	Terr war	Total deaths	Deaths/month	Battle deaths	SSRI	TPG
		Start	End								
USSR I	Ukraine	1942	1950	0	1	1	17,569	195	—	0	0
Greece	Civil war	1944	1949	0	0	0	157,068	2,662	160,135	0	0
USSR II	Lithuania	1944	1952	0	1	1	8,620	85	—	0	0

(continued)

Cases (*continued*)

State	War	Start	End	War term	Recur	Identity	Terr war	Total deaths	Deaths/month	Battle deaths	SSRI	TPG
Israel/Palest	War of Independence	1945	1949	0	0	1	1	15,500	397	—	0	0
China I	Revolution: final phase	1945	1949	1	0	0	0	1,100,000	23,404	1,000,000	0	0
Indonesia I	War of Independence	1945	1949	1	0	1	1	5,937	116	1,400	0	0
Iran I	Kurds/Mahabad	1946	1946	0	0	1	1	14,500	1,208	25	0	0
Philippines I	Huks	1946	1954	0	0	0	0	9,000	96	9,000	0	0
Bolivia I	Popular revolt	1946	1946	1	0	0	0	1,000	1,000	1,000	0	0
Vietnam I	French-Indochina War	1946	1954	1	0	1	1	600,000	6,522	300,000	0	0
India Ia	Partition	1946	1949	3	1	1	1	759,500	24,500	316,479	0	0
Madagascar	MDRM/Independence	1947	1948	0	0	1	1	5,976	272	6,952	0	—
Paraguay	Coup attempt	1947	1947	0	0	0	0	2,500	417	1,000	0	0
Burma I	Communist revolt	1948	1989	0	0	0	0	—	—	—	0	0
India II	Hyderabad	1948	1948	0	0	1	1	2,180	2,180	2,000	0	0
Malaysia	Malayan Emergency	1948	1960	0	0	0	0	12,025	82	13,000	0	—

South Korea	Yosu Sunch'on revolt	1948	1948	0	0	0	16,392	16,392	16,392	0	—
Yemen, North I	Coup	1948	1948	0	0	0	4,000	2,000	4,000	0	0
Costa Rica	Civil war	1948	1948	1	0	0	2,000	667	2,000	0	0
Colombia I	La Violencia	1948	1958	2	0	0	300,000	2,400	300,000	0	0
China IIa	Tibet	1950	1951	0	1	1	5,000	417	1,000	0	0
Indonesia II	Ambon/Moluccans	1950	1950	0	1	1	5,000	833	5,000	0	0
Korea	Korean War	1950	1953	3	0	1	1,082,322	28,482	909,833	0	—
Kenya I	Mau Mau	1952	1956	0	0	0	11,978	240	12,955	0	—
Bolivia II	Bolivian Revolution	1952	1952	1	0	0	1,050	1,050	600	0	0
Egypt	Free Officers' Coup	1952	1952	1	0	0	1,000	1,000	—	0	0
Morocco I	War of Independence	1952	1956	1	1	1	3,000	75	3,000	0	—
Tunisia	War of Independence	1952	1956	1	1	1	2,500	51	3,000	0	—
Indonesia III	Aceh revolt	1953	1959	0	0	1	15,500	225	1,000	0	0
China IIb	Tibet	1954	1959	0	0	1	85,500	1,527	40,000	0	0
Algeria I	War of Independence	1954	1962	1	0	1	176,013	1,893	252,026	0	0
Argentina	Coup	1955	1955	1	0	0	1,950	1,950	900	0	0
Cameroon	War of Independence	1955	1960	1	1	1	32,000	582	4,270	0	—
Sudan Ia	Anya-Nya	1955	1972	2	1	1	250,000	1250	20,000	1	1

(continued)

Cases *(continued)*

State	War	Start	End	War term	Recur	Identity	Terr war	Total deaths	Deaths/month	Battle deaths	SSRI	TPG
Cuba	Cuban Revolution	1956	1959	1	0	0	0	5,000	185	5,000	0	0
India III	Naga revolt	1956	1997	3	0	1	1	3,500	7	3,500	0	0
Vietnam II	Vietnam War	1957	1975	1	0	0	0	2,097,705	9,942	1,321,442	0	0
Indonesia IV	PRRI revolt	1958	1961	0	0	0	0	31,722	774	33,444	0	0
Iraq I	Army revolt	1958	1958	1	0	0	0	2,000	2,000	25	0	0
Lebanon Ia	First Civil War	1958	1958	2	1	1	0	1,400	200	1,400	0	1
Iraq II	Mosul revolt	1959	1959	0	0	0	0	2,000	2,000	2,000	0	0
Laos	Pathet Lao	1959	1973	2	0	0	0	23,250	142	23,000	0	0
Burma IV	Kachins	1960	1994	0	0	1	1	9,000	22	9,000	0	0
Zaire/Congo I	Katanga/Stanleyville	1960	1965	0	0	1	1	65,499	992	30,948	0	0
Guatemala II	Civil war	1960	1996	2	0	0	0	147,278	339	46,300	1	1
Angola I	War of Independence	1961	1974	0	0	1	1	67,000	409	79,000	0	0
Ethiopia I	Eritrea	1961	1993	1	0	1	1	175,000	459	70,000	0	—
Iraq IIIa	Kurds	1961	1970	2	1	1	1	50,000	485	3,000	0	0
Yemen, North II	N. Yemeni civil war	1962	1970	1	0	0	0	75,500	821	101,000	0	0

Algeria II	Opposition to Bella	1963	1963	0	0	0	0	1,500	250	1,500	0	0
Rwanda Ia	First Tutsi invasion	1963	1964	0	1	1	0	20,000	10,000	2,500	0	0
GuineaBissau I	War of Independence	1963	1974	1	0	1	1	11,078	79	7,155	0	—
Cyprus Ia	Greek/Turk clashes	1963	1964	3	1	1	1	2,000	222	2,000	0	0
Mozambique I	War of Independence	1964	1975	1	0	1	1	33,375	257	5,000	0	0
Burundi Ia	Hutu coup attempt	1965	1965	0	1	1	0	5,000	5,000	50	0	0
Indonesia V	PKI coup attempt	1965	1966	0	0	0	0	400,000	57,143	—	0	0
Chad	FROLINAT	1965	1997	2	0	1	0	21,119	55	4,981	0	0
Domin Republic	Civil war	1965	1966	2	0	0	0	3,276	218	2,526	0	1
India Ib	Kashmir	1965	1965	3	1	1	1	6,000	3,000	—	0	0
Uganda I	Buganda	1966	1966	0	0	1	1	2,000	2,000	2,000	0	0
China III	Cultural Revolution	1966	1969	1	0	0	0	550,000	15,278	50,000	0	0
Namibia	War of Independence	1966	1990	2	0	1	1	22,500	79	1,000	1	—
Nigeria I	Biafra	1967	1970	0	0	1	1	87,500	2,734	100,000	0	0
Jordan	Palestinians	1970	1971	0	0	1	1	2,100	124	2,100	0	0
Cambodia Ia	Khmer Rouge	1970	1975	1	1	0	0	217,500	3,508	56,000	0	0

(continued)

Cases (*continued*)

State	War	Start	End	War term	Recur	Identity	Terr war	Total deaths	Deaths/ month	Battle deaths	SSRI	TPG
Sri Lanka Ia	JVP I	1971	1971	0	1	0	0	1,815	605	2,000	0	0
Pakistan I	Bangladesh	1971	1971	1	0	1	1	500,000	50,000	500,000	0	0
Burundi Ib	Hutu Rebellion	1972	1972	0	1	1	0	50,000	12,500	50,000	0	0
Bangladesh	Chittagong Hill	1972	1997	2	0	1	1	20,000	64	20,000	1	0
Philippines IIIa	Moro Rebellion	1972	1996	2	1	1	1	47,500	164	15,000	0	0
Zimbabwe	Front for Liberation of Zimbabwe	1972	1979	2	0	1	0	12,000	141	12,000	1	1
Pakistan II	Baluchi Rebellion	1973	1977	0	0	1	1	8,700	161	8,600	0	0
Chile	Army revolt	1973	1973	1	0	0	0	5,048	5,048	100	0	—
Iraq IIIb	Kurds	1974	1975	0	1	1	1	16,250	1,250	4,500	0	0
Cyprus Ib	Coup/Turk invasion	1974	1974	3	0	1	1	5,800	2,900	1,500	0	0
Lebanon Ib	Second civil war	1975	1990	0	0	1	0	155,500	832	43,800	0	0
Ethiopia II	Tigray	1975	1991	1	0	1	0	15,000	77	15,000	0	—
Angola IIa	Civil war	1975	1994	2	1	0	0	244,775	1,028	143,750	0	1
Indonesia VI	East Timor	1975	1999	2	0	1	1	33,525	116	30,000	0	0

Location	Name	Year			Year							
Morocco II	Western Sahara	1975	3	0	1991	1	1	14,500	76	12,000	0	—
Mozambique II	RENAMO	1976	2	0	1992	0	0	1,200,550	6,094	145,400	1	1
Ethiopia III	Ogaden	1977	0	0	1978	1	1	27,500	3,056	12,400	0	—
Afghanistan I	Mujahideen, Taliban	1978	1	0	2001	1	0	1,330,150	4,667	510,300	0	0
Iran IIa	Iranian Revolution	1978	1	1	1979	1	0	7,500	536	7,500	0	0
Cambodia Ib	Vietnamese intervention	1978	2	0	1991	0	0	200,000	1,290	40,300	0	1
Nicaragua	Revolution/Contras	1978	2	0	1990	0	0	59,000	396	78,000	0	1
Syria	Sunni v. Alawites	1979	0	0	1982	1	0	15,450	468	—	0	—
El Salvador	FMLN/FDR	1979	2	0	1992	0	0	62,000	392	75,000	1	1
Iraq IIc	Kurds	1980	0	0	1991	1	1	23,800	183	—	0	0
Nigeria II	Maitasine	1980	0	0	1984	1	1	6,000	150	6,000	0	0
Peru	Shining Path	1980	0	0	1999	0	0	30,435	132	30,000	0	0
Uganda II	War in the Bush	1980	1	0	1986	0	0	102,400	1,652	102,000	0	0
Iran IIb	NCR/Mojahedin	1981	0	0	1982	1	0	14,000	737	14,000	0	0
India IV	Sikh insurrection	1982	0	0	1993	1	1	24,438	194	30,000	0	0
South Africa	Racial violence	1983	2	0	1994	1	0	12,240	95	—	1	0

(continued)

Cases (continued)

State	War	Start	End	War term	Recur	Identity	Terr war	Total deaths	Deaths/month	Battle deaths	SSRI	TPG
Yemen South	Civil war	1986	1986	1	0	0	0	11,750	11,750	12,000	0	—
Sri Lanka Ib	JVP II	1987	1989	0	0	0	0	30,000	1,000	30,000	0	0
Burundi Ic	Hutu/Tutsi	1988	1988	0	1	1	0	22,000	22,000	5,000	0	0
Azerbaijan/USSR	Nagorno-Karabakh	1988	1994	3	0	1	1	20,000	263	3,250	0	0
Liberia	NPFL	1989	1997	1	0	0	0	163,000	1,772	23,000	0	0
Rwanda Ib	Tutsi invasion/genocide	1990	1994	1	0	1	0	502,000	10,913	5,500	0	0
Georgia I	South Ossetia	1990	1992	3	0	1	1	1,975	99	1,000	0	1
Burundi Id	Hutu/Tutsi	1991	1991	0	1	1	0	3,000	3,000	1,500	0	0
Iraq IV	Shi'ite insurrection	1991	1993	0	0	1	0	165,000	5,000	31,622	0	0
Sierra Leone	RUF	1991	2002	0	0	0	0	16,499	115	20,000	0	—
Yugoslavia I	Croatian secession	1991	1995	2	0	1	1	10,000	182	10,000	1	1
Moldova	Trans-Dniester Slavs	1991	1997	3	0	1	1	1,500	22	—	0	—
Tajikistan	Civil war	1992	1997	2	0	1	0	65,700	1,060	20,000	0	0

Yugoslavia II	Bosnian civil war	1992	1995	2	0	1	1	250,000	5,319	55,000	1	1
Georgia II	Abkhazia	1992	1993	3	0	1	1	2,500	179	3,000	0	1
Yemen	Southern revolt	1994	1994	0	0	1	1	6,250	2,083	7,000	0	—
Russia Ia	First Chechen War	1994	1996	3	1	1	1	68,250	3,250	30,000	0	0
Zaire/Congo II	Post-Mobutu	1996	2002	2	0	0	0	300,000	3,125	149,000	0	—
Brazzaville Ib	Factional warfare	1997	1997	1	0	1	0	8,500	1,700	4,000	0	—
GuineaBissau II	Coup	1998	1999	1	0	0	0	1,850	154	1,850	0	—
Yugoslavia III	Kosovo	1998	1999	1	0	1	1	10,000	625	3,000	0	1
Angola IIb	UNITA warfare	1998	2002	3	0	0	0	57,863	1,564	15,725	0	1

Wars ongoing as of 2003[b]

Burma II	Karens	1948
Burma III	Shan	1959
Colombia II	FARC	1964
Philippines II	NPA insurgency	1969
Sri Lanka II	Tamil insurgency	1983
Sudan Ib	SPLM	1983

(continued)

Wars ongoing as of 2003[b] (continued)

State	War	Start	End	War term	Recur	Identity	Terr war	Total deaths	Deaths/ month	Battle deaths	SSRI	TPG
Turkey	Kurds	1984										
India Ic	Kashmir	1988										
Somalia	Clan warfare	1988										
Algeria III	Fundamentalists	1992										
Burundi Ie	Hutu/Tutsi	1993										
Russia Ib	Second Chechen War	1999										
Philippines IIIb	Moro Rebellion	2000										

[a] Key variables

Warterm: 0—military victory/government; 1—military victory/rebels; 2—negotiated settlement; 3—stalemate/cease-fire

Recur: 0—war did not recur; 1—war did recur

Identity: 0—war was not identity-based; 1—war was identity-based

Terr War: 0—war was not fought over territory; 1—war was fought over territory

Total Deaths: total war-related deaths, including battle deaths

Deaths/Month: total war-related deaths, divided by months of conflict

Battle Deaths: total number of combatants killed

SSRI: 0—security sector reform was not implemented; 1—security sector reform was implemented

TPG: 0—third parties did not make security guarantees; 1—third parties made security guarantees

[b] Even though civil wars in Sudan and the Philippines ended after 2003, they were dropped from statistical analysis of war recurrence on the ground that not enough time had passed to determine whether those conflict could definitively be considered resolved.

Appendix 2

Data for Figures 4.1 and 4.2

DATA FOR FIGURE 4.1
Polity Score before and after Civil War, by Termination Type

	Victory	Negotiated settlement	Stalemate/ cease-fire	Government victory	Rebel victory
5 years before	−17	0.77	0	−0.29	0
Start year	−0.54	−1.56*	0.375	−0.06**	−1.8*
5 years after	-0.79***	6.12***	0.88	−1.13***	−0.13
10 years after	−0.98***	3.93**	2.00	−2.17***	1.19
15 years after	−1.16***	3.11**	2.60	−1.35*	−0.73
20 years after	−0.91	−5.75*	−0.25	−2.86**	2.67***

*** p < .01, ** p < .05, * p < .10
One-tailed t-tests

DATA FOR FIGURE 4.2
Per Capita GDP before and after Civil War, by Termination Type

	Victory	Negotiated settlement	Stalemate/ cease-fire	Government victory	Rebel victory	Average
5 years before	−0.12	−0.12	0.05**	−0.1	−0.14	0.13
Start year	−0.01**	−0.05	−0.11**	0.02***	−0.07	−0.03
5 years after	0.29	0.63	−0.04*	0.42	0.03*	0.57
10 years after	0.7	0.57	0.26	0.75	0.50	1.08
20 years after	1.92	1.72	1.12	1.82	2.16	1.85

*** p < .01, ** p < .05, * p < .10
One-tailed t-tests

Notes

Chapter 1. Introduction

1. This is Edward Luttwak's argument in his article "Give War a Chance." See Edward N. Luttwak, "Give War a Chance," *Foreign Affairs*, Vol. 78, No. 4 (July/August 1999): pp. 36–44.

2. Laurie Nathan, "Obstacles to Security Sector Reform in New Democracies," Berghof Research Center for Constructive Conflict Management, 2004; and Gavin Cawthra and Robin Luckham, eds, *Governing Insecurity: Democratic Control of Military and Security Establishments in Transitional Societies* (London: Zed Books, 2003). See also Charles T. Call and William T. Stanley, "Protecting the People: Public Security Choices After Civil Wars," *Global Governance*, Vol. 7, No. 2 (April–June 2001): pp. 151–172.

3. Matthew Hoddie and Caroline Hartzell conclude that out of sixteen peace agreements between 1980 and 1996, the ones that completely implemented a provision for military power sharing among former combatants held the greatest prospects for maintaining peace. See Matthew Hoddie and Caroline Hartzell, "Civil War Settlements and the Implementation of Military Power-Sharing Agreements," *Journal of Peace Research*, Vol. 40, No. 3 (May 2003): pp. 303–320. In a later work, they further show that implementation of institutional reform in political, economic, and territorial power sharing are crucial components of a lasting peace. They also have similar tables with the number of civil wars per decade. See Caroline A. Hartzell and Matthew Hoddie, *Crafting Peace: Power Sharing and the Negotiated Settlement of Civil Wars* (University Park: Pennsylvania State University Press, 2007).

4. A more formal definition of civil war is presented later in this chapter. For now, it is enough to understand that civil wars are marked by large-scale violence that takes place within the borders of a state, among at least two groups of organized combatants, each of whom has the capacity to inflict casualties on the other.

5. The start of the war is the first year and month in which the combatants engaged in their first public act of violence, as reported in news accounts in Lexis Nexis or such publications as *Keesing's Contemporary Archives*. The end date of the war was coded with the defeat of one side that resulted in surrender, or the cessation of large-scale violence for at least five years (resulting in fewer than 100 war-related deaths for five years), or the formal signing of a cease-fire agreement or negotiated settlement.

6. The seventeen ongoing wars are excluded here.

7. Roy Licklider, "The Consequences of Negotiated Settlements in Civil Wars, 1945-1993," *American Political Science Review,* Vol. 89, No. 3 (September 1995): p. 684.

8. One might assume in such cases that the rebels are most likely to flee when they surrender because traditionally (that is, especially prior to 1977) rebels have never enjoyed the full protections of International Humanitarian Law. Victorious

incumbent governments have tended to deal harshly with surviving rebels, who most often face exile and imprisonment at best, and torture and murder at worst.

9. The rise of private military corporations in recent interventions serves as strong support for this argument. States such as the United States appear to calculate that although expensive in terms of cash, private security contractors are cheap compared to the political liability of armed forces killed or maimed in vague contingencies.

10. See generally James D. Fearon, "Rationalist Explanations for War," *International Organization*, Vol. 49, No. 3 (Summer 1995): pp. 379–414. For more on the topic, see Barbara F. Walter, including *Committing to Peace: The Successful Settlement of Civil Wars* (Princeton: Princeton University Press, 2002); "The Critical Barrier to Civil War Settlement," *International Organization*, Vol. 51, No. 3 (Summer 1997): pp. 335–364; and "Civil War Resolution: What We Know and Don't Know," *Annual Review of Political Science*, Vol. 12 (June 2009). See also Suzanne Werner and Amy Yuen, "Making and Keeping Peace," *International Organization*, Vol. 59, No. 2 (Spring 2005): pp. 261–292; Virginia Page Fortna, *Peace Time: Cease-Fire Agreements and the Durability of Peace* (Princeton: Princeton University Press, 2004); Fortna, "Does Peacekeeping Keep Peace? International Intervention and the Duration of Peace After Civil War," *International Studies Quarterly*, Vol. 48, No. 2 (June 2004): pp. 269–292; and Michael W. Doyle and Nicholas Sambanis, "International Peacebuilding: A Theoretical and Quantitative Analysis," *American Political Science Review*, Vol. 94, No. 4 (December 2000): pp. 779–801.

11. Doyle and Sambanis (2000) found a related but contradictory finding: settlements enhanced peace building between the combatants. While the quality of peace is generally related to its absence and duration, this finding would more directly support a discussion specifically on quality of peace. As the scope of the present work does not leave room for such a discussion, this finding will not be treated in detail.

12. See, for example, Hartzell and Hoddie, *Crafting Peace*.

13. Meredith Reid Sarkees, "The Correlates of War Data on War: An Update to 1997," *Conflict Management and Peace Science*, Vol. 18, No. 1 (Fall 2000): pp. 123–144.

14. Peter Wallensteen and Margareta Sollenberg, "Armed Conflicts, Conflict Termination, and Peace Agreements, 1989–1996," *Journal of Peace Research*, Vol. 34, No. 3 (August 1997): p. 342.

15. The argument about the willingness to resume violence could apply to negotiated settlements as well as military victories.

16. UNDP, "Security Sector Reform and Transitional Justice: A Crisis Post-Conflict Programmatic Approach," March 2003. Available at http://www.undp .org/bcpr/we_do/security_reform.shtml (accessed June 21, 2007).

17. Nicole Ball, J. Kayode Fayemi, Funmi Olonisakin, and Rocklyn Williams with Martin Rupiya, *Security Sector Governance in Africa*, CDD Occasional Paper, forthcoming. As found in UNDP Bureau for Crisis Prevention and Recovery (BCPR), "Justice and Security Sector Reform: BCPR's Programmatic Approach," November 2002, appendix B, p. 8.

18. Owen Greene, "Security Sector Reform, Conflict Prevention and Regional Perspectives," *Journal of Security Sector Management*, Vol. 1, No. 1 (March 2003): p. 2.

19. BCPR, "Justice and Security Sector Reform," appendix B, p. 8.

20. Michael Brzoska, "Introduction: Criteria for Evaluating Post-Conflict Reconstruction and Security Sector Reform in Peace Support Operations," *International Peacekeeping*, Vol. 13, No. 1 (March 2006): p. 3.

21. I updated Walter's data to 2005 as hers included wars that were initiated between 1940 and 1992. For an accounting of Walter's methods, see Walter, *Committing to Peace*.

22. On the advantages of mixed methods for assessing causal inference and conditionality, See Gary King, Robert O. Keohane, and Sidney Verba, *Designing Social Inquiry: Scientific Inference in Qualitative Research* (Princeton: Princeton University Press, 1994); Stephen Van Evera, *Guide to Methods for Students of Political Science* (Ithaca: Cornell University Press, 1997); and Alexander L. George and Andrew Bennett, *Case Studies and Theory Development in the Social Sciences* (Cambridge: MIT Press, 2005).

23. This is the basic premise of John E. Mueller's *Remnants of War* (Ithaca: Cornell University Press, 2004). For a contrary opinion that stresses the importance of civil wars, their ability to undermine international security, and a rebuke of scholars for underestimating the relevance of civil wars, see Andrew Mack, "Civil War: Academic Research and the Policy Community," *Journal of Peace Research*, Vol. 39, No. 5 (September 2002): pp. 515–525.

24. This is the central thesis of Robert Kaplan's widely read essay, "The Coming Anarchy." See Robert D. Kaplan, "The Coming Anarchy: How Scarcity, Crime, Overpopulation, Tribalism, and Disease Are Rapidly Destroying the Social Fabric of Our Planet," *Atlantic Monthly*, Vol. 273, No. 2 (February 1994): pp. 44–76.

Chapter 2. Civil War Termination in Perspective

1. Caroline Hartzell and Matthew Hoddie record four areas of power sharing in negotiated settlements between 1946 and 1999: political, military, economic, and territorial. See Hartzell and Hoddie, *Crafting Peace*.

2. Development Assistance Committee, Organization for Economic Cooperation and Development, *Security System Reform and Governance*, DAC Guidelines and Reference Series (Paris: OECD, 2005), p. 57.

3. Ibid., pp. 83–84.

4. What little academic research exists on SSR is largely hooked into current policy practices. See, for example, Nicole Ball, "Transforming Security Sectors: The IMF and World Bank Approaches," *Conflict, Security, and Development*, Vol. 1, No. 1 (2001): pp. 45–66; Dylon Hendrickson, "A Review of the Security Sector Reform," Working Paper no. 1 (London: King's College London, Centre for Defence Studies, 1999); and Chris Smith, "Security Sector Reform: Development Breakthrough or Institutional Engineering?" *Conflict, Security & Development*, Vol. 1, No. 1 (April 2001): pp. 5–20.

5. The name of this fund is the Law and Order Trust Fund for Afghanistan (LOTFA), and it is administered by the United Nations Development Programme (UNDP). Interview with German ambassador Michael Schmunk, Cambridge, MA (December 2005). Schmunk has been one of the principle German officials in charge of postconflict operations in Afghanistan.

6. World Bank, "Sub-Saharan Africa: From Crisis to Sustainable Growth: A Long-Term Perspective Study" (Washington, DC: World Bank, 1989).

7. Michel Camdessus, transcript of a September 28, 1989, press conference (Washington, DC: International Monetary Fund, 1989), p. 1.

8. Ball, "Transforming Security Sectors."

9. Cawthra and Luckham, eds., *Governing Insecurity*, p. 16.

10. Ibid.

11. Development Assistance Committee, Organization for Economic Cooperation and Development, *The DAC Guidelines: Helping Prevent Violent Conflict* (Paris: OECD, 2001).

12. Development Assistance Committee, *Security System Reform and Governance*.

13. *Peace Support Operations: A Working Draft Manual for African Military Practitioners* (Pretoria, South Africa: Institute for Security Studies, February 1, 2000).

14. Boutros Boutros-Ghali, *Supplement to an Agenda for Peace: Position Paper of the Secretary General on the Occasion of the Fiftieth Anniversary of the United Nations*, UN Document A/50/60-S/1995/1 (New York: United Nations, Department of Public Information, January 3, 1995).

15. Lakhdar Brahimi, *Report of the Panel on United Nations Peace Operations*, UN Document A55/305-S/2000/809 (New York: United Nations, August 17, 2000).

16. United Nations Development Program Bureau for Crisis Prevention and Recovery web site, http://www.undp.org/bcpr/documents/jssr/ssr/UNDP_2003_JSSR_Approach.doc (accessed September 1, 2008).

17. Ibid.

18. Other motivations include revenge and bloodlust. Nevertheless, because the literature does not address these factors, and because greed and fear seem to be the dominant reasons for fighting, I leave them aside for now. I do deal with revenge in the case studies, however, when I discuss notions of justice in the termination of individual civil wars. For an article that discusses these and other motivations, see Peter Uvin, "Ethnicity and Power in Burundi and Rwanda: Different Paths to Mass Violence," *Comparative Politics*, Vol. 31, No. 3 (April 1999): pp. 253–271.

19. On a theoretical level, James Davies and Ted Gurr were two of the main contributors to the civil war fields of resource inequality. See James C. Davies, "Toward a Theory of Revolution," *American Sociological Review*, Vol. 27, No. 1 (February 1962): pp. 5–19; and Ted R. Gurr, *Why Men Rebel* (Princeton: Princeton University Press, 1970). I have summarized geography, representation, and other types of resource theories in civil war in *The Geography of Ethnic Violence: Identity, Interests, and the Indivisibility of Territory* (Princeton: Princeton University Press, 2003).

20. David A. Lake and Donald Rothchild, "Spreading Fear: The Genesis of Transnational Ethnic Conflict," in Lake and Rothchild, eds., *The International Spread of Ethnic Conflict: Fear, Diffusion, and Escalation* (Princeton: Princeton University Press, 1998), pp. 3–32.

21. Christopher Cramer (among many others) summarizes the literature on resources in his article "Does Inequality Cause Conflict?" *Journal of International Development*, Vol. 15, No. 4 (2003): pp. 397–412. For a good overall summary of the theoretical causes of civil wars, see Nils Petter Gleditsch and Ole Magnus Theisen, *Resources, the Environment, and Conflict* (Oslo: International Peace and Research Institute, 2006). Available at http://www.prio.no/files/file48356_gleditsch_theisen_160906.doc (accessed September 1, 2008).

22. James Robinson, Nicholas Sambanis, Marie Besançon, and Gudrun Østby identify differentiated causes for disaggregated civil wars. Besançon shows that the greed factor, or "natural resources," may in fact support such wars, but she also demonstrates that resource inequality is a stronger motivation. See Daron Acemoglu and James A. Robinson, "A Theory of Political Transitions," *American Economic Review*, Vol. 91, No. 4 (September 2001): pp, 938–963; Nicholas Sambanis, "Do Ethnic and Nonethnic Civil Wars Have the Same Causes?" *Journal of Conflict Resolution*, Vol. 45, No. 3 (June 2001): pp. 259–282; Marie Besançon, "Relative Resources: Inequality in Ethnic Wars, Revolutions, and Genocides," *Journal of Peace Research*, Vol. 42, No. 4 (July 2005): pp. 393–415; and Gudrun Østby, "Horizontal Inequalities and Civil Conflict," paper presented at the 46th Annual International Studies Association (ISA) Convention (Honolulu, March 2, 2005).

23. See Paul Collier and Anke Hoeffler, "Greed and Grievance in Civil War," *Oxford Economic Papers*, Vol. 56, No. 4 (October 2004): pp. 563–595; Paul Collier, "Doing Well Out of War: An Economic Perspective," in Mats Berdal and David M. Malone, eds., *Greed and Grievance: Economic Agendas in Civil Wars* (Boulder: Lynne Rienner, 2000), pp. 91–111; and Paul Collier, "On the Economic Consequences of Civil War," *Oxford Economic Papers*, Vol. 51, No. 1 (January 1999): pp. 168–183. For information on resources and war more generally, see Philippe Le Billon, *Fuelling War: Natural Resources and Armed Conflict*, Adelphi Paper no. 373 (London: Routledge, 2005); Michael L. Ross, "Oil, Drugs, and Diamonds: The Varying Roles of Natural Resources in Civil War," in Karen Ballentine and Jake Sherman, eds., *The Political Economy of Armed Conflict: Beyond Greed and Grievance* (Boulder: Lynne Rienner, 2003), pp. 47–70; and Charles L. Glaser, "Political Consequences of Military Strategy: Expanding and Refining the Spiral and Deterrence Models," *World Politics*, Vol. 44, No. 4 (July 1992): pp. 497–538.

24. Though it has not been definitively proven that greed for natural resources actually causes wars, natural resources do in fact help pay for war.

25. See Lake and Rothchild, eds., *The International Spread of Ethnic Conflict*.

26. John Herz is credited with the origins of the concept and Robert Jervis with its development and refinement. See John H. Herz, *Political Realism and Political Idealism: A Study in Theories and Realities* (Chicago: University of Chicago Press, 1951); Robert Jervis, "Cooperation under the Security Dilemma," *World Politics*, Vol. 30, No. 2 (January 1978): pp. 167–214; Robert Jervis,

Perception and Misperception in International Politics (Princeton: Princeton University Press, 1976); Barry R. Posen, "The Security Dilemma in Ethnic Conflict," in Michael E. Brown, ed., *Ethnic Conflict and International Security* (Princeton: Princeton University Press, 1993), pp. 103–124. Other works in which authors have applied the security dilemma to ethnic civil wars in particular include David A. Lake and Donald Rothchild, "Containing Fear: The Origins and Management of Ethnic Conflict," *International Security*, Vol. 21, No. 2 (Fall 1996): pp. 41–75; James D. Fearon, "Commitment Problems and the Spread of Ethnic Conflict," in Lake and Rothchild, eds., *The International Spread of Ethnic Conflict*, pp. 107–126; Stuart J. Kaufman, "Spiraling to Ethnic War: Elites, Masses, and Moscow in Moldova's Civil War," *International Security*, Vol. 21, No. 2 (Fall 1996): pp. 108–138; Russell Hardin, *One for All: The Logic of Group Conflict* (Princeton: Princeton University Press, 1995). For critiques on this matter, see Steven R. David, "Internal War: Causes and Cures," *World Politics*, Vol. 49, No. 4 (July 1997): pp. 552–576; and William Rose, "The Security Dilemma and Ethnic Conflict: Some New Hypotheses," *Security Studies*, Vol. 9, No. 4 (Summer 2000): pp. 1–51.

27. For an excellent extension of Jervis's model and one on which this discussion is based, see Glaser, "Political Consequences of Military Strategy."

28. See David Keen, "The Economic Functions of Violence in Civil Wars," Adelphi Paper no. 320 (London: International Institute for Strategic Studies, 1998).

29. For more on hatred, see, for example, Roger D. Petersen, *Understanding Ethnic Violence: Fear, Hatred, and Resentment in Twentieth-Century Eastern Europe* (New York: Cambridge University Press, 2002).

30. Those who take an optimistic view about how to fix or tweak agreements include Caroline Hartzell, Matthew Hoddie, and Donald Rothchild, "Stabilizing the Peace After Civil War: An Investigation into Some Key Variables," *International Organization*, Vol. 55, No. 1 (Winter 2001): pp. 183–208; and Virginia Page Fortna, "Scraps of Paper? Agreements and the Durability of Peace," *International Organization*, Vol. 57, No. 2 (Spring 2003): pp. 337–372. A pessimistic account of peace agreements can be found in Roland Paris, *At War's End: Building Peace After Civil Conflict* (New York: Cambridge University Press, 2004). For how the terms of a peace agreement led to renewed violence in Colombia, see Jonathan Hartlyn, "Civil Violence and Conflict Resolution: The Case of Colombia," in Roy Licklider, ed., *Stopping the Killing: How Civil Wars End* (New York: New York University Press, 1993), pp. 37–61.

31. Caroline Hartzell and Matthew Hoddie, "Institutionalizing Peace: Power Sharing and Post–Civil War Conflict Management," *American Journal of Political Science*, Vol. 47, No. 2 (April 2003): pp. 318–332.

32. Note that a perhaps stronger variant of this argument surrounds the issue of translating agreements. The most famous example still stands as UN Resolution 242, which in its Arabic version forbids Israel's continued occupation of all the territories it acquired following the 1967 cease-fire, but in its Hebrew version is far more ambiguous both about the requirement to withdraw and about the specific territories from which Israeli defense forces (or settlers) might be required to pull out. This ambiguity effectively destroyed any chance of peace, and func-

tionally the ambiguity itself meant there was no "resolution." Consequently, a state of war continued and has to the present day. I do not analyze this type of case because again, functionally, it cannot count as a peace agreements or a negotiated settlement and can therefore not be analyzed as having endured or failed in the way that other settlements can.

33. See Werner and Yuen, "Making and Keeping Peace"; and Bumba Mukherjee, "Why Political Power-Sharing Agreements Lead to Enduring Peaceful Resolution of Some Civil Wars, but Not Others?" *International Studies Quarterly*, Vol. 50, No. 2 (June 2006): pp. 479–504.

34. Terrence Lyons, "The Role of Postsettlement Elections," in Stephen John Stedman, Donald S. Rothchild, and Elisabeth M. Cousens, eds., *Ending Civil Wars: The Implementation of Peace Agreements* (Boulder: Lynne Rienner, 2002), p. 222.

35. See Werner and Yuen, "Making and Keeping Peace."

36. Charles Taylor (b. 1948) served as president of Liberia from 1997 to 2003. A prominent figure in that country's civil wars (1989–1996 and 1999–2003), Taylor was indicted for war crimes on June 4, 2003, by a United Nations Special Court for Sierra Leone.

37. Stedman, Rothchild, and Cousens, *Ending Civil Wars*.

38. Glaser, "Political Consequences of Military Strategy."

39. See Walter, "The Critical Barrier to Civil War Settlement." Fen Osler Hampson also developed a similar argument in *Nurturing Peace: Why Peace Settlements Succeed or Fail* (Washington, DC: United States Institute of Peace Press, 1996). For a nice overview of the subject see Fen Osler Hampson, "Parent, Midwife or Accidental Executioner? The Role of Third Parties in Ending Violence Conflicts," in Chester A. Crocker, Fen Osler Hampson, and Pamela R. Aall, eds., *Turbulent Peace: The Challenges of Managing International Conflict* (Washington, DC: U.S. Institute of Peace Press, 2001), pp. 387–406.

40. Walter, "The Critical Barrier to Civil War Settlement," pp. 345–47.

41. Ibid., p. 340.

42. A more recent addition is Kimberly Zisk Marten, *Enforcing the Peace: Learning from the Imperial Past* (New York: Columbia University Press, 2004). In this text, Marten advances the idea of "security-keeping" as opposed to peacekeeping. According to Marten, "security-keeping" is a more manageable and achievable objective than is the attempt to push political change on a foreign country. See especially chapter 6, "Security as a Step to Peace," pp. 145–166.

43. Thomas C. Schelling, *The Strategy of Conflict* (Cambridge: Harvard University Press, 1960); Paul R. Pillar, *Negotiating Peace: War Termination as a Bargaining Process* (Princeton: Princeton University Press, 1983); and Robert Powell, "Bargaining and Learning While Fighting," *American Journal of Political Science*, Vol. 48, No. 2 (April 2004): pp. 344–361.

44. Suzanne Werner, "The Precarious Nature of Peace: Resolving the Issues, Enforcing the Settlement, and Renegotiating the Terms," *American Journal of Political Science*, Vol. 43, No. 3 (July 1999): pp. 912–934; Caroline Hartzell, "Explaining the Stability of Negotiated Settlements to Intrastate Wars," *Journal of Conflict Resolution*, Vol. 43, No. 1 (February 1999): pp. 3–22; Hartzell and Hoddie, *Crafting Peace*.

45. Stephen John Stedman, "International Implementation of Peace Agreements in Civil Wars: Findings from a Study of Sixteen Cases," in Chester A. Crocker, Fen Osler Hampson, and Pamela Aall, eds., *Turbulent Peace: The Challenges of Managing International Conflict* (Washington DC: United States Institute of Peace Press, 2001), p. 746.

46. Robert Harrison Wagner makes this case with regard to the destruction of organizations in "The Causes of Peace," in Licklider, *Stopping the Killing*, pp. 235–268. For a discussion of multiple actors (veto players) in civil war settlement, see David E. Cunningham, "Veto Players and Civil War Duration," *American Journal of Political Science*, Vol. 50, No. 4 (October 2006): pp. 875–892.

47. On this point in particular, see Ivan Arreguín-Toft, "Crossing the Line: The Problem of Interstate Boundaries as Insurgent Sanctuary," paper presented at the Annual Convention of the American Political Science Association, Washington, DC, September 2005.

48. Note that when James Fearon introduces "private" information as an obstacle to nonviolent conflict resolution, he is referring to the information each side has about its true intentions or stake in the fight (or even capabilities). Here, I use the term in a slightly different sense, which is to emphasize capabilities and to suggest that such information can be "private" because actors are very often unclear about their own capabilities until they are tested. See Fearon, "Rationalist Explanations for War"; and Stephen Van Evera, "Why States Believe Foolish Ideas," manuscript.

49. Geoffrey Blainey, *The Causes of War*, 3rd ed. (New York: Free Press, 1988).

50. See Chaim D. Kaufmann, "Possible and Impossible Solutions to Ethnic Civil Wars," *International Security*, Vol. 20, No. 4 (Spring 1996): pp. 136–175; Chaim D. Kaufmann, "Intervention in Ethnic and Ideological Civil Wars: Why One Can Be Done and the Other Can't," *Security Studies*, Vol. 6, No. 1 (Autumn 1996): pp. 62–103; and Chaim D. Kaufmann, "When All Else Fails: Evaluating Population Transfers and Partition as Solutions to Ethnic Conflict," in Barbara F. Walter and Jack Snyder, eds., *Civil Wars, Insecurity, and Intervention* (New York: Columbia University Press, 1999), pp. 221–260. Other proponents of the tactic include John Mearsheimer, "Shrink Bosnia to Save It," *New York Times*, March 31, 1993; John Mearsheimer and Stephen Van Evera, "When Peace Means War," *New Republic*, December 18, 1995, pp. 16–21; Leslie H. Gelb, "The Three-State Solution," *New York Times*, November 25, 2003; and Donald L. Horowitz, *Ethnic Groups in Conflict* (Berkeley: University of California Press, 1985), pp. 588-591.

51. A recent compilation of responses to Kaufmann is Roy Licklider and Mia Bloom, eds., *Living Together After Ethnic Killing: Exploring the Chaim Kaufmann Argument* (London: Routledge, 2006).

52. Nicholas Sambanis, "Partition as a Solution to Ethnic War: An Empirical Analysis of the Theoretical Literature," *World Politics*, Vol. 52, No. 4 (July 2000): pp. 437–483.

53. The 2008 declaration of independence by Kosovo facilitated by international intervention is a rare exception.

54. Paris, *At War's End*, pp. 97–111.

55. Data are from the International Institute for Strategic Studies (IISS) Armed Conflict database, http://acd.iiss.org (accessed September 1, 2008).

56. See Horowitz, *Ethnic Groups in Conflict*, pp. 588-591; Radha Kumar, "The Troubled History of Partition," *Foreign Affairs*, Vol. 76, No. 1 (January/ February 1997): pp. 22–34; Sambanis, "Partition as a Solution to Ethnic War"; and Toft, *The Geography of Ethnic Violence*, pp. 144–145.

Chapter 3. Securing the Peace

1. Charles Tilly, "Reflections on the History of European State Making," in Charles Tilly, ed., *The Formation of National States in Western Europe* (Princeton: Princeton University Press, 1975), pp. 3–84.

2. See Barrington Moore, *Social Origins of Dictatorship and Democracy: Lord and Peasant in the Making of the Modern World* (Boston: Beacon Press, 1966); Samuel P. Huntington, *Political Order in Changing Societies* (New Haven: Yale University Press, 1968); and Dankwart Rustow, "Transitions to Democracy: Toward a Dynamic Model," *Comparative Politics*, Vol. 2, No. 3 (April 1970): pp. 337–363.

3. Eric A. Nordlinger, "Political Development: Time Sequences and Rates of Change," *World Politics*, Vol. 20, No. 3 (April 1968): p. 500. Similar arguments have re-emerged in the literature on democratic transitions of the late 1980s and 1990s. Later transition theorists rejected these arguments on the grounds that they were teleological, setting forth trajectories for states that could not be escaped or designed around. The more recent theorists have argued instead that democratic institutions could be fashioned regardless of a state's historical experience. On this matter, the basic difference between the old and the new schools seems to boil down to disagreements about the relative role of structure versus agency. While the old school stressed structure, the new school stressed agency. Not surprisingly, the pendulum is swinging somewhat in the direction of structure again in recognition of the many stalled and failed transitions, especially since the end of the Cold War. See Adam Przerworski et al., *Democracy and Development: Political Institutions and Well-Being in the World, 1950–1990* (New York: Cambridge University Press, 2000); Juan J. Linz and Alfred C. Stepan, *Problems of Democratic Tradition and Consolidation: Southern Europe, South America, and Post-Communist Europe* (Baltimore: Johns Hopkins University Press, 1996); Guillermo O'Donnell, Philippe C. Schmitter, and Laurence Whitehead, *Transitions from Authoritarian Rule: Comparative Perspectives* (Baltimore: Johns Hopkins University Press, 1986); and Giuseppe Di Palma, *To Craft Democracies: An Essay on Democratic Transitions* (Berkeley: University of California Press, 1990).

4. Terrence Lyons, "The Role of Postsettlement Elections," p. 222.

5. Ibid., p. 226.

6. Larry Diamond, *Developing Democracy: Toward Consolidation* (Baltimore: Johns Hopkins University Press, 1999), p. 114.

7. This argument follows Charles Tilly's about the monopolization of violence in state formation. See Tilly, *The Formation of National States in Europe*; and Charles Tilly, "War Making and State Making as Organized Crime," in Peter B. Evans, Dietrich Rueschemeyer, and Theda Skocpol, eds., *Bringing the State Back In* (New York: Cambridge University Press, 1985), pp. 169–191.

8. This is a classically "statist" way of framing the issue. "Peace" and "stability" have often been used by tyrants as rhetorical proxies for injustice and oppression. Again, this analysis will force us to consider the extent to which we may determine a general policy prescription regarding intervention in civil wars.

9. Adam Przeworski, "The Games of Transition," in Scott Mainwaring, Guillermo O'Donnell, and J. Samuel Valenzuela, eds., *Issues in Democratic Consolidation: The New South American Democracies in Comparative Perspective* (Notre Dame: University of Notre Dame Press, 1992), pp. 105–153.

10. In much of the world, political power and personal wealth are closely linked. One reason for this is that political offices allow office holders—as a political economist might put it—to "extract rents" (a practice that in the West is known more commonly as "corruption"). This often obviates the need for a direct transfer of wealth as a precondition to supporting a cease-fire.

11. Key examples include Rwanda's Hutu president, Juvénal Habyarimana, in 1994, and contemporary Kenya's president, Mwai Kibaki. For both men, sharing power with opposition leaders amounted to an unacceptable cost and one that each ultimately rejected in favor of civil war.

12. Nicole Ball, "The Challenge of Rebuilding War-Torn Societies," in Chester A. Crocker, Fen Osler Hampson, and Pamela Aall, eds., *Turbulent Peace: The Challenges of Managing International Conflict* (Washington, DC: U.S. Institute of Peace Press, 2001), p. 725.

13. Ibid.

14. Ibid., p. 726. For a more general analysis of the need for security sector reform in developing countries, see Development Assistance Committee, *Security System Reform and Governance*.

15. One study found that demobilization was by far the most important subgoal of peace implementation and that disarmament was *not* crucial to implementation success. See Stedman, "International Implementation of Peace Agreements."

16. Charles T. Call and William Stanley, "Civilian Security," in Stedman, Rothchild, and Cousens, eds., *Ending Civil Wars*, pp. 303–326.

17. For background reading on the history and war in Colombia, see David Bushnell, *The Making of Modern Colombia: A Nation in Spite of Itself* (Berkeley: University of California Press, 1993); Bert Ruiz, *The Colombian Civil War* (Jefferson, NC: McFarland, 2001); and Frank Safford and Marco Palacios, *Colombia: Fragmented Land, Divided Society* (New York: Oxford University Press, 2002).

18. William Avilés, "Institutions, Military Policy, and Human Rights in Colombia," *Latin American Perspectives*, Vol. 28, No. 1 (January 2001): pp. 31–55.

19. Development Assistance Committee, *Security System Reform and Governance*, p. 11.

20. Ibid., p. 23.

21. Ibid., p. 28.

22. Ibid., p. 46.

23. Osman Gbla, "Security Sector Reform under International Tutelage in Sierra Leone," *International Peacekeeping*, Vol. 13, No. 1 (March 2006): pp. 78–93.

24. For an analysis of implementing negotiated settlements following three centralist civil wars, see Dorina Akosua Odoraa Bekoe, "After the Peace Agree-

ment: Lessons for Implementation from Mozambique, Angola, and Liberia,"
Ph.D. Dissertation, Harvard University, 2002.

25. Walter, "The Critical Barrier to Civil War Settlement."

26. For the most comprehensive treatment of UN peacekeeping operations, see
Michael W. Doyle and Nicholas Sambanis, *Making War and Building Peace:
United Nations Peace Operations* (Princeton: Princeton University Press, 2006).
Doyle and Sambanis do an excellent job of showing the success of the United Nations in peacekeeping operations. However, their research cannot overcome such
fundamental issues as states' interests (or lack thereof) in getting involved in civil
wars, the size of the countries receiving UN operations (which tends to be small),
and the scale of operations—factors that limit where and the conditions under
which the United Nations is willing to be engaged. For another study of UN multidimensional peacekeeping, see Lise Morjé Howard, *UN Peacekeeping in Civil
Wars* (New York: Cambridge University Press, 2007).

27. See Max Weber, *From Max Weber: Essays in Sociology*, trans. H. H. Gerth
and C. Wright Mills (New York: Oxford University Press, 1946).

28. Such support can range from apathy, at a minimum, to active support of
rebels and mass uprisings, at the high end. For an extended discussion of the
importance of social support in asymmetric conflicts, see Gil Merom, *How Democracies Lose Small Wars: State, Society, and the Failures of France in Algeria,
Israel in Lebanon, and the United States in Vietnam* (New York: Cambridge University Press, 2003); and Ivan Arreguín-Toft, *How the Weak Win Wars: A Theory
of Asymmetric Conflict* (New York: Cambridge University Press, 2005).

29. Here, one might consider Kosovar Albanians in Kosovo from 1990 to
1998. A later example would be the situation of Serbs in Kosovo following Ser-
bia's NATO-supervised retreat in 1999.

30. The notable historical exception is Marxists, who by doctrine must consider
all opposition to single-party rule anathema. Victorious Marxist rebels in Russia,
China, Cuba, Vietnam, and Afghanistan are representative cases. The distribution
of Marxist rebels has declined to nearly zero since 1991. Nepal is exceptional.

31. For the best short discussion of this problem in a setting of asymmetric
conflict, see Michael Walzer, *Just and Unjust Wars: A Moral Argument with Historical Illustrations*, 3rd ed. (New York: Basic Books, 2000), pp. 195–196.

32. There exists an extensive body of literature that examines the preference of
the international community (or at least the "Western international community")
for liberal values and institutions. See, for example, Michael N. Barnett, "Bringing
in the New World Order: Liberalism, Legitimacy, and the United Nations," *World
Politics*, Vol. 49, No. 4 (July 1997): pp. 526–551; Andrew Moravcsik, "Taking
Preferences Seriously: A Liberal Theory of International Politics," *International
Organization*, Vol. 51, No. 4 (Autumn 1997): pp. 513–553; and Martha Finnemore
and Kathryn Sikkink, "International Norm Dynamics and Political Change," *International Organization*, Vol. 52, No. 4 (Autumn 1998): pp. 887–917.

33. The most famous relevant example of this was Batista's Cuba in 1959.

34. For a timely analysis of states and statelike entities that result from such
ambiguous settlements, see Charles King, "The Benefits of Ethnic War: Understanding Eurasia's Unrecognized States," *World Politics*, Vol. 53, No. 4 (July 2001):
pp. 524–552.

35. William Stanley and David Holiday, "Broad Participation, Diffuse Responsibility: Peace Implementation in Guatemala," in Stedman, Rothchild, and Cousens, eds., *Ending Civil Wars*, pp. 421–462.

36. Glaser, "Political Consequences of Military Strategy."

37. Shantayanan Devarajan, David Dollar, and Torgny Holmgren, eds., *Aid and Reform in Africa: Lessons from Ten Case Studies* (Washington, DC: World Bank Publications, 2001). Also see Joan M. Nelson with Stephanie J. Eglington, *Encouraging Democracy: What Role for Conditioned Aid?* Policy Essay no. 4 (Washington, DC: Overseas Development Council, 1992).

38. John Mearsheimer, "Back to the Future: Instability in Europe After the Cold War," *International Security*, Vol. 15, No. 4 (Summer 1990): pp. 5–56.

39. In the United States, for example, the increasing challenges presented by military intervention—and the logical policy implication, nonintervention—were codified twice following U.S. failure in the American intervention in the Vietnamese civil war. This occurred first in the context of the Weinberger Doctrine (1984) and later in the Powell Doctrine (1992). See Caspar W. Weinberger, "The Uses of Military Power," (remarks prepared for delivery to the National Press Club, Washington, DC, November 28, 1984); and Colin L. Powell, "U.S. Forces: Challenges Ahead," *Foreign Affairs*, Vol. 71, No. 5 (Winter 1992/1993): pp. 32–51. On the theoretical and policy implications of the trend toward increasing failures in military interventions following World War II, see Arreguín-Toft, *How the Weak Win Wars*; and Ivan Arreguín-Toft, "Unconventional Deterrence: How the Weak Deter the Strong," in T. V. Paul, James Wirtz, and Patrick Morgan, eds., *Complex Deterrence: Strategy in the Global Era* (Chicago: University of Chicago Press, 2009).

40. Kaplan, "The Coming Anarchy."

41. Roland Paris, *At War's End: Building Peace after Civil Conflict* (New York: Cambridge University Press, 2004), p. 19.

42. Mark Peceny and William Stanley, "Liberal Social Reconstruction and the Resolution of Civil Wars in Central America," *International Organization*, Vol. 55, No. 1 (Winter 2001): p. 150.

43. For a critical assessment of peace agreements and peace-building efforts in their stress on markets and democracy, see Paris, *At War's End*.

Chapter 4. Statistical Analysis of War Recurrence and Longer-Term Outcomes

1. While the logit analysis allows us to see whether the types of war outcomes are associated with the recurrence of war, hazard models (also called duration or event history models) allow us to determine the impact of independent variables on the probability that peace will fail at a given time. I tested the argument using both methods and found similar results. Because logit models are easier to present and interpret, I report only the logit results here.

2. See Toft, *The Geography of Ethnic Violence*; Licklider, "The Consequences of Negotiated Settlements" p. 684; Kaufmann, "Possible and Impossible Solutions to Ethnic Civil Wars"; and Kaufmann, "Intervention in Ethnic and Ideo-

logical Civil Wars." Nicholas Sambanis found that partition is more likely to follow ethnic and/or religious wars, in "Partition as a Solution to Ethnic War."

3. See data set in appendix 1: IDENTITY (identity-based war) and TERRWAR (territorial war).

4. I. William Zartman, *Elusive Peace: Negotiating an End to Civil Wars* (Washington, DC: Brookings Institution Press, 1995).

5. See data set in appendix 1: LNTOTALDEATHS (log of total war-related deaths) and LNINTENSE (log of war-related deaths per month).

6. James Fearon and David Laitin, "Ethnicity, Insurgency, and Civil War," *American Political Science Review*, Vol. 97, No. 1 (February 2003): pp. 75–90; Besançon, "Relative Resources."

7. See data set in appendix: MILVIC (military victory); NEGSET (negotiated settlement); STALCEAS (stalemate/cease-fire); MVGOV (military victory by government); and MVREB (military victory by rebels).

8. First differences for nontermination type controls are given for model 2. First differences for casualty variables are taken for one standard deviation below the mean versus one standard deviation above the mean.

9. Frederic Pearson et al. reexamine the 2001 paper by Caroline Hartzell, Matthew Hoddie, and Donald Rothchild in terms of the duration of settlements. In this newer study, they use five years or greater as the test for stable outcomes (i.e., no recurrence), looking at lower-intensity conflicts with fewer than one thousand battle deaths per year. For these lesser-intensity conflicts they do not find any significant difference between military victories and negotiated settlements. Pearson et al. also find no significant effect from the Cold War era. For them, the only significant variable is democracy. Countries that were democratic or semidemocratic before the war have a significant chance of reaching a stable end to a civil war. See Frederic S. Pearson et al., "Rethinking Models of Civil War Settlement," International Interactions, Vol. 32, No. 2 (April–June 2006): pp. 109–128; and Hartzell, Hoddie, and Rothchild, "Stabilizing the Peace After Civil War."

10. The Sambanis/Doyle data set can be found at http://www.worldbank.org/research/conflict/papers/peacebuilding/, and the Fearon/Laitin data set can be found at http://www.stanford.edu/group/ethnic/publicdata/publicdata.html (accessed November 2008).

11. Cases included in my data set involve a casualty threshold of one thousand deaths on average per year of the war, while Fearon and Laitin's data set includes conflicts with a death count of at least 1,000 over the course of the conflict and at least 100 for each year of the conflict, and Doyle and Sambanis's data set includes cases that have at least 500 deaths (among other criteria). Note that casualty figures are notoriously difficult to ascertain given that most of these fights happen in impoverished and poorly governed countries with little to no reporting. This is another reason a higher threshold seems more appropriate for determining which cases should be included in the analysis. Ibid., and also Doyle and Sambanis, *Making War and Building Peace*, pp. 133–135.

12. I included wars of independence (or colonial/anticolonial wars) in my data set and analysis since it is not clear what differentiates them from some of their more contemporary counterparts. So, for example, what makes the Namibian

War of Independence qualitatively different from the war in Chechnya, in which the Chechens see themselves as trying to get out from under Moscow's imperial yoke? The central political question in all of these cases is the same: who would govern the state? Nevertheless, to assess whether anticolonial wars impact the analysis here, I ran the regressions without them, and the results changed little: victory by rebels remained statistically significant.

13. Walter, including *Committing to Peace.*

14. Ibid. The variable is coded as MILPACT in Walter's data set.

15. See ibid. The variable is coded as PEACEPROCESS in Walter's data set.

16. Ibid. This variable is coded as GUARDUM in Walter's data set.

17. Both models in table 4.2 were tested against all combinations of intensity measures, territorial war, and duration as measured in months: in no instance did the coefficients change in sign or relative magnitude, nor did these changes cause any variables to lose their significance as measured by one-tailed t-tests.

18. To conduct the duration tests, the values of duration for each country's civil wars were added together. If, for example, in the original data set there were two separate observations for Angola called "Angola IIa" (Angola civil war) and "Angola IIb" (UNITA warfare), the duration in months for each module was added to measure total hardship that a country endured as a result of both the initial war and its resumption. Where a recurred civil war is still ongoing, it is truncated in 2006, after which PRIO does not code fatalities data. See combined data set.

19. This finding holds even when excluding the most deadly of these civil wars—Sudan—as a potential outlier. When excluding Angola (another particularly deadly conflict), per capita battle deaths are similar to the global mean, but per capita total deaths remain higher for recurred negotiated settlements. To exclude both Sudan and Angola simultaneously—thus removing the two deadliest of five total failed negotiated settlements—makes little sense.

20. Polity IV Project, "Polity IV Data Set" (College Park: Center for International Development and Conflict Management, University of Maryland, 2000). Available at http://www.cidcm.umd.edu/polity/data. All of the results presented in this chapter are consistent using the "polity2" variable in the Polity IV data set as well. The polity2 variable uses "extrapolations and estimations" to fill in a large number of missing values in the main data, but the authors of the data set warn that these data are much less reliable than the original figures.

21. See data set in appendix for POL5AV, POL10AV, POL20AV, and POL30AV.

22. See data set in appendix for PREPOL1, POL5AVDIF, POL10AVDIF, and POL20AVDIF.

23. Changes in the level of democratization were estimated based on the POLITY variable from the Polity IV data. The POLITY variable ranges from −10 to 10, with a score of −10 corresponding to the most severe authoritarian regimes with no democratic qualities, while a score of 10 indicates the most democratic regimes with no authoritarian qualities.

24. Table 4.5 indicates a shift toward less repression as war approaches, although repression increases just slightly during the year in which the war breaks out. Such a decrease in authoritarianism might indicate these states' attempts to placate a discontented society. Nonetheless, this "loosening up" argument goes

only so far. As the war approaches, we do see the level of authoritarianism increasing ever so slightly. This dynamic lends credence to the idea that the "liberalization" of a system is precarious because it might stress that system too much, which would lead to additional calls for even more liberalization. Should these demands not be met, frustration will set in, repression will increase, and violence will ensue.

25. This figure was calculated by the author. It is interesting to note that a comparison of the average rates through this ten-year period shows that average polity scores increased two points, from 0.76 in 1990 to 2.29 in 1995 and 2.83 in 2000. Although these scores nevertheless indicate that democracy is not the norm (most scholars use a score of 6 as their cutoff point to indicate a true democracy), increasing levels of democratization in the last decade at the global level do seem to form a trend.

26. The table that follows presents t-tests for the significance of difference in means across the categories. Thus, for example, the upper-left cell addresses the question of whether the average polity score for cases of military victory differs statistically from those cases that did not end in military victory. See the appendix for supporting data.

27. Because there are so few cases of cease-fires/stalemates, we must carefully examine how we interpret the findings related to such situations. India and Cyprus account for five of fourteen observed cease-fires/stalemates in the data set.

28. Moreover, they do not answer whether democratization affects civil war recurrence. I included this factor in an earlier model and found that it had no effect.

29. Differences are measured in absolute terms. This is more appropriate than measuring percentage changes, for two reasons. First, when a state has a polity score of zero, it is impossible to define the relative magnitude of a change in any direction. Second, there is no reason to believe that a change from a polity score of 5 to 6 should be seen as five times less valuable than a change from a polity score of 0 to 1. See appendix for supporting data. The high democracy values for cease-fires/stalemates are due to the fact that nearly half of those observations come from India and Cyprus.

30. See appendix for supporting data. Because per capita GDP information is missing at the beginning of more than half of the conflicts in the data set, because the remaining information is parsed into several categories, and because many civil wars ended fewer than twenty years ago, some of the points in these trend lines are driven by a small number of cases. The "20 years after" figure for cease-fires, for instance, contains only India/Kashmir, and the corresponding data point for negotiated settlements measures only the Dominican Republic and Zimbabwe.

31. Wagner, "The Causes of Peace."

Chapter 5. El Salvador

1. Charles T. Call, "Assessing El Salvador's Transition from Civil War to Peace," in Stephen John Stedman, Donald Rothchild, and Elizabeth M. Cousens, eds., *Ending Civil Wars: The Implementation of Peace Agreements* (Boulder: Lynne Rienner, 2002), p. 383.

2. See Krishna Kumar and Marina Ottaway, *From Bullets to Ballots: A Synthesis of Findings from Six Evaluations* (Washington, DC: USAID, 1997).

3. Call, "Assessing El Salvador's Transition," p. 387. Call credits Terry Lynn Karl with the coining of the phrase "strategic stalemate" in Karl's "El Salvador's Negotiated Revolution," *Foreign Affairs*, Vol. 71, No. 2 (Spring 1992): p. 149.

4. See Luttwak, "Give War a Chance"; Licklider, "The Consequences of Negotiated Settlements"; and Wagner, "The Causes of Peace."

5. Call, "Assessing El Salvador's Transition," p. 389.

6. Roy Prosterman, Jeffrey Riedinger, and Mary Temple, "Land Reform and the El Salvador Crisis," *International Security*, Vol. 6, No. 1 (Summer 1981): pp. 53–74. According to these authors, 38 percent of El Salvadorans were landless, p. 54.

7. Elisabeth Jean Wood, *Forging Democracy from Below: Insurgent Transitions in South Africa and El Salvador* (New York: Cambridge University Press, 2000), p. 28.

8. Enrique A. Baloyra, *El Salvador in Transition* (Chapel Hill: University of North Carolina Press, 1982), p. 7.

9. William Stanley, "International Tutelage and Domestic Political Will: A New Civilian Police Force in El Salvador," in *Studies in Comparative International Development*, Vol. 30, No. 1 (Spring 1995): pp. 30–58.

10. Baloyra, *El Salvador in Transition*, p. 10. Also see Juhn, *Negotiating Peace in El Salvador: Civil Relations and the Conspiracy to End the War* (New York: St. Martin's, 1998), p. 31.

11. William Deane Stanley, *The Protection Racket State: Elite Politics Military Extortion, and Civil War in El Salvador* (Philadelphia: Temple University Press, 1996), p. 42.

12. Wood, *Forging Democracy from Below*, pp. 31–33.

13. Jeffery M. Paige, "History and Memory in El Salvador: Elite Ideology and the Insurrection and Massacre of 1932," paper presented at the Meetings of the Latin American Studies Association, Atlanta, March 1994. As quoted in Stanley, *The Protection Racket State*, p. 57.

14. Stanley, *The Protection Racket State*, p. 58.

15. Wood, *Forging Democracy from Below*, p. 33.

16. Walter Knut and Philip J. Williams, "The Military and Democratization in El Salvador," *Journal of Interamerican Studies and World Affairs*, Vol. 35, No. 1 (1993): pp. 39–88.

17. Wood, *Forging Democracy from Below*, p. 33.

18. Ibid., p. 39.

19. By the late 1970s it became apparent that land reform was absolutely vital, as the peasant insurgency was gaining ground. See Prosterman et al., "Land Reform," pp. 60–61.

20. Baloyra, *El Salvador in Transition*, p. 39.

21. Wood, *Forging Democracy from Below*, p. 42.

22. Stanley, *The Protection Racket State*, p. 71.

23. Call, "Assessing El Salvador's Transition," p. 385.

24. Stanley, *The Protection Racket State*, pp. 117, 118, 113–114.

25. Ibid., p. 168.

26. Ibid., p. 169.

27. Ibid., p. 206; and Baloyra, *El Salvador in Transition*, p. 130.

28. Call, "Assessing El Salvador's Transition," p. 385.

29. In 1981 the FMLN numbered less than 5,000, but by 1983 its membership had more than doubled to 12,000. The government's forces numbered about 14,000 in 1981 (these included firefighters, police, and soldiers). As stated in Edwin G. Corr, "Societal Transformation for Peace in El Salvador," *Annals of the American Academy of Political and Social Science*, Vol. 541 (September 1995): p. 152.

30. Although most analysts report 75,000 as the number of killed, Corr reports that Salvadoran official statistics put the number from January 1981 to July 1991 at 30,907. Ibid., p. 145.

31. Stanley, *The Protection Racket State*, p. 238.

32. Ibid., pp. 234–235.

33. Ibid., p. 240.

34. Call, "Assessing El Salvador's Transition," p. 387.

35. Stanley, *The Protection Racket State*, p. 242.

36. Ibid., pp. 245, 246–247.

37. Juhn, *Negotiating Peace in El Salvador*, p. 51.

38. Stanley, *The Protection Racket State*, pp. 246–247.

39. Michael W. Doyle, Ian Johnstone, and Robert C. Orr, eds., *Keeping the Peace: Multidimensional UN Operations in Cambodia and El Salvador* (New York: Cambridge University Press, 1997), p. 231.

40. Juhn, *Negotiating Peace in El Salvador*, p. 9. This is also a central thesis in Elisabeth Jean Wood, *Insurgent Collective Action and Civil War in El Salvador* (New York: Cambridge University Press, 2003). Wood demonstrates how domestic alliances were key, showing how the pressure of civil war and the insurgency forced new economic alliances and diminished the role of the military. See especially chapter 3.

41. Stanley, *The Protection Racket State*, p. 242.

42. On the role of the United States in ending the civil war in El Salvador, see especially Walter and Williams, "The Military and Democratization in El Salvador." For an excellent discussion of the limitations of the influence of the United States, see William Deane Stanley, "El Salvador: State-Building Before and After Democratisation, 1980–95," *Third World Quarterly*, Vol. 27, No. 1 (February 2006): pp. 101–114.

43. Stanley, *The Protection Racket State*, p. 259.

44. Wood, *Forging Democracy from Below*, pp. 71–75.

45. David Holiday and William Stanley, "Under the Best of Circumstances: ONUSAL and the Challenges of Verification and Institution Building in El Salvador" in Tommie Sue Montgomery, ed., *Peacemaking and Democratization in the Western Hemisphere* (Coral Gables: North South Center Press, 2000), p. 43.

46. Ibid., p. 39.

47. The earlier FMLN proposals can be found at http://www.envio.org.ni/articulo/2573 (accessed July 2007).

48. Stanley, "International Tutelage," p. 50.

49. As cited in Call, "Assessing El Salvador's Transition," p. 399.

50. Claude E. Welch, Jr., ed, *Civilian Control of the Military: Theory and Cases from Developing Countries* (Albany: SUNY Press, 1976) and Morris Janowitz, *The Military in Political Development of New Nations: An Essay in Comparative Analysis* (Chicago: University of Chicago Press, 1964).

51. The treaty calls for such proportions to be established in the future, and the exact figures were set after the treaty was signed. Ibid., p. 390.

52. Samuel Finer called this phenomenon the "Man on Horseback syndrome," noting that when the military becomes oversized and influential, it is increasingly drawn into political intervention that undermines civilian government. Samuel E. Finer, *The Man on Horseback: The Role of the Military in Politics* (London: Pall Mall Press, 1962).

53. Call, "Assessing El Salvador's Transition," pp. 410–412.

54. Morris Janowitz, in particular, stresses the importance of operational experience for creating an effective security sector. It was therefore wise of El Salvador to *reform* its military rather than completely rebuild it. Janowitz, *The Military in the Political Development of New Nations.*

55. Charles T. Call, *Challenges in Police Reform: Promoting Effectiveness and Accountability* (New York: International Peace Academy Policy Report, 2003).

56. Ibid., p. 6.

57. Call, "Assessing El Salvador's Transition," p. 397.

58. To further this argument, Call adds that the greatest failure of the police reform effort was the decision to maintain the existing Special Investigative Unit and Anti-Narcotics Unit within the otherwise entirely revamped National Police Force. The officials in these units, holdovers from the old regime, were extremely repressive, and were removed from power only after widespread hunger strikes. The devastating effects of maintaining even these two small units emphasize the importance of vetting the security sector in postconflict scenarios—something that was called for in the accords but not fully carried out in these units. Ibid., p. 401.

59. The term is taken from a medical term meaning the critical period following a trauma when action or inaction determines the fate of the victim.

60. Seth G. Jones et al., "Establishing Law and Order After Conflict,"(Santa Monica: RAND Corporation, 2005), pp. xi, p. xiii.

61. Call, "Assessing El Salvador's Transition," p. 389.

62. Ibid., p. 408.

63. Ibid., pp. 389, 392.

64. Elisabeth Jean Wood, "The Peace Accords and Postwar Reconstruction," in James K. Boyce, ed., *Economic Policy for Building Peace: The Lessons of El Salvador* (Boulder: Lynne Rienner, 1996), p. 79.

65. Walter Knut and Philip J. Williams, *Militarization and Demilitarization in El Salvador's Transition to Democracy* (Pittsburgh: University of Pittsburgh Press, 1997), pp. 152–154.

66. Wood, "The Peace Accords," p. 81.

67. One of the more contentious issues involved education. The military resisted civilian oversight in how its members were to be educated, which served as an important source of institutional autonomy.

68. James K. Boyce, "External Resource Mobilization," in Boyce, ed., *Economic Policy for Building Peace*, pp. 129–154.

69. Holiday and Stanley, "Under the Best of Circumstances," p. 395.

70. Alexander Segovia, "Domestic Resource Mobilization," in Boyce, ed., *Economic Policy for Building Peace* (Boulder: Lynne Rienner, 1996), pp. 107–127.

71. Holiday and Stanley, "Under the Best of Circumstances," p. 58. Juhn makes the same point; see especially *Negotiating Peace in El Salvador*, chap. 5.

72. Call, "Assessing El Salvador's Transition," Also Karl, "El Salvador's Negotiated Revolution."

73. For a detailed and critical assessment of El Salvador's economic policies following the peace agreement until 1995, see Alexander Segovia, "Macroeconomic Performance Policies Since 1989," in Boyce, ed., *Economic Policy for Building Peace*, pp. 51–72. Call's more recent assessment affirms these earlier trends. See "Assessing El Salvador's Transition," pp. 410–412.

74. The setback was due to delays in land and reintegration programs in 1992, as well as the need for reassurance that Cristiani was going to purge the officer corps as recommended by the Ad-Hoc Commission. Wood, "The Peace Accords," p. 92.

75. Holiday and Stanley, "Under the Best of Circumstances," pp. 37–53.

76. Ibid.

77. Wood, "The Peace Accords," p. 77.

78. Ibid., pp. 83–84.

79. Ibid., p. 95.

80. One of the debates is whether it was a lack of funding or a lack of political will that delayed the development of the police force. The consensus seems to be that it was lack of political will on the part of the government. See ibid., p. 102; Williams and Walter, *Militarization and Demilitarization*, pp. 178–180. More nuance can be found in Stanley, "International Tutelage," in which he balances political will with funding.

81. Stanley makes this point convincingly in "El Salvador," pp. 109–110. For a somewhat contrary assessment of the military's continued security role, if not political role, in the rural areas, see Walter and Williams, "The Military and Democratization in El Salvador," pp. 67–69.

82. Peceny and Stanley, "Liberal Social Reconstruction," p. 167.

83. Stanley, "El Salvador," p. 110.

84. Ibid., p. 111.

85. Victimization rates dropped again in 2001 but increased a bit in 2002. Nevertheless, the trend in crime rates have decreased substantially since the end of the war and mid-1990s. Edgardo Alberto Amaya, "Security Policies in El Salvador, 1992–2002," in John Bailey and Lucía Dammert, eds., *Public Security and Police Reform in the Americas* (Pittsburgh: University of Pittsburgh Press, 2006), p. 137.

86. See ibid. Also see Charles T. Call, "The Mugging of a Success Story: Justice and Security Reform in El Salvador," in Charles T. Call, ed., *Constructing Justice and Security After War* (Washington, DC: United States Institute of Peace Press, 2007), pp. 29–67.

87. "El Salvador at a Glance," World Bank Group, September 28, 2007. Available at http://devdata.worldbank.org/AAG/slv_aag.pdf (accessed October 1, 2008).

88. Data from World Bank, *World Development Indicators* (WDI), and *CIA World Factbook 2007*.

89. *United Nations Human Development Report*, various years; table: inequality in income or expenditure.

90. See Mitchell A. Seligson, "Thirty Years of Transformation in the Agrarian Structure of El Salvador, 1961–1991," *Latin American Research Review*, Vol. 30, No. 3 (1995): pp. 43–74; Martin Diskin, "Distilled Conclusions: The Disappearance of the Agrarian Question in El Salvador," *Latin American Research Review*, Vol. 31, No. 2 (1996): pp. 111–126; and Jeffery M. Paige, "Land Reform and Agrarian Revolution in El Salvador: Comment on Seligson and Diskin," *Latin American Research Review*, Vol. 31, No. 2 (1996): pp. 127–139.

91. The FMLN appears to have followed the logic that so long as the government and the army did not blatantly cheat, its broader social and economic agenda could eventually be enacted by means of ballot instead of bullet. After all, a majority of Salvadorans could see the benefits of an at least modest redistribution of land and wealth.

92. A concise overview of economic reforms can be found in Call, "Assessing El Salvador's Transition," pp. 410–412. Also see Paris, *At War's End*, pp. 124–128.

Chapter 6. Uganda

1. Paul Collier and Ritva Reinikka, eds., *Uganda's Recovery: The Role of Farms, Firms, and Government* (Washington, DC: World Bank, 2001).

2. Aili Mari Tripp, "The Changing Face of Authoritarianism in Africa: The Case of Uganda," *Africa Today*, Vol. 50, No. 3 (Spring 2004): p. 4.

3. A.B.K. Kasozi, *The Social Origins of Violence in Uganda: 1964-1985* (Montreal: McGill-Queen's University Press, 1994), p. 3.

4. Rita M. Byrnes, "The Society and Its Environment," in *Uganda: A Country Study* (Washington, DC: Government Printing Office for the Library of Congress, 1990), available at http://lcweb2.loc.gov/frd/cs/ugtoc.html (accessed October 1, 2008); Samwiri Karugire, *Roots of Instability in Uganda*, 2nd ed. (Kampala: Fountain, 1996); Kasozi, *The Social Origins*.

5. Uganda's name resulted from a British mistranslation of "Buganda," according to Karugire, *Roots of Instability in Uganda*, p. 13.

6. Ibid., p. 18.

7. Ibid., pp. 16–17.

8. Ibid., pp. 18–19.

9. Jeremy M. Weinstein, *Inside Rebellion: The Politics of Insurgent Violence* (New York: Cambridge University Press, 2007), p. 64.

10. Kasozi, *The Social Origins*, pp. 53-54.

11. Riccardo Orizio, *Talk of the Devil: Encounters with Seven Dictators*, trans. Avril Bardoni (New York: Walker, 2002), p. 24.

12. Figures are taken from the Polity IV database.

13. Kasozi, *The Social Origins*, p. 104.

14. Severine Rugumamu and Osman Gbla, *Studies in Reconstruction and Capacity-Building in Post-Conflict Countries in Africa: Some Lessons of Experience from Uganda* (Harare, Zimbabwe: African Capacity Building Foundation, 2003).

15. These figures come from my database, which includes figures from a variety of sources, such as the Correlates of War (COW) data set by J. David Singer and Melvin Small and reports found in the press.

16. Weinstein, *Inside Rebellion*, pp. 55, 67. The following account draws heavily on Weinstein, pp. 62–71 and 219–229; Ondoga Ori Amaza, *Museveni's Long March from Guerilla to Statesman* (Kampala: Fountain, 1998), pp. 23–38; and Onyango Odongo, *A Political History of Uganda: The Origin of Museveni's Referendum 2000* (Kampala: Monitor, 2000), pp. 67–68.

17. Amaza, *Museveni's Long March*, pp. 30–31.

18. Weinstein, *Inside Rebellion,* p. 71.

19. Kasozi, *The Social Origins*, p. 183.

20. Weinstein, *Inside Rebellion*, p. 220.

21. Ibid.

22. Amin had taken exile in Libya, and later in Saudi Arabia, where he died in 2003.

23. Dan M. Mudoola, "Institution Building: The Case of the NRM and the Military in Uganda, 1986-1989," in Holger Bernt Hansen and Michael Twaddle, eds., *Changing Uganda: The Dilemmas of Structural Adjustment and Revolutionary Change* (London: James Currey, 1991), p. 233.

24. Kasozi, *Social Origins*, p. 193.

25. John Kiyaga-Nsubuga, "Uganda: The Politics of 'Consolidation' under Museveni's Regime, 1996-2003," in Taisier M. Ali and Robert O. Matthews, eds., *Durable Peace: Challenges for Peacebuilding in Africa* (Toronto: University of Toronto Press, 2004), p. 89.

26. Kasozi, *Social Origins*, p. 196.

27. Joshua B. Rubongoya, *Regime Hegemony in Museveni's Uganda* (New York: Palgrave Macmillan, 2007), p. 86.

28. "Joint Assistance Strategy for the Republic of Uganda (2005-2009)," *Country Assistance Strategy* (Washington, DC: World Bank, May 2006).

29. Amaza, *Museveni's Long March*, p. 32.

30. Weinstein, *Inside Rebellion*, pp. 266, 269.

31. E. A. Brett, "Neutralising the Use of Force in Uganda: The Role of the Military in Politics," *Journal of Modern African Studies*, Vol. 33, No. 1 (March 1995): pp. 129–152.

32. Thomas P. Ofcansky, "National Security," in *Uganda: A Country Study*, p. 54.

33. Mudoola, "Institution Building."

34. Weinstein, *Inside Rebellion,* p. 142. This passage relies on Weinstein, pp. 140–145 and 268–270.

35. Rubongoya, *Regime Hegemony*, p. 59.

36. Mudoola, "Institution Building," p. 238. See also Brett, "Neutralising the Use of Force in Uganda."

37. Mudoola, "Institution Building," p. 237.

38. Amaza, *Museveni's Long March*, pp. 149–150.

39. Mudoola, "Institution Building," p. 237.

40. Ibid.; and Kiyaga-Nsubuga, "Uganda," p. 90.

41. Nelson Kasfir, "The Ugandan Elections of 1989: Power, Populism, and Democratization," in Hansen and Twaddle, eds., *Changing Uganda*, pp. 247–278.

42. This paragraph relies primarily on Collier and Reinikka, *Uganda's Recovery.*

43. Tim Carrington, "Poor Lands Try to Cope with Residue of War: Their Leftover Armies." *Wall Street Journal*, December 10, 1994, p. 1.

44. Michael Clark, "In the Spotlight: The Lord's Resistance Army (LRA)," Center for Defense Information, October 27, 2004, available at http://www.cdi .org/program/document.cfm?documentid=2606&programID=39&from_ page=../friendlyversion/printversion.cfm (accessed October 1, 2008).

45. "The Lord's Resistance Army (LRA)," GlobalSecurity.org, available at http://www.globalsecurity.org/military/world/para/lra.html (accessed October 1, 2008); Kevin C. Dunn, "Uganda: The Lord's Resistance Army," *Review of African Political Economy*, Vol. 31, No. 99, ICTs "Virtual Colonisation" and Political Economy (March 2004): p. 141; Steve Bloomfield, "Uganda and Rebels Set Truce After 100,000 Deaths," *Independent*, August 29, 2006.

46. See DeNeen L. Brown, "A Child's Hell in the Lord's Resistance Army," *Washington Post*, (May 10, 2006), p. C01.

47. Payam Akhavan, "The Lord's Resistance Army Case: Uganda's Submission of the First State Referral to the International Criminal Court," *American Journal of International Law*, Vol. 99, No. 2 (April 2005): p. 409.

48. Ibid., p. 407.

49. "In-Depth: Life in Northern Uganda; UGANDA: Nature, Structure, and Ideology of the LRA," IRIN, UNOCHA, available at http://www.irinnews.org/ InDepthMain.aspx?InDepthId=23&ReportId=65772 (accessed October 1, 2008).

50. Ibid.

51. "The Lord's Resistance Army (LRA)."

52. Clark, "In the Spotlight." See also Martin Plaut, "Profile: Uganda's LRA rebels," *BBC News*, February 6, 2004, available at http://news.bbc.co.uk/go/pr/ fr/-/2/hi/africa/3462901.stm (accessed October 1, 2008).

53. "In-Depth."

54. "Conflict History: Uganda," International Crisis Group, available at http:// www.crisisgroup.org/home/index.cfm?action=conflict_search&1=1&t=1&c_ country=111 (accessed October 1, 2008).

55. "Timeline: Uganda," *BBC News*, March 13, 2008, available at http://news .bbc.co.uk/go/pr/fr/-/2/hi/africa/country_profiles/1069181.stm (accessed October 1, 2008).

56. "Uganda: From Conflict to Sustained Growth and Deep Reductions in Poverty," Shanghai Poverty Conference: Case Study Summary, available at http:// info.worldbank.org/etools/docs/reducingpoverty/case/29/summary/Uganda Country%20Summary.pdf (accessed November 4, 2008).

57. The interim national government was later extended for an additional five years.

58. Mudoola, "Institution Building," p. 235.

59. Rubongoya, *Regime Hegemony*, p. 73.

60. Yoweri Museveni, *The Path of Liberation* (Kampala: Government Printer, 1989), p. 3.

61. Rugumamu and Gbla, *Studies in Reconstruction*; Brett, "Neutralising the Use of Force in Uganda."

62. Amaza, *Museveni's Long March*, p. 153.

63. The Resistance Councils were renamed Local Councils in 1995.

64. Weinstein, *Inside Rebellion*, p. 178.

65. Tarsis Bazana Kabwegyere, *People's Choice, People's Power: Challenges and Prospects of Democracy in Uganda* (Kampala: Fountain, 2000), p. 57.

66. Mudoola, "Institution Building."

67. Thomas P. Ofcansky, *Uganda: Tarnished Pearl of Africa* (Boulder: Westview Press, 1996).

68. Ofcansky, *Uganda*.

69. Amaza, *Museveni's Long March*, p. 156.

70. Justus Mugaju, "An Historical Background to Uganda's No-Party Democracy," in Justus Mugaju and J. Oloka-Onyango, eds., *No-Party Democracy in Uganda: Myths and Realities* (Kampala: Fountain, 1998), p. 8; and Kiyaga-Nsubuga, "Uganda," p. 89.

71. Rubongoya, *Regime Hegemony*, pp. 175–176.

72. Will Ross, "Museveni: Uganda's Fallen Angel," *BBC News*, November 30, 2005.

73. Rubongoya, *Regime Hegemony*, p. 4.

74. World Bank, *Uganda: Growing Out of Poverty*, 2nd ed. (Washington, DC: World Bank, 1997); and World Bank, *Uganda: The Challenge for Growth and Poverty Reduction*, Country Economic Memorandum, Report no. 14313-49 (Washington, DC: World Bank, 1995).

75. Petter Langseth and Justus Mugaju, eds., *Post-Conflict Uganda: Towards an Effective Civil Service* (Kampala: Fountain, 1996), p. 18.

76. Museveni, *The Path of Liberation*, p. 33.

77. Kiyaga-Nsubuga, "Uganda," p. 94. This paragraph relies on this source.

78. Rubongoya, *Regime Hegemony*, pp. 88-89.

79. Ross, "Museveni."

80. Amaza, *Museveni's Long March*, p. 162.

81. Collier and Reinikka, *Uganda's Recovery*.

82. Rubongoya, *Regime Hegemony*, p. 153.

83. Economist Intelligence Unit, *Country Data for Uganda*, based on World Bank data.

84. Rubongoya, *Regime Hegemony*, p. 154.

85. Ibid., p. 220. Note that Uganda was criticized in 2005 for shifting policies in favor of "abstinence-only" HIV/AIDS education programs.

Chapter 7. The Republic of Sudan: A Collapsed Negotiated Settlement

1. Donald Rothchild and Caroline Hartzell, "The Peace Process in Sudan, 1971-1972" in Licklider, ed., *Stopping the Killing*, pp. 63–93.

2. Monica Duffy Toft, "Getting Religion? The Puzzling Case of Islam and Civil War," *International Security*, Vol. 31, No. 4 (Spring 2007): pp. 97–131.

3. Ibid.

4. "Historic Sudan Peace Accord Signed," CNN, January 9, 2005, available at http://www.cnn.com/2005/WORLD/africa/01/09/sudan.signing/index.html (accessed October 1, 2008). A copy of the treaty can be found at the United States Institute of Peace website, http://www.usip.org/library/pa/sudan/cpa01092005/cpa_toc.html (accessed October 1, 2008).

5. Even though the rebel groups had different names, the second war could be labeled a recurrence of the first conflict. In any case, the two wars extended through every single regime in Sudan's independent history.

6. Sudan achieved independence from the Anglo-Egyptian "Condominium" in 1956.

7. CIA World Factbook 2006. Available at https://www.cia.gov/library/publications/the-world-factbook/index.html (accessed October 1, 2008).

8. Various sources and CIA Factbook 2006.

9. Donald Petterson, Inside Sudan: Political Islam, Conflict, and Catastrophe (Boulder: Westview Press, 1999), p. 5.

10. Besançon, "Relative Resources," p. 409.

11. Francis M. Deng, "Sudan—Civil War and Genocide," Middle East Quarterly, Vol. 8, No. 1 (Winter 2001): pp. 13–21.

12. Francis M. Deng, "Sudan's Struggle to Become One Nation," Christian Science Monitor, February 1, 1990, p. 19.

13. Deng, "Sudan—Civil War and Genocide."

14. Milton Viorst, "Fundamentalism in Power: Sudan's Islamic Experiment," Foreign Affairs, Vol. 74, No. 3 (May/June 1995): pp. 45–58.

15. Ibid.

16. H.A.R. Gibb, "Islam," in R. C. Zaehner, ed., Encyclopedia of the World's Religions (New York: Barnes and Noble, 1997), pp. 189–195.

17. Viorst, "Fundamentalism in Power."

18. Deng, "Sudan—Civil War and Genocide."

19. Ibid.

20. Deng notes that the Arabs were interested in the material value of blacks as slaves and thus had no wish to integrate with them. He also notes that had the Arabs and Muslims successfully converted southern Black Africans to Islam, they could no longer have engaged in legal slave raids against them, given Islam's prohibition of enslaving fellow Muslims. See ibid. Besides the slave trade, an additional incentive for northerners to dominate the South was that it was from the South that the Nile flowed.

21. Petterson, Inside Sudan, pp. 6–8.

22. Fergus Nicoll, The Mahdi of Sudan and the Death of General Gordon, new ed. (Gloucestershire, UK: Sutton, 2005).

23. Petterson, Inside Sudan, pp. 6–8.

24. Viorst, "Fundamentalism in Power."

25. International Crisis Group (ICG), "God, Oil, and Country: Changing the Logic of War in Sudan," ICG Africa Report, No. 39 (January 28, 2002), p. 8, available at: http://www.crisisgroup.org/projects/africa/sudan/reports/A400534_28012002.pdf (accessed October 1, 2008).

26. Francis M. Deng, "Scramble for Souls: Religious Intervention among the Dinka in Sudan," in Abdullahi Ahmed an-Na'im, ed., *Proselytizing and Communal Self-Determination in Africa* (New York: Orbis, 1999), pp. 191–227.

27. D. Michelle Domke, "Civil War in Sudan: Resources or Religion?" Inventory of Conflict and Environment (ICE) case study, American University, available at http://www.american.edu/ted/ice/sudan.htm (accessed October 1, 2008).

28. See Abu Bakar El Obeid, "The Political Consequences of the Addis Ababa Agreement," *Publications of the Political Science Association in Uppsala*, Vol. 86, No. 2 (1980): p. 69.

29. Rothchild and Hartzell, "The Peace Process in Sudan."

30. Francis M. Deng, *War of Visions: Conflict of Identities in the Sudan* (Washington, DC: Brookings Institution, 1995), cited in ICG, "God, Oil, and Country," p. 8.

31. Edgar O'Ballance, *The Secret War in the Sudan: 1955–1972* (Hamden, CT: Archon Books, 1977).

32. ICG, "God, Oil, and Country," p. 9.

33. The largest opposition movement was Sudan African National Union (SANU), which initially sought a peaceful solution to the Southern Sudan problem. As the civil war intensified, the SANU itself took up arms. See Dunstan Wai, *The African-Arab Conflict in Sudan* (New York: Africana, 1981), p. 90. For more on the Anya-Nya, see Cecil Eprile, *War and Peace in Sudan: 1955–1972* (London: David and Charles, 1974), pp. 90–102; and O'Ballance, *The Secret War in the Sudan*, pp. 57–67.

34. Rothchild and Hartzell, "The Peace Process in Sudan," p. 78. Sadiq el-Mandi's second period in office started in 1985, and he was ousted by Bashir in 1989.

35. After the June 1967 Six Day War, Israel was supporting Anya-Nya troops militarily and financially. See, e.g., Eprile, *War and Peace in Sudan*, pp. 140–41; O'Ballance, *The Secret War in the Sudan*, pp. 126–28; and ICG, "God, Oil, and Country," p. 10.

36. Rothchild and Hartzell, "The Peace Process in Sudan"; and ICG, "God, Oil, and Country," p. 11.

37. El Obeid, "The Political Consequences," p. 104.

38. See ibid., p. 101; Nelson Kasfir, "Southern Sudanese Politics since the Addis Ababa Agreement," *African Affairs*, Vol. 76, No. 303 (April 1977): p. 145; and O'Ballance, *The Secret War in the Sudan*, p. 26. On the problem of a gap between policy and political utility generally, see Ivan Arreguín-Toft, "How to Lose a War on Terror: A Comparative Analysis of a Counterinsurgency Success and Failure," in Jan Ångström and Isabelle Duyvesteyn, eds., *Understanding Victory and Defeat in Contemporary War* (London: Routledge, 2007), pp. 142–167. Arreguín-Toft introduces the concept of "cross-audience utility" to explain why historically ineffective (or counterproductive) strategies or policies nevertheless find repeated support from political elites.

39. El Obeid, "The Political Consequences," p. 81.

40. Kasfir in fact attributes both the success of the agreement as a cease-fire and its duration (his essay predates the collapse of the agreement in 1983) to the leadership and personality of Nimeiri, Alier, and Lagu. See Kasfir, "Southern Sudanese Politics," p. 145; and O'Ballance, *The Secret War in the Sudan*, p. 78.

41. As quoted in El Obeid, "The Political Consequences," p. 37.

42. Kasfir, "Southern Sudanese Politics," p. 148.

43. Ibid., p. 149.

Chapter 8. The Republic of Sudan: Prospects for Peace

1. Interestingly, one interpretation that gained respectability and support after 1973 was Salafism, or the view that the humiliation of the Arab peoples at the hands of Israel (and the West more broadly) could only be explained as a collective punishment by God against a people who had fallen from the true faith. Once Muslims returned to the true practice—as interpreted by these conservative clerics—God would reward the Arab people with a civilization akin to that of ancient times and Arab humiliation would end. For a short introduction to Salafism as it relates to terrorism and conflict with the "West," see Marc Sageman, "Statement of Marc Sageman to the National Commission on Terrorist Attacks upon the United States," July 9, 2003.

2. See O'Ballance, *The Secret War in the Sudan*, pp. 100–101.

3. Ibid., p. 105.

4. Chevron discovered oil in Southern Sudan in 1974 and began drilling in 1977. In 1980 major finds were made at the company's Unity Field near Bentiu in Aali an Nil province. See Helen Chapin Metz, ed., *Sudan: A Country Study* (Washington, DC: GPO for the Library of Congress, 1991), available at http://countrystudies.us/sudan (accessed October 1, 2008).

5. Garang, as a Sudanese army officer, had been absorbed into the government after the implementation of the agreement and was sent to dispose of five hundred mutineers at Bor. But instead of crushing the rebels, he joined them. See John Garang: 1945–2005," *Times*, August 2, 2005, available at http://www.timesonline.co.uk/tol/comment/obituaries/article550465.ece (accessed October 1, 2008). Garang fled with other rebel leaders to Itang, Ethiopia, where they delegated responsibility for the SPLM/A. See Gatkuoth Dak Lam, "Dialogue with the Armed Groups in the South" (http://www.southsudan.net/gatkuoth.html, no longer active). The SPLA is the military wing of the Sudanese People's Liberation Movement (SPLM). Henceforth the two entities will be referred to as SPLM/A. In 1991 the leadership of the SPLA split, with a new faction led by an ethnic Nuer, Riek Machar, dubbing itself SPLA-United, which split itself numerous times thereafter. According to one study, the ensuing "internecine fighting soon became more terrible than the war between Sudanese army and the rebels," and "such inter-group strife has become the favored activity of the various rebel factions." See "The Self-Mutilation of Sudan," *Swiss Review of World Affairs* (July 3, 1995).

6. Administratively, this redivision of the South made little sense, due to the lack of adequate personnel to administer even a single administrative unit. J. Millard Burr and Robert O. Collins, *Requiem for the Sudan: War, Drought, and Disaster Relief on the Nile* (Boulder: Westview Press, 1995), p. 15.

7. Ibid. See also ICG, "God, Oil, and Country."

8. The simultaneous amputation of a person's right hand and left foot.

9. R. K. Badal, "The Addis Ababa Agreement Ten Years After: An Assessment," in Mom Kou Nhail Arou and Benaiah Yongo-Bure, eds., *North-South Relations in Sudan Since the Addis Ababa Agreement* (Khartoum: Khartoum University Press, 1988), p. 32. Cited in Burr and Collins, *Requiem for the Sudan*, p. 16.

10. ICG, "God, Oil, and Country," p. 13.

11. O'Ballance, *The Secret War in the Sudan*, p. 139.

12. Ibid., p. 142.

13. Andrew McGregor, "Terrorism and Violence in Sudan: The Islamist Manipulation of Darfur," *Jamestown Foundation, Terrorism Monitor*, Vol. 3, No. 12 (June 17, 2005): pp. 3–5.

14. Burr and Collins, *Requiem for the Sudan*, p. 157.

15. Timothy Carney, "The Sudan: Political Islam and Terrorism," in Robert I. Rotberg, ed., *Battling Terrorism in the Horn of Africa*, new ed. (Washington, DC: Brookings Institution Press, 2005), pp. 119-140. The Muslim members of the coup authority, the Revolutionary Command Council, all subsequently made Qur'anic allegiance to Turabi. Turabi is widely believed to have been the key figure behind most of Sudan's policy initiatives until his ousting late in 1999 and his arrest in 2001. After mid-1993, U.S. embassy reporting explicitly acknowledged Turabi's preeminence in the power structure. See Petterson, *Inside Sudan*, p. 85. Burr and Collins, writing about the 1989 coup, say that the coup was carried out by "unsophisticated brigadiers of Sudan army, supported financially by members of the National Islamic Front. They were soldiers, but the policy decisions were made by the Islamic politicians and polemicists led by Hassan el-Turabi." Burr and Collins, *Requiem for the Sudan*, pp. 2–3.

16. Prior to the 1989 coup, the NIF had not fared particularly well in the country's only national election of 1986, gaining only 6 percent of the vote. See Randolph Martin, "Sudan's Perfect War," *Foreign Affairs*, Vol. 81, No. 2 (March/April 2002): p. 111.

17. ICG, "God, Oil, and Country," p. 14.

18. O'Ballance, *The Secret War in the Sudan*, p. 168.

19. "Islam's Dark Side: The Orwellian State of Sudan," *Economist*, June 24, 1995, p. 21.

20. O'Ballance, *The Secret War in the Sudan*, p. 179.

21. Ibid., p. 184.

22. Ibid., p. 185.

23. Ibid., p. 188.

24. Ibid., p. 189.

25. Ibid., p. 192.

26. "Sudan Oil and Conflict Timeline," *Sudan Update*, available at http://www.sudanupdate.org/REPORTS/Oil/21oc.html (accessed October 1, 2008).

27. See "Pointers: Egypt-Sudan," *Africa Confidential*, Vol, 42, No. 2 (January 26, 2001): p. 8. Other reports have the North using new helicopter gunships, not in coordinated offensives against the SPLM/A, but to assault noncombatants in oil development areas. See "Sudan: Delusions of Peace," *Africa Confidential*, Vol. 42, No. 16 (August 10, 2001): p. 3.

28. "Sudan: Opening New Fronts in the Oil War," *Africa Confidential*, Vol, 42, No. 6 (March 23, 2001): p. 2.

29. Ibid., p. 3.

30. "East Africa: Conflicting Agendas," *Africa Confidential*, Vol. 43, No. 1 (January 11, 2002): pp. 5–6.

31. "Sudan: Unconstructive Engagement," *Africa Confidential*, Vol. 43, No. 4 (February 22, 2002): p. 4.

32. "Sudan: The Fire Does Not Cease," *Africa Confidential*, Vol. 43, No. 10 (May 17, 2002): p. 4. Although this initiative at first succeeded and later failed, it did facilitate eventual negotiations and U.S. involvement.

33. "Sudan: Calling the Shots at Machakos," *Africa Confidential*, Vol. 43, No. 15 (July 26, 2002): p. 1.

34. "Pointers: Sudan/Iraq," *Africa Confidential*, Vol. 44, No. 5 (March 7, 2003): p. 8.

35. "Sudan: Desperate Darfur," *Africa Confidential*, Vol. 45, No. 10 (May 14, 2004): p. 2.

36. Ibid., p. 3; "Sudan: Joy in the South, Silence in the North," *Africa Confidential*, Vol. 46, No. 2 (January 12, 2005): p. 1.

37. "Sudan: Mass Murder," *Africa Confidential*, Vol. 45, No. 9 (April 30, 2004): p. 2.

38. "Sudan: Joy in the South," p. 2.

39. Ibid., p. 3.

40. Ibid.

41. Ibid.

42. On this point, see Toft, "Getting Religion?"

43. "The Comprehensive Peace Agreement between the Government of the Republic of the Sudan and the Sudan People's Liberation Movement/Sudan People's Liberation Army," January 9, 2005, p. 88, available at http://www.relief web.int/rw/RWB.NSF/db900SID/EVIU-6AZBDB?OpenDocument (accessed October 1, 2008), henceforth CPA 2005.

44. Ibid., p. 87.

45. It is actually not clear whether the establishment of Sharia throughout Sudan is sought for its own sake or as a way to enhance the legitimacy and resources available to Bashir and the NIF. Alternately, political elites who have attempted over the years to qualify the application of Sharia—either its scope or its content—have suffered as a result. Thus, on this policy as elsewhere, elites in Khartoum appear to be most interested in acquiring and maintaining their power, and least interested in any outcomes beyond that. On the importance of Islamic legitimacy as tenure support, see Toft, "Getting Religion?" On the problem of the separation of real-world and tenure utility, see Arreguín-Toft, "How to Lose a War on Terror."

46. United Nations Mission in the Sudan, "Report to the Secretary-General on the Sudan," S/2007/500 (August 20, 2007), p. 3.

47. Ibid., p. 2.

48. Adam O'Brien, "Peace on the Rocks: Sudan's Comprehensive Peace Agreement," Enough Project, Washington, DC: Center for American Progress, February 19, 2009, available at http://www.enoughproject.org/files/publications/sudan_peace_agreement_revised_0.pdf.

49. Ban Ki-moon, "Report of the Secretary-General on the Sudan," New York: United Nations Security Council, January 30, 2009, available at http://www .reliefweb.int/rw/rwb.nsf/db900SID/EGUA-7KUMQQ?OpenDocument.

50. UNMIS, "Report to the Secretary-General on the Sudan," p. 16.

51. Ibid., pp. 4–5.

52. See, e.g., "Sudan: Delusions of Peace," p. 2.

Chapter 9. Conclusion

1. Ali Allawi makes it quite clear that sectarian divisions were real in Iraq, but that the policy decisions, especially the lack of planning and the general ignorance and incompetence of the Coalition Provisional Authority, did little to dampen those tensions and in fact exasperated them. See Ali A. Allawi, *The Occupation of Iraq: Winning the War, Losing the Peace* (New Haven: Yale University Press, 2007).

2. Since the invasion and occupation of Iraq, there have been a number of books detailing the lead-up to and the near-term consequences of the American invasion and occupation. The best accounts and those that informed this analysis include Allawi, *The Occupation of Iraq*; George Packer, *The Assassin's Gate: America in Iraq* (New York: Farrar, Straus and Giroux, 2005); Michael R. Gordon and General Bernard E. Trainor, *Cobra II: The Inside Story of the Invasion and Occupation of Iraq* (New York: Pantheon, 2006), Thomas E. Ricks, *Fiasco: The American Military Adventure in Iraq* (New York: Penguin, 2007); James Fallows, *Blind into Baghdad: America's War in Iraq* (New York: Vintage, 2006). On the decision-making process within the Bush Administration itself, see Ron Suskind, *The Price of Loyalty: George W. Bush, the White House and the Education of Paul O'Neill* (New York: Simon and Schuster, 2004); and Ron Suskind, *The One Percent Doctrine: Deep Inside America's Pursuit of Its Enemies Since 9/11* (New York: Simon and Schuster, 2006).

3. For a scholarly assessment of the Bush administration's foreign policy, see Robert Jervis, "Understanding the Bush Doctrine," *Political Science Quarterly*, Vol. 118, No. 3 (2003): pp. 365–388.

4. For a contrary view, see John J. Mearsheimer and Stephen M. Walt, *Can Saddam Be Contained? History Says Yes*, Research Paper, Belfer Center for Science and International Affairs, John F. Kennedy School of Government, Harvard University, November 12, 2002.

5. See especially Gordon and Trainor, *Cobra II*, chapter 8 on the planning for the postwar occupation period.

6. Many documents from these early State Department efforts have since been released to the public under the U.S. Freedom of Information Act (FOIA) and can be downloaded from the National Security Archive at George Washington University, available at http://www.gwu.edu/~nsarchiv/NSAEBB/NSAEBB198/index. htm (accessed November 2008).

7. See Office of Reconstruction and Humanitarian Assistance, *Unified Mission Plan for Post Hostilities Iraq*, Draft, Version 2 (April 3, 2003).

8. Allawi, *The Occupation of Iraq*, p. 444.

9. On the politics of Garner's appointment, his team, and their efforts, see Ricks, *Fiasco*, pp. 80–81 and 101–111; Packer, *The Assassin's Gate*, pp. 120–135; Gordon and Trainor, *Cobra II*, pp. 152–160.

10. The Bush administration was no doubt dedicated to the idea of not being bound by history and was determined to make its own. Suskind develops this theme most fully in a 2004 *New York Times Magazine* article and includes an aide claiming, "We're history's actors . . . and you, all of you, will be left to just study what we do" as *they* create new realities. Ron Suskind, "Faith, Certainty and the Presidency of George W. Bush," *New York Times Magazine*, October 17, 2004. Available at http://www.nytimes.com/2004/10/17/magazine/17BUSH.html ?ex=1255665600&en=890a96189e162076&ei=5090&partner=rssuserland (accessed November 2008).

11. In January 2008 the Iraqi Parliament passed "a bill allowing for the reinstatement of low-level Baath Party members for certain government jobs. The legislation also allows for those former Baathists with high-level jobs to receive a pension." See Michael E. O'Hanlon and Jason H. Campbell, *Iraq Index: Tracking Variables of Reconstruction and Security in Post-Saddam Iraq* (Washington, DC: Brookings Institution, August 28, 2008), p. 13. Available at http://www .brookings.edu/saban/iraq-index.aspx (accessed November 2008).

12. CPA orders 1 and 2 dismissed at least 400,000 people from both the armed forces and the intelligence services. Allawi, *The Occupation of Iraq*, p. 157.

13. For a recent scholarly account of occupation in theory and practice, see David M. Edelstein, "Occupational Hazards: Why Military Occupations Succeed or Fail," *International Security*, Vol. 29, No. 1 (Summer 2004): pp. 49–91.

14. One measure of this continued lack of security is the number of internally displaced persons (IDPs) in Iraq. An August 2008 report shows that 2,770,000 individuals have thus far been displaced since April 2003—an increase from previous years. See O'Hanlon and Campbell, *Iraq Index*, p. 32. Additionally, the International Organization of Migration reported that only 1 percent of all displaced Iraqis (including figures prior to April 2003) had returned to their homes by March 31, 2008. Kim Gamel, "Many Iraqis Just Want to Go Home," *Washington Times*, May 28, 2008. Cited in O'Hanlon and Campbell, *Iraq Index*, p. 32.

15. See Allawi, *The Occupation of Iraq*, especially chapters 2 and 21 on the perils of identity and daily life in postwar occupied Iraq. Additionally, the Independent Commission on the Security Forces of Iraq, headed by retired Marine General Jim Jones, argued in 2007 that "long-term security advances are impossible without political progress" and political reconciliation. See Karen DeYoung, "Iraqi Army Unable to Take Over within a Year, Report Says," *Washington Post*, September 6, 2007, p. A01. Available at http://www.washingtonpost.com/wp-dyn/ content/article/2007/09/05/AR2007090501282.html (accessed November 2008).

16. March 2008 survey data show an increase in Iraqis who thought that the security situation in Iraq had improved in the previous six months. Responding to a more general question in February 2008 ("How would you say things are going in Iraq overall these days?"), opinions differed depending on whether the individual was Shi'a, Sunni, or Kurd. Whereas the Shi'a had the most favorable response to the question, Sunnis held the most negative opinion on the situation in Iraq, and Kurds were in the middle. This appears to show improvement from a September

2006 survey, where 75 percent of Iraqis surveyed rated security conditions in the country as "poor." See O'Hanlon and Campbell, *Iraq Index*, pp. 50, 59.

17. While there appears to have been a spike in fatalities and numbers of persons wounded around April and May 2008, data available from the *Iraq Report* (updated August 28, 2008) show that for several months thereafter, levels of violence largely decreased, returning to the lower intensity of November 2007. See, for example, ibid., various charts.

18. A July 2007 article reported that retired Marine General Jim Jones thought that Iraq looked "better than he expected" when he visited the country. See "U.S. Observers Note Progress in Iraq Surge," *CBS News*, July 30, 2007. Available at http://www.cbsnews.com/stories/2007/07/30/iraq/main3109236.shtml (accessed November 2008). In addition, the 2007 Jones Commission report stated that "U.S. and Iraqi alliances with Sunni tribal forces in Anbar province have produced 'real and encouraging' military progress and intelligence cooperation, and there are promising signs they can be replicated elsewhere. Such relationships, however, 'will have to be managed very carefully in order for them to contribute to Iraq's long-term security.'" See DeYoung, "Iraqi Army Unable to Take Over within a Year, Report Says."

19. Further *Iraq Index* data tells us that the insurgency experienced an overall decline between November 2007 and May 2008, with the largest numbers of daily attacks during that period taking place in Baghdad, Ninawa, and Salah ad Din. See O'Hanlon and Campbell, *Iraq Index*, p. 27.

20. Another option, of course, is the legal partition of Iraq into three states, resulting essentially in a victory for the Kurds and Shi'a and a defeat for the Sunnis, but in all likelihood a robust peace. However, this policy would never be advocated or supported by the United States, the region, or the international community. One need only consider the historical record of partition or the current stalemate over Kosovo's status. A strong moral case for partition can be found in Peter W. Galbraith, *The End of Iraq: How American Incompetence Created a War without End* (New York: Simon and Schuster, 2006).

21. Assessments of reconstruction efforts since 2003 can be found in the quarterly and semiannual reports submitted to Congress by the Special Inspector General for Iraq Reconstruction (SIGIR). The January 30, 2009, report indicates that progress is being made but that security and integration of Sunnis into security institutions remain central concerns. Available at http://www.sigir.mil/reports/quarterlyreports/Jan09/pdf/Report_-_January_2009_LoRes.pdf. For an overall assessment of Iraq reconstruction efforts since 2003, see Special Inspector General for Iraq Reconstruction, *Hard Lessons: The Iraq Reconstruction Experience* (Washington, DC: U.S. Government Printing Office, 2009), available at http://www.sigir.mil/hardlessons/pdfs/Hard_Lessons_Report.pdf.

22. The Security Agreement (SA) was signed on January 1, 2009. The SA defines the legal basis for the continued U.S. military presence in Iraq until December 31, 2011, at which time U.S. troops are supposed to depart (unless the Iraqi government requests their earlier departure or an extension beyond that date, and the United States agrees).

23. Sectarian divisions remain a critical problem, especially in the Ministry of Interior, which is responsible for the various police forces (the regular police ser-

vice assigned to the eighteen provinces, national police, and border troops). As of October 21, 2008, there were roughly 566,000 members of the security forces, with 209,000 regular police and 53,000 national police subordinate to the Ministry of Interior and 263,000 forces under the Ministry of Defense. For a recent assessment, see Anthony H. Cordesman, "The Iraq War: Progress in the Fighting and Security," Center for Strategic and International Studies, February 21, 2009, available at http://www.csis.org. For general statistics on Iraq, including the security forces, see Michael O'Hanlon and Jason Campbell, *The Iraq Index* (multiple issues since November 2003), available at http://www.brookings.edu/iraqindex.

24. Thomas Hobbes lived through both the Thirty Years' War (1618–1648) and, closer to home, the English civil war (1642–1651). His now famous description of life under anarchy—his characterization of the political environment of civil war—is recorded in his most influential text, *Leviathan*, which he published in 1651. See Thomas Hobbes, *Leviathan*, ed. Richard Tuck (New York: Cambridge University Press, 1991), p. 89.

25. See Arreguín-Toft, *How the Weak Win Wars*; and Arreguín-Toft, "Unconventional Deterrence."

26. Richard N. Falk, "Hard Choices and Tragic Dilemmas," *Nation,* Vol. 257, No. 21 (December 1993): p. 757.

27. Weinberger, "The Uses of Military Power"; and Powell, "U.S. Forces."

28. The most recent International Crisis Group assessment of security in Afghanistan states: "Seven years after the U.S.-led intervention in Afghanistan the country is still at war against extremists and has developed few resilient institutions." See "Security in Afghanistan," International Crisis Group, updated April 2009. Available at http://www.crisisgroup.org/home/index.cfm?id=3071 (accessed June 2009).

Bibliography

Acemoglu, Daron, and James A. Robinson. "A Theory of Political Transitions." *American Economic Review*, Vol. 91, No. 4 (September 2001): pp. 938–963.

Akhavan, Payam. "The Lord's Resistance Army Case: Uganda's Submission of the First State Referral to the International Criminal Court." *American Journal of International Law*, Vol. 99, No. 2 (April 2005): pp. 403–421.

Allawi, Ali A. *The Occupation of Iraq: Winning the War, Losing the Peace.* New Haven: Yale University Press, 2007.

Amaya, Edgardo Alberto. "Security Policy in El Salvador, 1992–2002." IN John Bailey and Lucía Dammert, eds., *Public Security and Police Reform in the Americas.* Pittsburgh: University of Pittsburgh Press, 2006, pp. 132–147.

Amaza, Ondoga Ori. *Museveni's Long March from Guerilla to Statesman.* Kampala: Fountain, 1998.

Arreguín-Toft, Ivan. "Crossing the Line: The Problem of Interstate Boundaries as Insurgent Sanctuary." Paper presented at the Annual Convention of the American Political Science Association, Washington, DC, September 2005.

———. *How the Weak Win Wars: A Theory of Asymmetric Conflict.* New York: Cambridge University Press, 2005.

———. "How to Lose a War on Terror: A Comparative Analysis of a Counterinsurgency Success and Failure." In Jan Ångström and Isabelle Duyvesteyn, eds., *Understanding Victory and Defeat in Contemporary War.* London: Routledge, 2007, pp. 142–167.

———. "Unconventional Deterrence: How the Weak Deter the Strong." In T. V. Paul, James Wirtz, and Patrick Morgan, eds., *Complex Deterrence: Strategy in the Global Era.* Chicago: University of Chicago Press, 2009.

Avilaés, William. "Institutions, Military Policy, and Human Rights in Colombia." *Latin American Perspectives*, Vol. 28, No. 1 (January 2001): pp. 31–55.

Badal, RK, "The Addis Ababa Agreement Ten Years After: An Assessment." In Mom Kou Nhail Arou and Benaiah Yongo-Bure, eds., *North-South Relations in Sudan Since the Addis Ababa Agreement.* Khartoum: Khartoum University Press, 1988.

Ball, Nicole. "The Challenge of Rebuilding War-Torn Societies." In Chester A. Crocker, Fen Osler Hampson, and Pamela R. Aall, eds., *Turbulent Peace: The Challenges of Managing International Conflict.* Washington, DC: U.S. Institute of Peace Press, 2001, pp. 719–736.

———. "Transforming Security Sectors: The IMF and World Bank Approaches." *Conflict, Security, and Development*, Vol. 1, No. 1 (2001): pp. 45–66.

Ball, Nicole, et al. *Security Sector Governance in Africa.* CDD Occasional Paper, forthcoming.

Baloyra, Enrique A. *El Salvador in Transition.* Chapel Hill: University of North Carolina Press, 1982.

Ban Ki-Moon. "Report of the Secretary-General on the Sudan." New York: United Nations Security Council, January 30, 2009. Available at http://www.reliefweb .int/rw/rwb.nsf/db900SID/EGUA-7KUMQQ?OpenDocument.

Barnett, Michael N. "Bringing in the New World Order: Liberalism, Legitimacy, and the United Nations." *World Politics,* Vol. 49, No. 4 (July 1997): pp. 526–551.

BCPR. "Justice and Security Sector Reform: BCPR's Programmatic Approach," November 2002.

Bekoe, Dorina Akosua Odoraa, "After the Peace Agreement: Lessons for Implementation from Mozambique, Angola, and Liberia." Ph.D. Dissertation, Harvard University, 2002.

Besançon, Marie L. "Relative Resources: Inequality in Ethnic Wars, Revolutions, and Genocides." *Journal of Peace Research*, Vol. 42, No. 4 (July 2005): pp. 393–415.

Blainey, Geoffrey. *The Causes of War*. 3rd edition. New York: Free Press, 1988.

Boutros-Ghali, Boutros. *Supplement to an Agenda for Peace: Position Paper of the Secretary General on the Occasion of the Fiftieth Anniversary of the United Nations*. UN Document A/50/60-S/1995/1. New York: United Nations, Department of Public Information, January 3, 1995.

Boyce, James K. "External Resource Mobilization." In James K. Boyce, ed., *Economic Policy for Building Peace: The Lessons of El Salvador*. Boulder, CO: Lynne Rienner, 1996, pp. 129–154.

Brahimi, Lakhdar. *Report of the Panel on United Nations Peace Operations*. UN Document A55/305-S/2000/809. New York: United Nations, August 17, 2000.

Brett, E. A. "Neutralising the Use of Force in Uganda: The Role of the Military in Politics." *Journal of Modern African Studies*, Vol. 33, No. 1 (March 1995): pp. 129–152.

Brzoska, Michael. "Introduction: Criteria for Evaluating Post-Conflict Reconstruction and Security Sector Reform in Peace Support Operations." *International Peacekeeping*, Vol. 13, No. 1 (March 2006): pp. 1–13.

Burr, J. Millard, and Robert O. Collins. *Requiem for the Sudan: War, Drought, and Disaster Relief on the Nile* (Boulder: Westview, 1995).

Bushnell, David. *The Making of Modern Colombia: A Nation in Spite of Itself*. Berkeley: University of California Press, 1993.

Byrnes, Rita M. "The Society and Its Environment." In *Uganda: A Country Study*. Washington, DC: Government Printing Office for the Library of Congress, 1990.

Call, Charles T. "Assessing El Salvador's Transition from Civil War to Peace." In Stephen John Stedman, Donald Rothchild and Elizabeth M. Cousens, eds., *Ending Civil Wars: The Implementation of Peace Agreements*. Boulder: Lynne Rienner, 2002.

———. *Challenges in Police Reform: Promoting Effectiveness and Accountability*. New York: International Peace Academy Policy Report, 2003.

———. "The Mugging of a Success Story: Justice and Security Reform in El Salvador." In Charles T. Call, ed., *Constructing Justine and Security After War*, Washington, DC: United States Institute of Peace Press, 2007, pp. 29–67.

Call, Charles T., and William Stanley. "Civilian Security." In Stephen John Stedman, Donald Rothchild, and Elizabeth M. Cousens, eds., *Ending Civil Wars:*

The Implementation of Peace Agreements. Boulder: Lynne Rienner, 2002, pp. 303–326.

———. "Protecting the People: Public Security Choices After Civil Wars." *Global Governance*, Vol. 7, No. 2 (April–June 2001): pp. 151–172.

Camdessus, Michel. Transcript of a September 28, 1989, press conference. Washington, DC: International Monetary Fund, 1989.

Carney, Timothy. "The Sudan: Political Islam and Terrorism." In Robert Rotberg, ed., *Battling Terrorism in the Horn of Africa.* Washington, DC: Brookings Institution Press, 2005, pp. 119–140.

Carrington, Tim. "Poor Lands Try to Cope with Residue of War: Their Leftover Armies," *Wall Street Journal*, December 10, 1994, p. 1.

Cawthra, Gavin, and Robin Luckham, eds. *Governing Insecurity: Democratic Control of Military and Security Establishments in Transitional Societies.* London: Zed Books, 2003.

CIA World Factbook 2006. Available at https://www.cia.gov/library/publications/the-world-factbook/index.html.

Collier, Paul. "Doing Well Out of War: An Economic Perspective." in Mats Berdal and David M. Malone, eds., *Greed and Grievance: Economic Agendas in Civil Wars.* Boulder: Lynne Rienner, 2000, pp. 91–111.

———. "On the Economic Consequences of Civil War." *Oxford Economic Papers*, Vol. 51, No. 1 (January 1999): pp. 168–183.

Collier, Paul, and Anke Hoeffler, "Greed and Grievance in Civil War." *Oxford Economic Papers*, Vol. 56, No. 4 (October 2004): pp. 563–595.

Collier, Paul, and Ritva Reinikka, eds. *Uganda's Recovery: The Role of Farms, Firms, and Government* (Washington, DC: World Bank, 2001.

The Comprehensive Peace Agreement between the Government of the Republic of the Sudan and the Sudan People's Liberation Movement/Sudan People's Liberation Army, January, 2005. Available at http://www.un.org/chinese/ha/issue/sudan/docs/cpa-1.pdf.

Cordesman, Anthony H. "The Iraq War: Progress in the Fighting and Security." Center for Strategic and International Studies, February 21, 2009. Available at http://www.csis.org.

Corr, Edwin G. "Societal Transformation for Peace in El Salvador." *Annals of the American Academy of Political and Social Science*, Vol. 541 (September 1995): pp. 144–156.

Cramer, Christopher. "Does Inequality Cause Conflict?" *Journal of International Development*, Vol. 15, No. 4 (2003): pp. 397–412.

Cunningham, David E. "Veto Players and Civil War Duration." *American Journal of Political Science*, Vol. 50, No. 4 (October 2006): pp. 875–892.

David, Stephen R. "Internal War: Causes and Cures." *World Politics*, Vol. 49, No. 4 (July 1997): pp. 552–576.

Davies, James C. "Toward a Theory of Revolution." *American Sociological Review*, Vol. 27, No. 1 (February 1962): pp. 5–19.

Deng, Francis M. "Scramble for Souls: Religious Intervention among the Dinka in Sudan." In Abdullahi an-Na'im, ed., *Proselytizing and Communal Self-Determination in Africa.* New York: Orbis, 1999, pp. 191–227.

———. "Sudan—Civil War and Genocide." *Middle East Quarterly*, Vol. 8, No. 1 (Winter 2001): pp. 13–21.

———. "Sudan's Struggle to Become One Nation." *Christian Science Monitor*, February 1, 1990.

———. *War of Visions: Conflict of Identities in the Sudan*. Washington, DC: Brookings Institution, 1995.

Department of Defense. "Measuring Stability and Security in Iraq." Report to Congress in accordance with the Department of Defense Supplemental Appropriations Act 2008. December 2008. Available at http://www.defenselink.mil/pubs/pdfs/9010_Report_to_Congress_Dec_08.pdf.

Devarajan, Shantayanan, David Dollar, and Torgny Holmgren, eds. *Aid and Reform in Africa: Lessons from Ten Case Studies*. Washington, DC: World Bank Publications, 2001.

Development Assistance Committee, Organization for Economic Cooperation and Development. *The DAC Guidelines: Helping Prevent Violent Conflict*. Paris: OECD, 2001.

———. *Security System Reform and Governance*. DAC Guidelines and Reference Series. Paris: OECD, 2005. Available at http://www.oecd.org/dataoecd/8/39/31785288.pdf.

Diamond, Larry. *Developing Democracy: Toward Consolidation*. Baltimore: Johns Hopkins University Press, 1999.

Di Palma, Giuseppe. *To Craft Democracies: An Essay on Democratic Transitions*. Berkeley: University of California Press, 1990.

Diskin, Martin. "Distilled Conclusions: The Disappearance of the Agrarian Question in El Salvador." *Latin American Research Review*, Vol. 31, No. 2 (1996): pp. 111–126.

Domke, D. Michelle. "Civil War in Sudan: Resources or Religion?" Inventory of Conflict and Environment (ICE) case study, American University. Available at http://www.american.edu/ted/ice/sudan.htm.

Doyle, Michael W., Ian Johnstone, and Robert C. Orr, eds. *Keeping the Peace: Multidimensional UN Operations in Cambodia and El Salvador*. New York: Cambridge University Press, 1997.

Doyle, Michael W., and Nicholas Sambanis. "International Peacebuilding: A Theoretical and Quantitative Analysis." *American Political Science Review*, Vol. 94, No. 4 (December 2000): pp. 779–801.

Doyle, Michael W., and Nicholas Sambanis. *Making War and Building Peace: United Nations Peace Operations*. Princeton: Princeton University Press, 2006.

Dunn, Kevin C. "Uganda: The Lord's Resistance Army." *Review of African Political Economy*, Vol. 31, No. 99, ICTs "Virtual Colonisation" and Political Economy (March 2004): pp. 139–142.

"East Africa: Conflicting Agendas." *Africa Confidential*, Vol. 43, No. 1 (January 11, 2002).

Edelstein, David M. "Occupational Hazards: Why Military Occupations Succeed or Fail." *International Security*, Vol. 29, No. 1 (Summer 2004): pp. 49–91.

Eglington, Stephanie J., and Joan M. Nelson. "Encouraging Democracy: What Role for Conditioned Aid?" Policy Essay no. 4. Washington, DC: Overseas Development Council, 1992.

"Egypt-Sudan: Pharaoh Speaks." *Africa Confidential*, Vol. 42, No. 2 (January 26, 2001).

El Obeid, Abu Baker. *The Political Consequences of the Addis Ababa Agreement*, Publications of the Political Science Association in Uppsala. Stockholm: Liber Tryck, 1980.

"El Salvador at a Glance." World Bank Group, September 28, 2007. Available at http://devdata.worldbank.org/AAG/slv_aag.pdf.

Eprile, Cecile. *War and Peace in Sudan: 1955–1972*. London: David and Charles, 1974.

Falk, Richard N. "Hard Choices and Tragic Dilemmas." *Nation*, Vol. 257, No. 21 (December 2003): p. 757.

Fallows, James. *Blind into Baghdad: America's War in Iraq*. New York: Vintage, 2006.

Fearon, James D. "Commitment Problems and the Spread of Ethnic Conflict." In David A. Lake and Donald Rothchild, eds., *The International Spread of Ethnic Conflict: Fear, Diffusion, and Escalation*. Princeton: Princeton University Press, 1998, pp. 107–126.

———. "Rationalist Explanations for War." *International Organization*, Vol. 9, No. 3 (Summer 1995): pp. 379-414.

Fearon, James, and David Laitin. "Ethnicity, Insurgency, and Civil War." *American Political Science Review*, Vol. 97, No. 1 (February 2003): pp. 75–90.

Finer, Samuel. *The Man on Horseback: The Role of the Military in Politics*. London: Pall Mall Press, 1962.

Finnemore, Martha, and Kathryn Sikkink. "International Norm Dynamics and Political Change." *International Organization*, Vol. 52, No. 4 (Autumn 1998): pp. 887–917.

Fortna, Virginia Page. "Does Peacekeeping Keep Peace? International Intervention and the Duration of Peace After Civil War." *International Studies Quarterly*, Vol. 48, No. 2 (June 2004): pp. 269–292.

———. *Peace Time: Cease-Fire Agreements and the Durability of Peace*. Princeton: Princeton University Press, 2004.

———. "Scraps of Paper? Agreements and the Durability of Peace." *International Organization*, Vol. 57, No. 2 (Spring 2003): pp. 337–372.

Galbraith, Peter W. *The End of Iraq: How American Incompetence Created a War without End*. New York: Simon and Schuster, 2006.

Gbla, Osman. "Security Sector Reform under International Tutulage in Sierra Leone." *International Peacekeeping*, Vol. 13, No. 1 (March 2006): pp 78–93.

Gelb, Leslie H. "The Three-State Solution." *New York Times*, November 25, 2003.

George, Alexander L., and Andrew Bennett. *Case Studies and Theory Development in the Social Sciences*. Cambridge: MIT Press, 2005.

Gibb, H.A.R. "Islam." In R. C. Zaehner, ed., *Encyclopedia of the World's Religions*. New York: Barnes and Noble, 1997, pp. 166–199.

Glaser, Charles L. "Political Consequences of Military Strategy: Expanding and Refining the Spiral and Deterrence Models." *World Politics*, Vol. 44, No. 4 (July 1992): pp. 497–538.

Gleditsch, Nils Petter, and Ole Magnus Theisen. In *Resources, the Environment, and Conflict*. Oslo: International Peace and Research Institute, 2006. Available at http://www.prio.no/files/file48356_gleditsch_theisen_160906.doc.

Gordon, Michael R., and General Bernard E. Trainor. *Cobra II: The Inside Story of the Invasion and Occupation of Iraq*. New York: Pantheon Books, 2006.

Greene, Owen. "Security Sector Reform, Conflict Prevention and Regional Perspectives." *Journal of Security Sector Management*, Vol. 1, No. 1 (March 2003): pp. 1–15.

Gurr, Ted R. *Why Men Rebel*. Princeton: Princeton University Press, 1970.

Hampson, Fen Osler. *Nurturing Peace: Why Peace Settlements Succeed or Fail*. Washington, DC: United States Institute of Peace Press, 1996.

———. "Parent, Midwife or Accidental Executioner? The Role of Third Parties in Ending Violence Conflicts." In Chester A. Crocker, Fen Osler Hampson, and Pamela R. Aall, eds., *Turbulent Peace: The Challenges of Managing International Conflict*. Washington, DC: U.S. Institute of Peace Press, 2001: pp. 387–406.

Hardin, Russell. *One for All: The Logic of Group Conflict*. Princeton: Princeton University Press, 1995.

Hartlyn, Jonathan. "Civil Violence and Conflict Resolution: The Case of Colombia." In Roy Licklider, ed., *Stopping the Killing: How Civil Wars End*. New York: New York University Press, 1993, pp. 37–61.

Hartzell, Caroline. "Explaining the Stability of Negotiated Settlements to Intrastate Wars." *Journal of Conflict Resolution*, Vol. 43, No. 1 (February 1999): pp. 3–22.

Hartzell, Caroline, and Matthew Hoddie. *Crafting Peace: Power Sharing and the Negotiated Settlement of Civil Wars*. University Park: Pennsylvania State University Press, 2007.

———. "Institutionalizing Peace: Power Sharing and Post–Civil War Conflict Management." *American Journal of Political Science*, Vol. 47, No. 2 (April 2003): pp. 318–332.

Hartzell, Caroline, Matthew Hoddie, and Donald Rothchild. "Stabilizing the Peace After Civil War: An Investigation into Some Key Variables." *International Organization*, Vol. 55, No. 1 (Winter 2001): pp. 183–208.

Hendrickson, Dylon. "A Review of the Security Sector Reform." Working Paper no. 1. London: King's College London, Centre for Defence Studies, 1999.

Herz, John H. *Political Realism and Political Idealism: A Study in Theories and Realities*. Chicago: University of Chicago Press, 1951.

"Historic Sudan Peace Accord Signed." CNN, January 9, 2005. http://www.cnn.com/2005/WORLD/africa/01/09/sudan.signing/index.html.

Hobbes, Thomas. *Leviathan*, ed. Richard Tuck. New York: Cambridge University Press, 1991.

Hoddie, Matthew, and Caroline Hartzell. "Civil War Settlements and the Implementation of Military Power-Sharing Agreements." *Journal of Peace Research*, Vol. 40, No. 3 (May 2003): pp. 303–320.

Holiday, David, and William Stanley. "Broad Participation, Diffuse Responsibility: Peace Implementation in Guatamela." In Stephen John Stedman, Donald Rothchild, and Elizabeth M. Cousens, eds., *Ending Civil Wars: The Implementation of Peace Agreements*. Boulder: Lynne Rienner, 2002, pp. 421–462.

———. "Under the Best of Circumstances: ONUSAL and the Challenges of Verification and Institution Building in El Salvador." In Tommie Sue Montgomery, ed., *Peacemaking and Democratization in the Western Hemisphere*. Coral Gables: North South Center Press, 2000.

Horowitz, Donald L. *Ethnic Groups in Conflict*. Berkeley: University of California Press, 1985, pp. 588–591.

Hovil, Lucy, and Zachary Lomo. "Behind the Violence: Causes, Consequences and the Search for Solutions to the War in Northern Uganda." Refugee Law Project Working Paper no. 11. Kampala, Uganda: Refugee Law Project, February 2004.

Howard, Lise Morjé. *UN Peacekeeping in Civil Wars*. New York: Cambridge University Press, 2007.

Huntington, Samuel P. *Political Order in Changing Societies*. New Haven: Yale University Press, 1968.

International Crisis Group (ICG). "God, Oil and Country: Changing the Logic of War in Sudan." *ICG Africa Report*, No. 39, January 28, 2002, p. 8. Available at http://www.crisisweb.org/projects/africa/sudan/reports/A400534_28012002.pdf.

———. "Northern Uganda: Understanding and Solving the Conflict." *ICG Africa Report*, No. 77 (April 14, 2004).

International Institute for Strategic Studies (IISS) Armed Conflict database. Available at http://acd.iiss.org.

"Islam's Dark Side: The Orwellian State of Sudan." *Economist*, June 24, 1995, p. 21.

Janowitz, Morris. *The Military in the Political Development of New Nations: An Essay in Comparative Analysis*. Chicago: University of Chicago Press, 1964.

Jervis, Robert. "Cooperation under the Security Dilemma." *World Politics*, Vol. 30, No. 2 (January 1978): pp. 167–214.

———. *Perception and Misperception in International Politics*. Princeton: Princeton University Press, 1976.

Jervis, Robert. "Understanding the Bush Doctrine." *Political Science Quarterly*, Vol. 118, No. 3 (2003): pp. 365–388.

"Joint Assistance Strategy for the Republic of Uganda (2005–2009)." *Country Assistance Strategy*. Washington DC: World Bank, May 2006.

Jones, Seth G., et al. "Establishing Law and Order After Conflict." Santa Monica: RAND Corporation, 2005.

Juhn, Tricia. *Negotiating Peace in El Salvador: Civil-Military Relations and the Conspiracy to End the War*. New York: St. Martin's, 1998.

Kabwegyere, Tarsis Bazana. *People's Choice, People's Power: Challenges and Prospects of Democracy in Uganda*. Kampala: Fountain, 2000.

Kaplan, Robert D. "The Coming Anarchy: How Scarcity, Crime, Overpopulation, Tribalism, and Disease Are Rapidly Destroying the Social Fabric of Our Planet." *Atlantic Monthly*, Vol. 273, No. 2 (February 1994): pp. 44–76.

Karl, Terry Lynn. "El Salvador's Negotiated Revolution." *Foreign Affairs*, Vol. 71, No. 2 (Spring 1992): pp. 147–164.

Karugire, Samwiri. *Roots of Instability in Uganda*. 2nd edition. Kampala: Fountain, 1996.

Kasfir, Nelson. "Southern Sudanese Politics since the Addis Ababa Agreement." *African Affairs*, Vol. 76, No. 303 (April 1977): pp. 143–166.

———. "The Ugandan Elections of 1989: Power, Populism, and Democratization." In Holger B. Hansen and Michael Twaddle, eds., *Changing Uganda: The Dilemmas of Structural Adjustment and Revolutionary Change*. Athens: Ohio University Press, 1991, pp. 247–278.

Kasozi, A.B.K. *The Social Origins of Violence in Uganda, 1964–1985*. Montreal: McGill-Queen's University Press, 1994.

Kaufman, Stuart J. "Spiraling to Ethnic War: Elites, Masses, and Moscow in Moldova's Civil War." *International Security*, Vol. 21, No. 2 (Fall 1996): pp. 108–138.

Kaufmann, Chaim D. "Intervention in Ethnic and Ideological Civil Wars: Why One Can Be Done and the Other Can't." *Security Studies*, Vol. 6, No. 1 (Autumn 1996): pp. 62–103.

———. "Possible and Impossible Solutions to Ethnic Civil Wars." *International Security*, Vol. 20, No. 4 (Spring 1996): pp. 136–175.

———. "When All Else Fails: Evaluating Population Transfers and Partition as Solutions to Ethnic Conflict." In Barbara F. Walter and Jack Snyder, eds., *Civil Wars, Insecurity, and Intervention*. New York: Columbia University Press, 1999, pp. 221–260.

Keen, David. "The Economic Functions of Violence in Civil Wars." Adelphi Paper no. 320. London: International Institute for Strategic Studies, 1998.

King, Charles. "The Benefits of Ethnic War: Understanding Eurasia's Unrecognized States." *World Politics*, Vol. 53, No. 4 (July 2001): pp. 524–552.

Kiyaga-Nsubuga, John. "Uganda: The Politics of 'Consolidation' under Museveni's Regime, 1996–2003." In Taiser M. Ali and Robert O. Matthews, eds., *Durable Peace: Challenges for Peacebuilding in Africa*. Toronto: University of Toronto Press, 2004, pp. 86–113.

Knut, Walter, and Philip J. Williams. *Militarization and Demilitarization in El Salvador's Transition to Democracy*. Pittsburgh: University of Pittsburgh Press, 1997.

———. "The Military and Democratization in El Salvador." *Journal of Interamerican Studies and World Affairs*, Vol. 35, No. 1 (1993): pp. 39–88.

Kumar, Krishna, and Marina Ottaway. *From Bullets to Ballots: A Synthesis of Findings from Six Evaluations*. Washington, DC: USAID, 1997.

Kumar, Radha. "The Troubled History of Partition." *Foreign Affairs*, Vol. 76, No. 1 (January/February 1997): pp. 22–34.

Lake, David A., and Donald Rothchild. "Containing Fear: The Origins and Management of Ethnic Conflict," *International Security*, Vol. 21, No. 2 (Fall 1996): pp. 41–75.

———. "Spreading Fear: The Genesis of Transnational Ethnic Conflict." In David A. Lake and Donald Rothchild, eds., *The International Spread of Ethnic Conflict: Fear, Diffusion, and Escalation*. Princeton: Princeton University Press, 1998: pp. 3–32.

Langseth, Peter, and Justus Mugaju, eds. *Post-Conflict Uganda: Towards an Effective Civil Service*. Kampala: Fountain, 1996.

Le Billon, Philippe. *Fuelling War: Natural Resources and Armed Conflict*, Adelphi Paper no. 373. London: Routledge, 2005.

Licklider, Roy. "The Consequences of Negotiated Settlements in Civil Wars, 1945–1993." *American Political Science Review,* Vol. 89, No. 3 (September 1995): pp. 681–690.

Licklider, Roy, and Mia Bloom, eds. *Living Together After Ethnic Killing: Exploring the Chaim Kaufmann Argument.* London: Routledge, 2006.

Linz, Juan J., and Alfred C. Stepan. *Problems of Democratic Tradition and Consolidation: Southern Europe, South America, and Post-Communist Europe.* Baltimore: Johns Hopkins University Press, 1996.

Lounsbery, Marie Olson, et al. "Rethinking Models of Civil War Settlement." *International Interactions,* Vol. 32, No. 2 (April–June 2006): pp. 109–128.

Luttwak, Edward N. "Give War a Chance." *Foreign Affairs,* Vol. 78, No. 4 (July/August 1999): pp. 36–44.

Lyons, Terrence. "The Role of Postsettlement Elections." In Stephen John Stedman, Elisabeth M. Cousens, and Donald Rothchild, eds., *Ending Civil Wars: The Implementation of Peace Agreements.* Boulder: Lynne Rienner, 2002, pp. 215–236.

Mack, Andrew. "Civil War: Academic Research and the Policy Community." *Journal of Peace Research,* Vol. 39, No. 5 (September 2002): pp. 515–525.

Marten, Kimberly Zisk. *Enforcing the Peace: Learning from the Imperial Past.* New York: Columbia University Press, 2004.

Martin, Randolph. "Sudan's Perfect War," *Foreign Affairs,* Vol. 81, No. 2 (March/April 2002): pp. 111–127.

McGregor, Andrew. "Terrorism and Violence in Sudan: The Islamist Manipulation of Darfur." *Terrorism Monitor,* Vol. 3, No. 12 (June 17, 2005): pp. 3–5.

Mearsheimer, John. "Back to the Future: Instability in Europe After the Cold War." *International Security,* Vol. 15, No. 4 (Summer 1990): pp. 5–56.

———. "Shrink Bosnia to Save It." *New York Times,* March 31, 1993.

Mearsheimer, John, and Stephen Van Evera. "When Peace Means War." *New Republic,* December 18, 1995: pp. 16–21.

Mearsheimer, John, and Stephen M. Walt. *Can Saddam Be Contained? History Says Yes.* Research Paper, Belfer Center for Science and International Affairs, John F. Kennedy School of Government, Harvard University, November 12, 2002.

Metz, Helen Chapin, ed. *Sudan: A Country Study.* Washington, DC: GPO for the Library of Congress, 1991. Available at http://countrystudies.us/sudan.

Moore, Barrington. *Social Origins of Dictatorship and Democracy: Lord and Peasant in the Making of the Modern World.* Boston: Beacon Press, 1966.

Moravscik, Andrew. "Taking Preferences Seriously: A Liberal Theory of International Politics." *International Organization,* Vol. 51, No. 4 (Autumn 1997): pp. 513–553.

Mudoola, Dan M. "Institution-Building: The Case of NRM and the Military in Uganda, 1986–1989." In Holger Bernt Hansen and Michael Twaddle, eds., *Changing Uganda: The Dilemmas of Structural Adjustment and Revolutionary Change.* London: James Currey, 1991, pp. 230–246.

Mueller, John E. *Remnants of War.* Ithaca: Cornell University Press, 2004.

Mugaju, Justus. "An Historical Background to Uganda's No-Party Democracy." In Justus Mugaju and J. Oloka-Onango, eds., *No-Party Democracy in Uganda: Myths and Realities.* Kampala: Fountain, 2000.

Mukherjee, Bumba. "Why Political Power-Sharing Agreements Lead to Enduring Peaceful Resolution of Some Civil Wars, but Not Others?" *International Studies Quarterly*, Vol. 50, No. 2 (June 2006): pp. 479–504.

Museveni, Yoweri. *The Path of Liberation*. Kampala 1989.

Nathan, Laurie. "Obstacles to Security Sector Reform in New Democracies." Berghof Research Center for Constructive Conflict Management, 2004.

Nelson, Joan M., with Stephanie J. Eglington. *Encouraging Democracy: What Role for Conditioned Aid?* Policy Essay no. 4. Washington, DC: Overseas Development Council, 1992.

Nicoll, Fergus. *The Mahdi of Sudan and the Death of General Gordon*. Gloucestershire, UK: Sutton, 2005.

Nordlinger, Eric A. "Political Development: Time Sequences and Rates of Change." *World Politics*, Vol. 20, No. 3 (April 1968): pp. 494–520.

O'Ballance, Edgar. *The Secret War in Sudan: 1955–1972*. Hamden, CT: Archon Books, 1977.

O'Brien, Adam. "Peace on the Rocks: Sudan's Comprehensive Peace Agreement." Enough Project. Washington, DC: Center for American Progress, February 19, 2009. Available at http://www.enoughproject.org/files/publications/sudan_peace_agreement_revised_0.pdf.

Odongo, Onyango. *A Political History of Uganda: The Origin of Museveni's Referendum 2000*. Kampala: Monitor, 2000.

O'Donnell, Guillermo, Philippe C. Schmitter, and Laurence Whitehead. *Transitions from Authoritarian Rule: Comparative Perspectives*. Baltimore: Johns Hopkins University Press, 1986.

Ofcansky, Thomas P. "National Security." In *Uganda: A Country Study*. Washington DC: Government Printing Office for the Library of Congress, 1990.

———. *Uganda: Tarnished Pearl of Africa*. Boulder: Westview, 1996.

Office of Reconstruction and Humanitarian Assistance. *Unified Mission Plan for Post Hostilities Iraq*. Draft, Version 2, April 3, 2003.

O'Hanlon, Michael, and Jason Campbell. *The Iraq Index* (multiple issues since November 2003). Available at www.brookings.edu/iraqindex.

Omach, Paul, "Civil War and Internal Displacement in Northern Uganda: 1986–1998." Poverty Policy Perspectives Working Paper 26. Network of Ugandan Researchers and Research Users, 2002.

Orizio, Riccardo. *Talk of the Devil: Encounters with Seven Dictators*. New York: Walker, 2002.

Østby, Gudrun. "Horizontal Inequalities and Civil Conflict." Paper presented at the 46th Annual International Studies Association (ISA) Convention, Honolulu, March 2, 2005.

Packer, George. *The Assassin's Gate: America in Iraq*. New York: Farrar, Straus and Giroux, 2005.

Paige, Jeffery M. "History and Memory in El Salvador: Elite Ideology and the Insurrection and Massacre of 1932." Paper presented at the Meetings of the Latin American Studies Association, Atlanta, March 1994.

———. "Land Reform and Agrarian Revolution in El Salvador: Comment on Seligson and Diskin." *Latin American Research Review*, Vol. 31, No. 2 (1996): pp. 127–139.

Paris, Roland. *At War's End: Building Peace After Civil Conflict.* New York: Cambridge University Press, 2004.

Peace Support Operations: A Working Draft Manual for African Military Practitioners. Pretoria, South Africa: Institute for Security Studies, February 1, 2000.

Pearson, Frederic S., et al. "Rethinking Models of Civil War Settlement." *International Interactions*, Vol. 32, No. 2 (April–June 2006): pp. 109–128.

Peceny, Mark, and William Stanley. "Liberal Social Reconstruction and the Resolution of Civil Wars in Central America." *International Organization*, Vol. 55, No. 1 (Winter 2001): pp. 149–182.

Petersen, Roger D. *Understanding Ethnic Violence: Fear, Hatred, and Resentment in Twentieth-Century Eastern Europe.* New York: Cambridge University Press, 2002.

Petterson, Donald. *Inside Sudan: Political Islam, Conflict, and Catastrophe* Boulder: Westview Press, 1999.

Pillar, Paul R. *Negotiating Peace: War Termination as a Bargaining Process.* Princeton: Princeton University Press, 1983.

"Pointers: Egypt-Sudan." *Africa Confidential*, Vol. 42, No. 2 (January 26, 2001): p. 8.

"Pointers: Somalia, Sudan/Iraq, Algeria & Ethiopia." *Africa Confidential*, Vol. 44, No. 5 (March 7, 2003).

"Pointers: Sudan/Iraq." *Africa Confidential*, Vol. 44, No. 5 (March 7, 2003): p. 8.

Polity IV Project. "Polity IV Data Set." College Park, MD: Center for International Development and Conflict Management, University of Maryland, 2000. Available at http://www.cidcm.umd.edu/polity/data.

Posen, Barry R. "The Security Dilemma in Ethnic Conflict." In Michael Brown, ed., *Ethnic Conflict and International Security.* Princeton: Princeton University Press, 1993, pp. 103–124.

Powell, Colin L. "U.S. Forces: Challenges Ahead." *Foreign Affairs*, Vol. 71, No. 5 (Winter 1992/1993): pp. 32–51.

Powell, Robert. "Bargaining and Learning While Fighting." *American Journal of Political Science*, Vol. 48, No. 2 (April 2004): pp. 344–361.

Prosterman, Roy L., Jeffrey M. Riedinger, and Mary N. Temple. "Land Reform and the El Salvador Crisis," *International Security*, Vol. 6, No. 1 (Summer 1981): pp. 53–74.

Przeworski, Adam. "Games of Transition." In Scott Mainwaring, Guillermo O'Donnell, and J. Samuel Valenzuela, eds., *Issues in Democratic Consolidation: The New South American Democracies in Comparative Perspective.* Notre Dame: University of Notre Dame Press, 1992, pp. 105–153.

Przerworski, Adam, et al. *Democracy and Development: Political Institutions and Well-Being in the World, 1950–1990.* Cambridge: Cambridge University Press, 2000.

Ricks, Thomas E. *Fiasco: The American Military Adventure in Iraq.* 2nd edition. New York: Penguin, 2007.

Rose, William. "The Security Dilemma and Ethnic Conflict: Some New Hypotheses." *Security Studies*, Vol. 9, No. 4 (Summer 2000): pp. 1–51.

Ross, Michael L. "Oil, Drugs, and Diamonds: The Varying Roles of Natural Resources in Civil War." In Karen Ballentine and Jake Sherman, eds., *The Po-*

litical Economy of Armed Conflict: Beyond Greed and Grievance. Boulder: Lynne Rienner, 2003, pp. 47–70.

Ross, Will. "Museveni: Uganda's Fallen Angel." *BBC News,* November 30, 2005.

Rothchild, Donald, and Caroline Hartzell. "The Peace Process in Sudan, 1971– 1972." In Roy Licklider, ed., *Stopping the Killing: How Civil Wars End.* New York: New York University Press 1993, pp. 63–93.

Rubongoya, Joshua B. *Regime Hegemony in Museveni's Uganda.* New York: Palgrave Macmillan, 2007.

Rugumanu, Severine, and Osman Gebla. *Studies in Reconstruction and Capacity-Building in Post-Conflict Countries in Africa: Some Lessons of Experience from Uganda.* Harare, Zimbabwe: African Capacity Building Foundation, 2003.

Ruiz, Bert. *The Colombian Civil War.* Jefferson, NC: McFarland, 2001.

Rustow, Dankwart. "Transitions to Democracy: Toward a Dynamic Model." *Comparative Politics,* Vol. 2, No. 3 (April 1970): pp. 337–363.

Safford, Frank, and Marco Palacios. *Colombia: Fragmented Land, Divided Society.* New York: Oxford University Press, 2002.

Sageman, Marc. "Statement of Marc Sageman to the National Commission on Terrorist Attacks upon the United States," July 9, 2003.

Sambanis, Nicholas. "Do Ethnic and Nonethnic Civil Wars Have the Same Causes?" *Journal of Conflict Resolution,* Vol. 45, No. 3 (June 2001): pp. 259–282.

———. "Partition as a Solution to Ethnic War: An Empirical Analysis of the Theoretical Literature." *World Politics,* Vol. 52, No. 4 (July 2000): pp. 437–483.

Sarkees, Meredith Reid. "The Correlates of War Data on War: An Update to 1997." *Conflict Management and Peace Science,* Vol. 18, No. 1 (Fall 2000): pp. 123–144.

Schelling, Thomas C. *The Strategy of Conflict.* Cambridge: Harvard University Press, 1960.

Segovia, Alexander. "Domestic Resource Mobilization." In James K. Boyce, ed., *Economic Policy for Building Peace: The Lessons of El Salvador* (Boulder: Lynne Rienner, 1996: pp. 107–127.

———. "Macroeconomic Performance Policies Since 1989." In James K. Boyce, ed., *Economic Policy for Building Peace: The Lessons of El Salvador.* Boulder: Lynne Rienner, 1996: pp. 51–72.

"The Self-Mutilation of Sudan." *Swiss Review of World Affairs,* July 3, 1995.

Seligseon, Mitchell A. "Thirty Years of Transformation in the Agrarian Structure of El Salvador, 1961–1991." *Latin American Research Review,* Vol. 30, No. 3 (1995): pp. 43–74.

Shanker, Thom. "Minister Sees Need for U.S. Help in Iraq Until 2018." *New York Times,* January 15, 2008.

Smith, Chris. "Security Sector Reform: Development Breakthrough or Institutional Engineering?" *Conflict, Security & Development,* Vol. 1, No. 1 (April 2001): pp. 5–20.

Special Inspector General for Iraq Reconstruction. *Hard Lessons: The Iraq Reconstruction Experience.* Washington, DC: U.S. Government Printing Office, 2009. Available at http://www.sigir.mil/hardlessons/pdfs/Hard_Lessons_Report.pdf.

Stanley, William Deane. "El Salvador: State-Building before and after Democratisation, 1980–95." *Third World Quarterly*, Vol. 27, No. 1 (February 2006): pp. 101–114.

———. "International Tutelage and Domestic Political Will: A New Civilian Police Force in El Salvador." In *Studies in Comparative International Development*, Vol. 30, No. 1 (Spring 1995): pp. 30–58.

———. *The Protection Racket State: Elite Politics, Military Extortion, and Civil War in El Salvador*. Philadelphia: Temple University Press, 1996.

Stanley, William, and David Holiday. "Broad Participation, Diffuse Responsibility: Peace Implementation in Guatemala." In Stephen John Stedman, Donald Rothchild, and Elisabeth M. Cousens, eds., *Ending Civil Wars: The Implementation of Peace Agreements*. Boulder: Lynne Rienner, 2002, pp. 421–462.

Stedman, Stephen John. "International Implementation of Peace Agreements in Civil Wars: Findings from a Study of Sixteen Cases." In Chester A. Crocker, Fen Osler Hampson, and Pamela Aall, eds., *Turbulent Peace: The Challenges of Managing International Conflict* Washington, DC: United States Institute of Peace Press, 2001, pp. 737–752.

Stedman, Stephen John, Donald Rothchild, and Elisabeth M. Cousens, eds., *Ending Civil Wars: The Implementation of Peace Agreements*. Boulder: Lynne Rienner, 2002.

"Sudan: Calling the Shots at Machakos." *Africa Confidential*, Vol. 43, No. 15 (July 26, 2002).

"Sudan: Delusions of Peace." *Africa Confidential*, Vol. 42, No. 16 (August 10, 2001).

"Sudan: Desperate Darfur." *Africa Confidential*, Vol. 45, No. 10 (May 14, 2004).

"Sudan: Joy in the South, Silence in the North." *Africa Confidential*, Vol. 46, No. 2 (January 12, 2005): p. 1.

"Sudan: Mass Murder." *Africa Confidential*, Vol. 45, No. 9 (April 30, 2004).

"Sudan Oil and Conflict Timeline." *Sudan Update*. Available at http://www.sudanupdate.org/REPORTS/Oil/21oc.html.

"Sudan: Opening New Fronts in the Oil War." *Africa Confidential*, Vol. 42, No. 6 (March 23, 2001).

"Sudan: The Fire Does Not Cease." *Africa Confidential*, Vol. 43, No. 10 (May 17, 2002).

"Sudan: Unconstructive Engagement." *Africa Confidential*, Vol. 43, No. 4 (February 22, 2002).

"Sudan: West of the Border," *Africa Confidential*, Vol. 46, No. 2 (January 21, 2005).

Suskind, Ron A. "Faith, Certainty and the Presidency of George W. Bush," *New York Times Magazine*, October 17, 2004.

———. *The One Percent Doctrine: Deep Inside America's Pursuit of Its Enemies Since 9/11*. New York: Simon and Schuster, 2006.

———. *The Price of Loyalty: George W. Bush, the White House and the Education of Paul O'Neill*. New York: Simon and Schuster, 2004.

Tilly, Charles. "Reflections on the History of European State Making." In Charles Tilly, ed., *The Formation of National States in Europe*. Princeton: Princeton University Press, 1975, pp. 3–84.

————. "War Making and State Making as Organized Crime." In Peter R. Evans, Dietrich Rueschemeyer, and Theda Skocpol, eds., *Bringing the State Back In.* Cambridge: Cambridge University Press, 1985, pp. 169–191.

Toft, Monica Duffy. *The Geography of Ethnic Violence: Identity, Interests, and the Indivisibility of Territory.* Princeton: Princeton University Press, 2003.

————. "Getting Religion? The Puzzling Case of Islam and Civil War." *International Security*, Vol. 31, No. 4 (Spring 2007): pp. 97–131.

Tripp, Aili Mari. "The Changing Face of Authoritarianism in Africa: The Case of Uganda." *Africa Today*, Vol. 50, No. 3 (Spring 2004): pp. 3–36.

United Nations Development Programme (UNDP). "Security Sector Reform and Transitional Justice: A Crisis Post-Conflict Programmatic Approach." March 2003. Available at http://www.undp.org/bcpr/we_do/security_reform.shtml (accessed June 21, 2007).

United Nations Development Program Bureau for Crisis Prevention and Recovery Web site: http://www.undp.org/bcpr/documents/jssr/ssr/UNDP_2003_JSSR_Approach.doc.

United Nations Mission in Sudan. "Report to the Secretary-General on the Sudan," S/2007/500, August 20, 2007.

Uvin, Peter. "Ethnicity and Power in Burundi and Rwanda: Different Paths to Mass Violence." *Comparative Politics*, Vol. 31, No. 3 (April 1999): pp. 253–271.

Van Evera, Stephen. "Why States Believe Foolish Ideas." Manuscript.

Viorst, Milton. "Fundamentalism in Power: Sudan's Islamic Experiment." *Foreign Affairs*, Vol. 74, No. 3 (May/June 1995): pp. 45–58.

Wagner, Robert Harrison. "The Causes of Peace." In Roy Licklider, ed., *Stopping the Killing: How Civil Wars End.* New York: New York University Press, 1994, pp. 235–268.

Wai, Dunstan. *The African-Arab Conflict in Sudan.* New York: Africana, 1981.

Wallensteen, Peter, and Margaret Sollenberg. "Armed Conflicts, Conflict Termination, and Peace Agreements, 1989–1996." Journal of Peace Research, Vol. 34, No. 3 (August 1997): pp. 339–368.

Walter, Barbara F., "Civil War Resolution: What We Know and Don't Know." *Annual Review of Political Science*, Vol. 12 (June 2009).

————. *Committing to Peace: The Successful Settlement of Civil Wars.* Princeton: Princeton University Press, 2002.

————. "The Critical Barrier to Civil War Settlement." *International Organization*, Vol. 51, No. 3 (Summer 1997): pp. 335–364.

Walzer, Michael, *Just and Unjust Wars: A Moral Argument with Historical Illustrations.* 3rd edition. New York: Basic Books, 2000.

Weber, Max. *From Max Weber: Essays in Sociology*, trans. H. H. Gerth and C. Wright Mills. New York: Oxford University Press, 1946.

Weinberger, Casper W. "The Uses of Military Power." Remarks prepared for the National Press Club, Washington, DC, November 28, 1984.

Weinstein, Jeremy M., *Inside Rebellion: The Politics of Insurgent Violence.* New York: Cambridge University Press, 2007.

Welch, Claude E., ed., *Civilian Control of the Military: Theory and Cases from Developing Countries* Albany: SUNY Press, 1976.

Werner, Suzanne. "The Precarious Nature of Peace: Resolving the Issues, Enforcing the Settlement, and Renegotiating the Terms." *American Journal of Political Science*, Vol. 43, No. 3 (July 1999): pp. 912–934.

Werner, Suzanne, and Amy Yuen. "Making and Keeping Peace." *International Organization*, Vol. 59, No. 2 (Spring 2005): pp. 261–292.

Wood, Elisabeth J. *Forging Democracy from Below: Insurgent Transitions in South Africa and El Salvador*. New York: Cambridge University Press, 2000.

———. *Insurgent Collective Action and Civil War in El Salvador*. New York: Cambridge University Press, 2003.

———. "The Peace Accords and Postwar Reconstruction." In James K. Boyce, ed., *Economic Policy for Building Peace: The Lessons of El Salvador*. Boulder: Lynne Rienner, 1996.

World Bank. "Sub-Saharan Africa: From Crisis to Sustainable Growth: A Long-Term Perspective Study." Washington, DC: World Bank, 1989.

———. *Uganda: Growing Out of Poverty*. 2nd edition. Washington, DC: World Bank, 1997.

———. *Uganda: The Challenge for Growth and Poverty Reduction*. Country Economic Memorandum, Report no. 1413-549. Washington, DC: World Bank, 1995.

Zaehner, R. C. ed. *Encyclopedia of the World's Religions*. New York: Barnes and Noble, 1997.

Zartman, I. William. *Elusive Peace: Negotiating an End to Civil Wars*. Washington, DC: Brookings Institution Press, 1995.

Zisk, Kimberly Marten. *Enforcing the Peace: Learning from the Imperial Past*. New York: Columbia University Press, 2004.

Index

Note: Page numbers with an *f* indicate figures; those with a *t* indicate tables.